AN APPROACH TO CHRISTIAN DOCTRINE

AN APPROACH TO CHRISTIAN DOCTRINE

edited by

GREVILLE P. LEWIS
B.A., B.D.

WIPF & STOCK · Eugene, Oregon

Wipf and Stock Publishers
199 W 8th Ave, Suite 3
Eugene, OR 97401

An Approach to Christian Doctrine
By Lewis, Grevile P.
Copyright©1954 Methodist Publishing - Epworth Press
ISBN 13: 978-1-5326-3072-9
Publication date 4/6/2017
Previously published by Epworth Press, 1954

Every effort has been made to trace the current copyright
owner of this publication but without success. If you have
any information or interest in the copyright, please contact the publishers.

TO THE STUDENT

As the title indicates, this book offers you *An Approach to Christian Doctrine*. You will note that this is *an* approach; it does not claim to be *the* approach, as if only one way of coming to grips with Christian belief were possible.

So it is that, while we hope and believe that this book will help the thinking Christian to understand, and the seeker to find, we do not claim that the deep truths of our faith have always got to be expressed in just this manner, nor insist that you must come to them in this way. In what follows, you will find many signposts, but not a set of tram-lines; we want to stimulate your thinking, not to restrict it.

Ultimately, this book and all other helps must take 'a third place' in your quest. On the one hand, your Christian faith must be much more than something you read in a book; it must be something *you yourself* understand and believe and live by. On the other hand, your supreme Teacher must be *God*. It is His Spirit who will 'guide you into all the truth'; and His truth will make you, not a prisoner, but free.

DAVID N. FRANCIS,
Secretary, The Local Preachers Department,
1 *Central Buildings, S.W.*1.

PREFACE

THE purpose of this text-book is to help Methodist Local Preachers on Trial as they pursue their prescribed studies of Christian Doctrine. It is hoped, however, that it will prove in value to the students of other denominations who are seeking a simple and positive statement of the Christian Faith which takes into account the modern approach to theology and the present world situation.

The book has been written by a group of ten theologians, all of whom entered the Methodist Ministry between 1922 and 1937. The disadvantages of a theological symposium are obvious, but the editor hopes that they are more than balanced by the freshness which is given to the book by the varied styles and viewpoints of the writers. It should be made clear, however, that no writer must be held responsible for the opinions of a fellow-contributor, or for his method of presentation.

If there are any glaring omissions, unintentional duplications, or avoidable discrepancies, the editor must accept responsibility for them.

GREVILLE P. LEWIS.

CONTENTS

STUDY 1. INTRODUCTION TO THEOLOGY, by Alfred C. Lamb

A. THE IMPORTANCE OF THEOLOGY	1
1. It helps you become an intelligent Christian	1
2. It expands and deepens your Experience	1
3. It gives you the essential message for your Preaching	2
4. It makes your preaching relevant to Modern Need	3
5. It gives conviction and authority to your Preaching	3
6. It enables you to defend the Christian Faith against opponents	4
7. It provides the only sound basis for Moral Conduct	4
B. REVELATION	5
1. General Revelation	5
2. The Special Revelation	6
3. Inspiration	7
4. The unifying Theme	8
5. The End of Revelation	9
C. THE SOURCES OF CHRISTIAN DOCTRINE	9
Introduction	9
1. The Bible	10
2. The Church	10
3. Personal religious experience	11
4. The world of Nature	12
D. NOTE ON 'REVELATION AND REASON'	12
Introduction	12
a. The two sides to our thinking	13
b. The relation between Revelation and Reason	14

WESLEY'S SERMONS, by John Lawson . . 15
SERMON I. SALVATION BY FAITH 16
   I. What faith is 16
   II. What salvation is 17
   III. Common Objections to the Methodist Preaching answered 17

STUDY 2. GOD'S SELF-REVELATION THROUGH NATURE, by Alfred C. Lamb 19
A. THE NATURE OF GOD 20
   1. God is Personal 20
   2. The Orderliness of God 21

B. MIRACLE 23

C. THE PROVIDENCE OF GOD 25
   1. God's purposes for us are spiritual and moral . 25
   2. God is working in and through the world . 26
   3. The world of nature is one in which our moral and spiritual growth is possible . . . 26
   4. In the interplay of human life, it is possible for one to influence another 26

D. PHYSICAL EVILS 26
   1. The moral neutrality of Nature . . . 27
   2. Human suffering 27
   3. The fact of Death 29
   Conclusion 29

SERMON 2. THE ALMOST CHRISTIAN . . . 30
   I. A Portrait of the 'Almost Christian' . . 30
   II. The Religion of the Heart 31

STUDY 3. GOD IN THE OLD TESTAMENT, by Horace Cleaver 32
A. THE RULING CONCEPTION OF GOD . . . 32
   Introduction 32
   1. God is Personal 33
   2. God is Holy 34
   3. God is Righteous 36
   4. God is Love 36
   5. There is only One God 37

CONTENTS ix

  6. God is the Creator of all things . . . 38
  7. God is the God of all Nations . . . 39

B. THE SEARCH FOR REDEMPTION . . . 40
  Introduction 40
  1. Redemption by the provision of a Better Covenant 41
  2. Redemption by Reconciliation effected between God and man 42
    a. The priest 42
    b. The system of Sacrifices . . . 43
  3. Redemption by an Act of Divine Deliverance 43
    a. The Saving Remnant 46
    b. The Kingdom of a Messiah . . . 46
    c. The Suffering Servant 47
    d. The Son of Man 47

SERMON 44. THE USE OF MONEY . . . 48
  I. 'Gain all you can' 49
  II. 'Save all you can' 49
  III. 'Give all you can' 49

STUDY 4. MAN, SIN AND GRACE, *by Rupert E. Davies* 51
A. THE INCOMPLETENESS OF THE OLD TESTAMENT REVELATION 51

B. THE RIDDLE OF MAN'S NATURE, AND HIS RELATIONSHIP TO GOD 52
  Introduction 52
  1. The materialistic view of Man . . . 52
  2. The Christian view of Man . . . 53
    a. Conscious of himself 55
    b. As Persisting through time . . . 55
    c. Power of abstract thought . . . 55
    d. He can create 56
    e. He is free 56
    f. Power of personal relationship . . 56

C. THE FAILURE OF MAN; ORIGINAL AND ACTUAL SIN 57
  Introduction 57
  1. The nature of Sin 58
    a. Against all comers 59
    b. Against God 60

2. Original and Actual Sin	60
a. Original Sin as Corporate	61
b. Original Sin as Personal	62
3. The Fall of Man, corporate and personal	63
a. The Fall of Man as corporate	63
b. The Fall of Man as personal	64
D. THE GRACE OF GOD AND JUSTIFICATION	65
Introduction	65
1. By Grace	65
a. God takes the initiative	66
b. The grace of God is entirely undeserved	66
c. It is a personal relationship	67
2. Through Faith	67
SERMON 9. THE SPIRIT OF BONDAGE AND OF ADOPTION	68
I. The Natural Man	68
II. God's Rude Awakening	69
III. God's Merciful Release	70
IV. A Guide to Self-analysis	70

STUDY 5. THE WORK OF CHRIST, *by Rupert E. Davies*   72

A. THE FACT OF SALVATION THROUGH THE CROSS	72
B. THE PREACHING OF THE CROSS	72
Introduction	72
1. The Cross of Christ is the Work of God	73
2. Jesus did not come to earth simply and solely to die	73
3. The Cross of Jesus must not be separated from His Resurrection	74
4. The Blame for the Cruxifixion	75
C. THE DOCTRINE OF THE ATONEMENT	76
Introduction	76
1. Is it true to the Biblical Revelation?	76
2. Is it wholly consistent with the nature and character of God as revealed to us by and in Jesus Christ?	77
3. Does it show the Work of Christ as something done once and for all?	77

CONTENTS xi

 4. Does it show the Death of Christ as available or me? 78

D. THE HISTORIC THEORIES OF THE ATONEMENT . 78
 Introduction 78
 1. Christ our Champion against the hosts of evil 79
 2. The satisfaction of God's honour and justice . 81
 3. The moral influence of the Cross . . . 82
 4. The Sacrifice once offered 83
 5. The completion of our Penitence . . . 85
 6. We deserve Punishment, but we receive Forgiveness 86

E. THE PROBLEM OF SUFFERING 88

F. THE HOPE OF GLORY 89

G. NOTE ON 'THE DEVIL' 89

SERMON 8. THE FIRST-FRUITS OF THE SPIRIT . . 91
 I. The Life 'In Christ' and 'In the Spirit' . . 91
 II. The Good Conscience of the Christian before God 91
 III. The Subject Applied to the Enquiring Hearer 93

STUDY 6. THE PERSON OF CHRIST, *by Frederic Greeves* 94
A. THE SAVIOUR KNOWN THROUGH HIS WORK . 95
 Introduction 95
 1. The Apostolic Preaching 95
 2. Jesus reveals and reconciles 97

B. TRULY GOD 98
 Introduction 98
 1. Jesus' words about Himself 98
 2. Jesus' other teaching 100
  a. The Sermon on the Mount . . . 100
  b. The Miracles 100
  c. The Parables 101
  d. The Kingdom of God 101
 3. The Unexpected Messiah 101
 4. The faith of the first Christians . . . 102

xii AN APPROACH TO CHRISTIAN DOCTRINE

C. TRULY MAN 103
   Introduction 103
   1. The significance of the Humanity of Jesus . 103
   2. Jesus was not 'two persons' 105

D. TRULY GOD, TRULY MAN 107
   Introduction 107
   1. The Definition of Chalcedon . . . 108
   2. Why this matters 110

E. NOTE ON 'THE VIRGIN BIRTH' 111

SERMON 15. THE GREAT PRIVILEGE OF THOSE THAT ARE BORN OF GOD 112
   I. The New Birth Explained 112
   II. The Problem of Sin in Believers . . . 113
   III. The Process of Temptation, and its Prevention 113

STUDY 7. THE HOLY SPIRIT, *by A. Raymond George* 115

A. SALVATION 115
   1. What is Salvation? 115
     a. Past, present and future . . . 115
     b. What does God do when He saves us? . 116
       i. Conversion 116
       ii. Forgiveness 116
       iii. Justification 116
       iv. Adoption 117
       v. Redemption 117
       vi. Reconciliation 117
       vii. Dying and Rising with Christ . . 117
       viii. Regeneration 117
       ix. Sanctification 117
   2. How is Salvation obtained? . . . 119
     a. Grace 119
     b. Faith 120
     c. Repentance 120
     d. How can God justify us? . . . 121
     e. What is the status of those who cannot make even this simple response of repentance and faith? 121
   3. What follows from Salvation? . . . 122
     a. Fellowship with God 122

CONTENTS

b. Fellowship with each other	122
c. Loving our neighbour	123
d. Assurance	123
e. Christian Perfection	123
B. THE HOLY SPIRIT	124
1. The spirit in the Old Testament	125
2. The Spirit in the New Testament	126
3. Conclusions	129
a. Was the Holy Spirit operative among men before Pentecost?	130
b. Is sanctification the special work of the Holy Spirit?	130
c. The work of the Holy Spirit summarized	131
SERMON 10. THE WITNESS OF THE SPIRIT	132
I. The Two 'Witnesses'	133
II. How the 'Fully Assured' may guard against Fanaticism	134

STUDY 8. GOD THE HOLY TRINITY, *by Alfred H. S. Pask*

	136
A. THE NATURE OF GOD	136
1. Christ the Revealer of God	136
2. Christ accepts the Old Testament	137
3. The Teaching of Jesus on the Nature of God	137
4. Jesus, by His life, death and resurrection, shows us the character of God	139
5. God in action, in the Incarnate Son and in the Holy Spirit	142
B. GOD, THREE IN ONE	143
1. The inescapable facts of experience	143
2. The Church begins to preach the Triune God	144
3. Avoiding the facts	145
4. The Trinity and Saving Faith	146
5. The Doctrine of the Trinity and Theology	146
6. The Search for a 'form of sound words'	148
7. The Communion of God	151
8. The Mystery remains	151
9. The Trinity and Worship	152

SERMON 5. 'JUSTIFICATION BY FAITH'	153
I. Man's Need of a Saviour	154
II. What is Justification?	155
III. Can Man Earn Forgiveness?	155
IV. The Nature of Saving Faith	155

STUDY 9. THE CHURCH (1), *by Norman P. Goldhawk* — 157

A. THE CHURCH IN THE BIBLE	157
Introduction	157
1. The Teaching of Jesus	159
a. The Kingdom of God	159
b. The idea of Messiahship	159
c. Shepherd and flock	159
d. The new Israel	160
i. He called twelve disciples	160
ii. He taught them	160
iii. He sent them out	160
iv. He established a covenant	161
2. The Primitive Church	161
a. The new Israel	162
b. Confession of the Lordship of Christ	162
c. The Church shares in the gifts and fellowship of the Spirit	163
d. The Church is a missionary Church	164
3. The Remainder of the New Testament	164
B. THE CHURCH'S LIFE AND SERVICE	165
Introduction	165
1. What the Church is	165
a. A Fellowship of Believers	165
b. A Fellowship which transcends death	166
c. A Fellowship created by the Gospel	167
2. The purpose of the Church's existence	168
C. THE CHURCH'S MINISTRY	169
SERMON 12. THE MEANS OF GRACE	173
I. The Use and Abuse of the Means of Grace	174
II. Divine Grace and the Means of Grace	174
III. A Guide to Prayer, Bible Study, and the Holy Communion	175

IV. Quietist Objections Overturned	176
V. The Form of Christian Discipline	176

STUDY 10. THE CHURCH (2), *by Norman P. Goldhawk* 177

A. THE CHURCH'S WORSHIP 177
  1. What worship is 178
  2. The Bible 179
  3. Preaching 179
  4. The Sacraments 180
     a. Baptism 180
     b. The Lord's Supper 182

B. THE CHURCH IN HISTORY 183

C. THE DIVISIONS IN THE CHURCH 186

D. THE METHODIST CHURCH 190
  1. Methodism is a communion within the Holy Catholic Church 192
  2. Methodism is a Protestant Evangelical Church 192
  3. Methodism is a distinctive community within the Church 193

E. THE CHURCH TODAY 193
  1. The broken fellowship of the Church 193
  2. The future lies under the Hand of God 194
  3. Unity is to be found in fellowship at the Lord's Table 194
  4. Some major unions already achieved 195

SERMON 18. UPON OUR LORD'S SERMON ON THE MOUNT: DISCOURSE III 196
  I. 'The Mind which was in Christ Impart' 196
  II. 'That all Mankind Thy Truth may see' 197
  III. 'From Doubt, and Fear, and Sorrow Free' 197
  IV. 'Now let me gain Perfection's Height' 198

STUDY 11. CHRISTIAN ETHICS, *by Edward Rogers* 199

A. WHAT IS ETHICS? 199
B. ETHICS DEPENDS ON THEOLOGY 200
C. CHRISTIAN FAITH AND CONDUCT 201
D. THE RANGE OF 'THE LAW OF CHRIST' 202

E. APPLICATION	204
1. Difficulties	204
2. Clear Judgements	206
a. The Christian Doctrine of Man	206
b. We are members one of another	207
c. The Christian's attitude to Work	207
d. The Christian's use of Time	208
e. The Christian's use of Sunday	208
f. The Christian's use of Money	209
g. Other questions	210
F. CONCLUSION	210
SERMON 19. UPON OUR LORD'S SERMON ON THE MOUNT: DISCOURSE IV	211
I. The Christian must go to the World	211
II. The Christian must make an Open Witness	212
III. Current Excuses for Secret Discipleship Exposed	212
IV. The Invitation to Christianity in Earnest	213
STUDY 12. THE LAST THINGS, *by Thomas C. Baird*	214
A. THE GOD WHO COMES	214
1. Time and Eternity	214
2. The God who will come—has come	214
a. The same God	215
b. The God who ever comes	215
B. THE FINAL COMING OF CHRIST	216
1. Maran Atha	216
2. Three difficulties	217
a. Why need Jesus come?	217
b. And what about Science?	217
c. Is not Adventist teaching unbalanced?	218
3. The New Testament's witness	218
a. He will come—to judge men	219
b. He judges—because He loves	219
c. He will come with glory	220
d. He will not come alone	221
4. A Humble, Vivid Certainty	222
C. HEAVEN	223
1. Heaven is the Presence of God	223

CONTENTS xvii

2. Heaven will mean unfettered Adoration . 224
3. Heaven will mean a deep fellowship with one another in Christ 224
4. Heaven will mean the perfect delight of doing God's Will 224
5. In Heaven, we shall have Spiritual Bodies . 225
   NOTE ON SPIRITUALISM 226
   NOTE ON IMMORTALITY 226

D. HELL 227
1. Hesitations about the Doctrine of Hell . . 227
   a. Preaching about Hell has often been exaggerated 227
   b. The word Hell (Gehenna) is not a common New Testament word 228
2. Four Truths about Hell 228
   a. A man faces his self-centredness after death . 228
   b. Hell is not the automatic destiny of the non-Christian 229
   c. The purpose of Hell is redemptive . . 230
   d. Hell may lead to spiritual death . . 231

E. LIVING IN THE LAST DAYS 232
1. Be ready! 232
2. Be Spirit-filled! 232
3. In the struggle with evil—rejoice! . . . 233
4. Expect problems of compromise . . . 233

SERMON 28. UPON OUR LORD'S SERMON ON THE MOUNT: DISCOURSE XIII 234
   I. What it is to say 'Lord, Lord!' . . . 234
   II. What it is to be 'Built upon the Rock.' . . 235
   III. A Summons to the Religion of the Heart . 235

APPENDIX: BELIEF IN GOD, *by Alfred C. Lamb* 236
1. The evidence from Nature 236
2. The existence and compulsion of Spiritual Values 238
   a. Their existence 238
   b. Their compulsion 239
3. The evidence of history 240

METHOD OF STUDY

1. Throughout these Studies there are *references* (in brackets) to important Scripture passages, to the prescribed O.T. and N.T. text-books, to Wesley's Sermons, etc. Do not ignore these references. Carefully study the passages referred to.
2. Each of the following Studies is planned as a *fortnight's work*. If you intend to complete the course within six months, you will find it desirable to keep to this timetable.
3. At the end of each Study you will find three *Test Questions*. Write your answers to these, without reference to the text-book; say, 200 words on each. If you are taking a Correspondence Course, send your answers as promptly as possible to your Tutor.
4. Before you finish these Studies, note 'To Be Continued' on p. 242.

ABBREVIATIONS

AOT = *An Approach to the Old Testament* (Horace Cleaver).

ANT = *An Approach to the New Testament* (Greville P. Lewis).

MHB = The Methodist Hymn Book (published in 1933).

CAT = The Senior Catechism (*Minutes*, 1952, pp. 216–224).

TWB = *A Theological Word Book of the Bible*, edited by Alan Richardson, D.D. (S.C.M.).

PH = *The Preacher's Handbook* (published by the Epworth Press, every two years). *Consult the Index in PH(4)*

STUDY ONE

Introduction to Theology

CHRISTIAN Theology is a reasoned statement of what the Christian believes about God, His being, character, and purpose for mankind. The Creeds are statements of these beliefs, but theology not only makes the statements, it also gives us the reasons why we hold them, and explains what they mean.

A. THE IMPORTANCE OF THEOLOGY

1. *It helps you to become an intelligent Christian*

If you are a thoughtful Christian, you will sooner or later have to face questions which go right down to the roots of your convictions. Is there really a God? What is He like? How do we know? Has He a purpose for us, His creatures? If so, has He made it known to us? How? What is that purpose? What and who was Jesus of Nazareth? Was He just a man, or was He truly 'Immanuel'—'God-with-us'? Can we be His disciples without joining the Church? If we are His disciples, what kind of lives ought we to live? Is there a life hereafter? If there is, has our conduct here anything to do with the life we shall know hereafter? So the questions arise, and we cannot simply dismiss them without trying to give a *reasoned* answer to them. As you study theology, you will find out the answers to such questions, helped by the convictions of countless other Christians who have faced the same questions and given their own answers to them.

At the same time, you must recognize that a thoughtful Christian needs more than the ability to answer these questions, if he is really to be a Christian. He must live by, and live out, what he believes in his daily life. He must have what theologians have long called 'saving faith': i.e. he must surrender his whole life to God, as well as learn about God.

2. *It expands and deepens your Experience*

As you study Christian Doctrine, you enter into a rich heritage which comes to you from the experience of a host of others.

When you learned the craft by which you earn your livelihood, you could not afford to rely on your own native skill, however clever you might be. If you had done so, you would not have got very far. You learned from others, and your immediate teachers were the channel through which the skill and knowledge of many people came to enrich your own skill and knowledge. Thus your own experience widened, and you became a better craftsman than you could possibly have been, had you depended only upon your own resources.

So, in your religious life, as you study the great essentials of the Christian Faith, your understanding will be deepened, and your experience made richer. As a Methodist, you will enter into the experience from which, under God, the Methodist Church grew, and which finds so constant an expression in the hymns of Methodism, especially in those of Charles Wesley. If you depend only upon your own meagre insight into Christian truth, your religion will be poverty-stricken. You enter into the riches of religious experience by learning from others of the 'deep things of God'.

3. *It gives you the essential message for your Preaching*

As a preacher, you must expound Christian Doctrine. Paul's words to Titus apply also to you: 'Speak thou the things which become sound doctrine' (Tit. 2¹). You cannot preach your own experience alone, although that personal experience will add conviction to what you say.

The Methodist Church turns to a volume of sermons as one of the sources of its doctrines—the *Forty-Four Sermons* of John Wesley. As Methodists, we believe that preaching and doctrine are inseparable. If you purpose to be a Methodist preacher, the basis of your sermons must be doctrinal (*see* the High Leigh Report on *Doctrinal Preaching*).

You cannot, indeed, preach with good conscience through the Christian Year, without dealing with those great doctrines which alone give meaning to the great Festivals of that Year: Advent and Christmas, Lent and Passiontide, Easter and Whitsuntide. Nor, indeed, can you be true to your calling as a preacher, if you do not proclaim the great doctrines which underlie those other Festivals which the insight of the Church has brought into use in more recent years; Covenant Sunday, Aldersgate Sunday, Harvest Festival and the like. At all times, therefore, you must seek to 'speak the things which become sound doctrine'.

4. *It makes your preaching relevant to Modern Need*

Preaching must apply the Gospel of the saving grace of God in Jesus Christ to the immediate needs and conditions of men and women. If it does not do so, the Gospel will seem remote and unreal to our hearers, for their conditions and needs are apparently so different from those of the people to whom Jesus spoke.

In thinking of human conditions, we can separate them into the temporal and the permanent conditions. In the *temporal*, we would include those constantly changing outward settings of our lives; the social, economic and political conditions in which we live. Often, indeed, when we speak of the conditions of men and women, it is only to these outward circumstances that we refer. We cannot ignore them, and however different our conditions may be from those of Palestine 1,900 years ago, our Gospel has got to be related to them. Our doctrine must have its meaning for our hearers as citizens. It is only as they are informed Christian citizens, that they can face the alien and godless forms of citizenship which strive for the mastery of the world today. Of these, the most militant and highly publicised is Communism; but there are more subtle, and perhaps more successful forms; in particular, the common assumption that material standards are the only ones by which aims and conduct are to be guided and judged.

The *permanent* conditions of human life are even more important. They are at once as old as man himself, and yet ever new and always modern. Only two salient features of these conditions call for our attention here: (*a*) Each of us is mortal, and some day will have to die. (*b*) Each of us is beset by sin and evil, both from within and without. The Christian Gospel must speak, through the voice of the preacher, to these permanent conditions under which all men and women live.

5. *It gives conviction and authority to your Preaching*

Only as you study theology can you learn to sift truth from error. As a Christian, and especially as a preacher, you will want to find your way with certainty through the confused thinking of today, when so many sects assert their own peculiar doctrines. It is only as you find your way that you can be a trustworthy guide to those who need help in this confusion. One of your responsibilities is to be such a guide; and a preacher can only be trusted, and his preaching be accepted as authoritative, when he has learned the way himself.

6. *It enables you to defend the Christian Faith against opponents*

We can look at the last statement from a different view-point. It is only as you come to have a sound understanding of the Faith, that you can defend it against its various opponents and detractors. Some of these opponents (i.e. the Communists) use the method of 'indoctrination' (the systematic teaching of their doctrine) as their most powerful weapon. These non-Christian systems have taught us that the study of doctrine is not something remote from the world, but that it is of tremendous significance in the shaping of the world's destiny. They have destroyed for ever the old foolish belief that 'it doesn't matter what a man believes'. It matters; it matters terribly—and that is why the Christian preacher must oppose false doctrines with the true, and vigorously defend the Christian Faith against all who deny it.

7. *It provides the only sound basis for Moral Conduct*

Theology includes within its scope, not only your relationship to God—God's word to *you*, and *your* response to God—but also your relationship to other people. That is why this text-book on Theology includes a Study on Christian Ethics. For the Christian, religion and morality must never be divorced, and for obvious reasons:

a. As a Christian, your own personal standards of behaviour, your motives and ambitions, will finally depend, not upon what your family, your local society, or your country demand from you, but upon what you believe that *God* requires of you.

b. Your individual life is bound up with complex circles of group life; the life of your family, your trade or profession, your club, your church, your town, your nation. In so far as your standards of conduct are held with conviction and proclaimed with courage, they will inevitably exercise a strong influence upon the groups of which you are a member. Since, therefore, your theology is the source of your own moral principles, it becomes an intensely practical force in social and political life.

c. But what happens when you fail to keep God's commands, and suffer moral defeat? Again, your theology is relevant, for it speaks to you of the fact and purpose of punishment, the necessity of repentance, and the promise and conditions of divine forgiveness.

d. But can we expect anything but moral defeat in our struggle against the world, the flesh and the devil? A quotation will point the way to our answer. 'Merely to hold up to people an ethical ideal may be just about as useful as to tell a cripple that he ought to run 100 yards in 10 seconds; perhaps he ought, but he can't, until he is cured. We need to give to people, not only the ethical ideal, but also the means of attaining it, and that drives us straight to Christian Doctrine.'* To Christian Doctrine, for it is there that we discover, not only the ideal of conduct, but also the divine power whereby we can realize the ideal.

B. REVELATION

When we set out to study theology, we obviously assume that we can get to know something about God and His ways with men. But how can we? To answer such a question brings us straight to the fundamental conviction of Christian people that we can know about God because, and only because, He has first made Himself known to us. This belief we express in the familiar word 'Revelation'. God, we say, has given us a revelation of Himself and His purposes and dealings with us. This belief we must now study.

1. *General Revelation*

For many centuries, theologians have held that it is possible for men to obtain a knowledge of God by the use of their own unaided reason, as they study the world of nature which God has created. This kind of knowledge was contrasted with the knowledge given by divine 'revelation' through Scripture.

We no longer think like that. We have come to see that all knowledge in every sphere of life comes from God, who alone is the author and source of all knowledge, as of all creation. Further, we realize more and more that there is no such thing as man's unaided reason, as he seeks for knowledge of God's creation. Our powers of understanding come, like the world we seek to understand, from the Creator of all. This is as true of the scientist, the historian, the craftsman, the artist, the musician, as of the theologian. In every branch of knowledge, religious included, our limited insight and experience narrow down what God can reveal to us; yet we believe that, as we conscientiously seek out

* *Doctrinal Preaching* (Local Preachers Dept), pp. 11–12.

God's truth in any realm, God the Holy Spirit can and does lead us into truth.

We can speak, therefore, of a *General Revelation* which God has given to *all* men, and which covers all the wide fields of human knowledge. This knowledge includes that insight into the being and nature of God which is given through the natural world, and which we shall discuss in the next *Study*.

However, whilst God has given us a measure of insight into some of the truths of religion through this general revelation, we Christians know that *we need something more*. The world of nature does not reveal to us the nature and consequences of sin; it does not disclose God's redemptive purposes to us; it does not interpret Jesus of Nazareth to us; it gives us no insight into the need for and the meaning of the Christian Church, and of worship; it does not give us clear guidance when we face moral issues, or give us conviction about the life after death and its nature—and so we could continue. These are our major religious concerns, and to find help in facing such issues we must turn to the *Special Revelation* which God has given to us, over and above all He has revealed to us through the world of nature, and which we find in the Scriptures of the Old and New Testaments.

2. *The Special Revelation*

The Special Revelation which God gave began when Abraham, convinced that God had called him to leave Haran, obeyed the call (Gen. 11^{31}–12^9; Heb. 11$^{8-12}$, *see AOT* and *ANT*). It was given in a unique way when God, through His servant Moses, led the Children of Israel out of Egypt at the Exodus, saved them from their foes at the crossing of the Red Sea, gave them the Law on Sinai, and made them into a nation. Within that nation there arose a long line of prophets, who sought to interpret the events of their times in the light of what they believed to be God's character and His purposes for their nation. The revelation came, not only in the actual *events* themselves, but also in the *meaning* these Hebrew preachers found in the events, as they sought to understand, proclaim and obey God's will. It is primarily to the prophets that we owe our knowledge of God's ways with His chosen people, but their work influenced in its turn the work of other religious leaders in Israel—priests, law-givers and psalmists. The same individual could play more than one of these parts; the prophet, e.g., might also be a priest or shape the people's laws, or make their songs.

The Special Revelation came to its climax when, under the procuratorship of Pontius Pilate over Judea, a new prophetic movement arose in Palestine. It began in the work of John the Baptist who, after a short ministry, was beheaded by Herod. It continued and broadened out in the work of John's kinsman, Jesus of Nazareth, whose brief ministry also ended in execution, this time by crucifixion on the orders of Pilate, and at the demand of the Jewish authorities. The Crucifixion had a startling sequel. Within a few days, the followers of Jesus boldly proclaimed the fact that He had risen from the dead. It was not long before those followers became convinced that God had given to men a unique revelation of Himself and of His purposes, through the life, teaching, deeds, passion, death and resurrection of Jesus. They came to believe that, because Jesus had been rejected by the Jews, acting through their leaders, God had in turn set the Jews on one side, and that henceforth the promises made to the old Israel of the flesh would now be transferred to the new Israel created through Jesus Christ, the Israel of the Spirit, the Church of Christ.

To Christians, then, God's special revelation embraces both the insight granted to the old Israel, and that supreme self-disclosure which He gave through the life, death and resurrection of Jesus and the birth of the Christian Church. The revelation given to the old Israel is recorded in the Old Testament; that to the new Israel in the New Testament. The New Testament is the climax and interpretation of the Old; the Old Testament remains for ever incomplete and unfulfilled apart from the New (*See Study Three,* later). In both, we read the record of the Mighty Acts of God, by which He ever expressed His gracious will and purpose in redemptive activity.

3. *Inspiration*

We have said that revelation did not come only in the events recorded in Scripture, but also through the interpretation put upon these events by the Biblical writers. The interpretation is an essential part of the revelation.

Now we firmly hold that it was under the influence of God's Holy Spirit that the different writers of Scripture were able to interpret God's Mighty Acts, and to set forth their meaning. This influence, by which events are interpreted and communicated to others, we believe to be the 'inspiration' behind and in Holy Scripture.

You will have realized from your studies in the Old and New

Testaments that the Biblical authors have left evidence in plenty that their own personal qualities and experiences have influenced their recording, and coloured their interpretation, of events. Different writers gave different accounts of the same event, and, at times, contradictory interpretations. It follows that we must reject the view which is still held today, though by a minority of Protestants, that the Holy Spirit endowed the sacred writers with complete infallibility, so that no error of any kind could be found in Scripture.*

Nor can we hold that each of the several writers had an equal degree of insight into God's dealings and purposes. Dr. John Baillie reminds us that we must 'distinguish the successive levels of understanding, both within the Old Testament and in the transition from that to the New'.† Especially in the earlier stages of Hebrew history, we find crude and immature ideas of God. They present us with the familiar 'moral difficulties' of Scripture. Some of these you will already have met in your O.T. studies; for instance, in the stories of Jephthah's daughter (Jges 11^{29-40}), of the destruction of Achan and his family (Josh. 7), and of the death of the seven sons of Saul (2 Sam. 21^9). We do not defend these conceptions of God, but frankly recognize them as primitive and characteristic of their day. They stand condemned in the light of the revelation of the character and purpose of God, made through Jesus Christ. As by the Holy Spirit's inspiration we see 'the light of the knowledge of the glory of God in the face of Jesus Christ', all else, in Scripture and out of it, must be judged by that light.

4. *The unifying Theme*

Throughout the long period of revelation, in which God inspired generation after generation of sacred writers, there was one unifying theme to the whole process. That theme was *the redemptive work of God*. At first, it was conceived as the redemption of a people from outward slavery and oppression. Finally, when Jesus came, it was conceived as redemption from sin and death. Though the outward setting of the message changed with the

---

* Because we are familiar with this way of thinking about Scripture, we must not think that it has always been held by the majority of Christians. It really developed in its *extreme* form after the Protestant Reformation in the 16th century, when some Protestants began to look for authority in religion to an infallible Bible, rather than to an infallible Church.

† *The Idea of Revelation in Recent Thought*, p. 120.

passing years, the theme itself, that God was His people's Redeemer, remained unchanged. *What* God redeems from, *why* God redeems, and *how* man can claim that redemption—these were questions which could only be fully answered when at last Jesus came; yet, from the beginning, the hope of Israel had been for a Redeemer. Jesus, we believe, is still the fulfilment of that hope, not only for the Gentiles—from whom most of the converts to Christianity now come—but also for His own people, the Jews.

5. *The End of Revelation*

The purpose of revelation is to awaken Christian faith in the heart of man. But what is Christian faith?

The word faith itself is capable of varied meanings, and we often confuse them. Let us unravel three different strands of meaning.

a. We can use 'faith', on the lowest plane, as meaning the same as 'assumption'; the act of assuming certain ideas to be true, and then testing them by experience.

b. We use 'Faith' (or, generally, '*The* Faith') to mean the whole body of convictions which, we believe, can be shown to be worthy of our acceptance, on the grounds of adequate evidence and trustworthy reasoning. In this sense, 'Faith' is used as an equivalent of 'Doctrine'.

c. Christian faith in its fullness, however, includes both these, and that 'saving faith' which we have already mentioned (p. 1). It is the complete committal of ourselves to Christ, to live and die by all we hold to be true of Him and through Him. Such a faith is akin to the personal trust in others, such as hallows the most sacred of our human relationships. It is not only of the mind, but is the committal of the whole self to a personal Lord.

For Christians, this personal committal is possible only because the Holy Spirit first awakens it, and afterwards constantly sustains it. It is under His influence that the convictions of the mind are fixed on Christ, and the surrender of the will called forth and sustained (1 Cor. 12^3).

C. THE SOURCES OF CHRISTIAN DOCTRINE

The theologian gathers his material from four principal sources, each of which has profoundly influenced the others.

1. *The Bible*

First and foremost is the special revelation given in the Scriptures of the Old and New Testaments. Today we know more than ever as to how the Bible came into being; of the circumstances in which its various strands and books were written, and of the characters and purposes of the many different writers. Yet all this is only preliminary to the use of the Bible by the theologian. It is the embodiment in literature of God's eternal message to mankind, given in Old Testament times little by little as men were able to comprehend it, and then given finally in all its splendour through Jesus Christ (Heb. 1$^{1-4}$).

The Bible is essential to the theologian. (i) It is the record of those events through which God's revelation came. More especially, it is *the* place where he can find the facts concerning the life, death and resurrection of Jesus, and the birth of the Church. (ii) It is only from the Bible that he can learn what Jesus taught by word and deed. (iii) The Bible gives him that knowledge of human nature in its sinfulness and rebelliousness against God which shows why God's redeeming work was necessary. (iv) In the Bible he finds the prophetic and apostolic teaching, and its interpretation of the nature and purposes of God. (v) As he holds on to the Bible, the theologian safeguards the ties which bind his convictions to those of the Church in apostolic times. (vi) The Bible is the starting point of the Christian's personal experience, and, further, it both illuminates that experience and disciplines it.

2. *The Church*

The Church itself provides the theologian with very important material. The fact that, so soon after Calvary, the Church came into being, that it declared that the Crucified Jesus was none other than God Incarnate, and that it offered Him to all as the Saviour of the world has a profound significance for the theologian. So also has the fact that the Christian Society so soon ceased to be a Jewish sect, and threw open its doors to the Gentiles.

The faith of the early Church was expressed in the Apostolic Preaching, in its worship and sacraments, and in its instruction to its converts. Within a few centuries, the Church embodied its convictions in carefully-phrased Creeds. These were short concise statements of its Faith; the Faith which was grounded in the

Scriptures and confirmed in its own experience. The Creeds (chief among them being the Apostles' Creed and the Nicene Creed) were formulated and used, partly as instruments for teaching the believer—especially in ages when comparatively few could read—and partly as a defence against heretical and unscriptural teaching.

When the Western Church was broken into two by the Protestant Reformation, the Reformers sought to recall the Church to Scripture as the sole foundation of its Faith. In so doing they retained the ancient Creeds, because these *did* sum up the Scriptural Faith of the Church.

When the Methodist Revival broke out in 18th-century England, its leaders framed no new Creed. They accepted the Creeds of the ancient Church, because they believed them to express the Faith which is contained in the Scriptures. Wesley and his preachers sought only to emphasise those evangelical doctrines which were being neglected by the Church in England, and to spread 'Scriptural Holiness' throughout the land.

We have said enough to show that the theologian must give special attention to the Creeds of the Church.

3. *Personal religious experience*

Methodists should need no reminder of the importance of personal religious experience. The Methodist Church owed its origin, under God, to the profound change which came in the religious experience of John and Charles Wesley at Whitsuntide, 1738. The Evangelical Revival, which deeply influenced the Church of England and created other religious communities besides Methodism, arose out of kindred experiences in the lives of others. Further, the quality of national life was in turn infused and changed by the moral outworking of those personal experiences. Christian experience is thus intensely individual, but also corporate. We know its power in ourselves as individuals, but through it we are made more surely 'members one of another' in the Body of Christ, His Church. In that wider setting of shared experience, our personal experience is informed, enriched and disciplined.

It follows that religious experience—personal, yet widely shared—is also a source of theology, and in several ways. (i) Religious experience is a stubborn fact of human life, and cannot be dismissed as an illusion. It has proved the most powerful of all driving forces in human behaviour. Its very existence must be explained, and can only be explained by a God from whom that experience has come, and to whom it points. (ii) Through his experience, the Christian knows that his redemption is not his own achievement, but the work of God's grace; a conviction which is often asserted by Paul (e.g., Eph. 2^{1-10}). (iii) Through his experience, the Christian receives assurance that he has been forgiven, and has received the gift of adoption by which he can claim to be a child of God (Rom. 8^{12-17}). (iv) The Christian's experience is shared by men and women of every race and tongue. He knows, therefore, that he cannot canalise God's redeeming love within any channels which human narrowness might dig for it. He knows that God's love is given to all, and that he is commissioned to offer Christ and the message of His redeeming love to every child of God.

4. *The world of Nature*

The world of nature can give its own testimony to the Creator. This testimony will be dealt with in the next Study.

It is from these varied sources that Christian theologians have taken their material. Their guiding principle, as they have gathered it together and welded it into doctrine, has been the conviction expressed by Paul: 'All things are of God, who hath reconciled us to himself by Jesus Christ, and hath given to us the ministry of reconciliation; to wit, that God was in Christ reconciling the world unto himself' (2 Cor. 5^{18-19}).

D. NOTE ON 'REVELATION AND REASON'

Some critics of Christian doctrine reject its truths *because* they are founded on revelation. They urge that we ought only to accept what we can prove by reason.

When they argue thus, these critics *assume* that, when we Christians say that God has revealed His truth to us, we mean that He has given us statements about Himself, the world of nature, and men, which we must always hold to be literally true, even though expanding knowledge shows that they are not true. We must admit that some Christians have adopted this attitude, and have gloried in believing in every detail of Scripture, even where the old Hebrew thought about the world of nature has been shown to be wrong in the light of newer knowledge. A simple instance may be quoted. When Copernicus, in 1543, published his book, in which he showed that the earth moves round the sun, and not the sun round the earth, Protestant Christians denounced it on the grounds that the Bible said that, in answer to the prayers of Joshua, the sun stood still (Josh. 10$^{12-14}$). Roman Catholics first accepted, and later rejected, the thought of Copernicus, not permitting it to be taught until 1822.

We have shown, however, that this attitude is not adopted by most thoughtful Christians today. Their idea of revelation is indeed very different. We have tried to show what it is. We must, however, go a little further, before we can finally answer those who condemn revelation on the ground that it is incompatible with reason.

a. *The two sides to our thinking.* In every act of thinking, there are two sides. Whatever subject we are dealing with, before we ever start to reason things out, we *assume* as the very basis of our reasoning that certain facts or ideas are true. The important thing to notice is that *an assumption is made, before we take steps to find out whether the assumption is justified.* It may, or may not be justified. When the assumption has been made, we use our powers of reasoning, either to see whether our assumption really fits in with the facts, or to describe, criticise, and change conditions in the light of what we assume to be true.

(i) For example, in the realm of science, the scientist will make a guess (he calls it a 'hypothesis') to explain the facts he observes, and to suggest further experiments or observations. He then tries to find out whether his guess is a good one; whether it does explain what he has observed. If it does not, and if he is an honest scientist, he will scrap his guess, and try to make a better one. If it proves reasonably good, he will use it to explore his own little part of nature more deeply, and will dignify his 'guess' with the name of 'theory' or 'law'. The important thing to notice is that his basic assumptions are guesses, and do not arise from reason. Reason is used, after the assumption is made, to justify and test it. So, in 1665–6, Sir Isaac Newton made a 'guess' that the same force held together and governed the planets in their movements round the sun, the moon in its motion round the earth, and the falling of bodies to the earth's surface; and he made a 'guess' as to how that force could be measured. His guess was supported by his observations, and became known as 'the law of gravity'. Though further observations of the planets have shown that it was not an absolutely accurate guess, it was so near the truth that it can still give a firm foundation for much science and engineering. Thus, in science, the results depend upon the assumptions, the guesses, and afterwards upon the reasoning by which they are tested or used.

(ii) A second example can be taken from the realm of politics. The Marxist assumes that certain principles, chiefly economic, govern human behaviour, and provide the only key by which past happenings can be accounted for, and future trends predicted. He finds the principles chiefly in the books of Marx and Engels. He ignores, or tries to abolish, the facts which do not fit in with his assumptions, and uses reasoning as he seeks to change conditions so that they will fit in with his assumptions. His reasonings, however, are founded on *assumptions*, and the assumptions are more important than the reasonings based upon them.

In all thinking, therefore, and in the very practical issues which follow from thinking, we first make assumptions and then try to reason out the consequences. When we say that an assumption is 'reasonable' or 'rational', we express our belief that it will best fit the facts we observe, and all the facts. The assumptions, however, are non-rational; whilst not being necessarily against reason, they are not made by any process of reasoning, but by guess, by flash of intuition, insight or imagination.

b. *The relation between Revelation and Reason.* Turning now to religion, we must assert that it is as absurd to oppose reason to revelation as it is to claim that in other spheres of thought reason alone counts.

In revelation itself, God has used the reasoning powers of the prophets and apostles, and enabled them thereby to interpret events. These men (to look at their work from the human side) made the supreme assumption that God was at work in the history of His chosen people. But assumption and reason worked together in showing how God worked, and what character and purpose were revealed to men as He worked through His people.

Further, Christians believe that the assumption that God is, and that He still works in creation and history, is the only adequate assumption on which we can explain this world's existence and destiny.

In all other branches of knowledge, assumptions play as great a part as reasoning. To condemn religion because it makes its great assumption—that God is, and rules over all things—and to imagine that all other kinds of knowledge are based on reasoning alone, is sheer moral blindness.

Wesley's Sermons

Why Wesley's Sermons? A very natural question in the mind of the new-comer to Methodist theology is why he should be asked to study sermons two centuries old, and which often require some explanation if they are to be understood today, even if they be by the great Wesley himself.

It follows a precedent set by Wesley that one clause of the *Model Deed*, which regulates the use of Methodist trust property, lays it down that in Methodist pulpits no person shall 'teach any Doctrine, or Practice, contrary to what is contained in certain Notes on the New Testament . . . of the said John Wesley, and in the First Four Volumes of Sermons . . . written and published by him'. This is the basis of the rule of our Church that all preachers shall read and give general approval to Wesley's *Forty-Four Sermons*. It is hoped that this explanation will help you to feel that this reading which you are required to undertake is not a dull piece of hide-bound tradition. It is part of a discipline which admirably expresses a very vital spiritual principle, namely, that the Church is no mere casual assembly of individuals. It is a disciplined body with a definite witness, and in it every member owes a glad allegiance to one Lord, to one Faith declared with divine authority, and to every other member. In addition, these Sermons are the work of one of the world's great men. There is bound to be a certain amount of effort required in following the mind of a great man who speaks to us from another age, but no one can make that effort without receiving a great blessing.

How to Use these Notes. The unfortunate impression seems to be widespread among Methodists that Wesley's Sermons are rather difficult, dull, and remote from our times. Nothing could be further from the facts, and you are urged to dismiss such notions, and to come to this study with an open mind. There are difficult passages in the Sermons, but few of them will be found in the twelve set for special study. In general, Wesley is a model for clarity of statement, and his subjects are important, practical, and ever-fresh. The difficulty is certainly not in what he says, but sometimes in the way he says it. At times his statements are set in the background of controversy with erroneous teaching, and the controversy in question has now ceased, or taken another form. A little explanation is then necessary, if the point of the argument is to be grasped. Still more, we today have to a large extent become unconsciously acclimatized to the 'snippet headline' style of writing in the newspapers and magazines, and Wesley by contrast appears solemn and 'high-flown'. The fault here is in ourselves! To make the effort required to follow a great mind expressing itself in a grand manner will do us a lot of good. To help the beginner through Wesley's Sermons there is provided: (i) For some of the Sermons, a short introductory note, which should first be read: (ii) A statement of the theme of the Sermon, in brief, which should be kept in mind as a leading thought as the Sermon is read: (iii) An explanatory outline. This is a condensation of Wesley's argument, put into modern speech. It should be read paragraph by paragraph with the Sermon. It will point out to the beginner what to look for in each paragraph, if Wesley is to speak for himself to us. At intervals there are the present writer's own comments (*in brackets*) on points which may require further explanation.

SERMON I. SALVATION BY FAITH

The student will observe that this is a real sermon, which was really preached. It is important to remember that this is the case with most of the '*Forty-Four Sermons*', though probably Wesley often employed illustrations and personal applications which are not included in the printed edition. Wesley was able to preach with tremendous interest and effect upon great themes like these, and even in the open-air.

Theme of the Sermon. To explain what the Methodist means by faith, and to answer objections to the Methodist preaching arising from the misunderstandings of conventional Christians.

EXPLANATORY OUTLINE OF THE SERMON

Introduction. (1) Man's creation is a work of divine grace, and (2, 3) so is his salvation.

I. *What Faith is.* (1) In the non-Christian world are to be found those who acknowledge that God is the just law-giver. (2) We may imagine that satanic intelligences can have a complete understanding of theological truth. (3) In the days of His flesh the Apostles sincerely followed Jesus. Saving Christian faith is more than any of these. (4) It acknowledges not merely

God, but God as made known in Jesus Christ. It is a movement of the heart in loving trustful obedience, and not just an intellectual assent. (5) In particular, Christian faith puts its sole hope for salvation in the atoning work of Christ.

(Try to learn the two grand key-passages, in (4) beginning 'it is not barely a speculative . . .' and in (5) 'Christian faith is then . . .'.)

II. *What Salvation is.* (1) Salvation is to be enjoyed now, and not, as some have said, only when we come to heaven. (2) The Christian is saved both from the guilt and the power of sin, alike from the sinful bias in human nature ('original sin'), and from individual sinful acts in which this bias can land him. (3) Man can do nothing to make amends for the guilt of past sin: the Atonement is his sole hope. (4) The Christian reverences God, but does not go in dread of Him, for he has an assurance of his salvation, and his heart is full of peace. However, he does not delude himself that it is impossible for him to fall again. (5) The true believer actually stops sinning, because God has conquered the power of sin also. (6) This victory extends to sinful habits, to individual wilful sinful acts, and to sinful desires as well as outward acts. Various human frailties remain, for which man is genuinely not responsible, but these are not sin. (7) This salvation is described as *Justification* (i.e. 'getting right with God') and as the *New Birth* (i.e. the beginning of a new Christ-like life).

III. *Common Objections to the Methodist Preaching answered.* (The objector in mind is the respectable and conventional churchgoer of the time, who trusts that a reasonable amount of church-attendance and good deeds will 'get him to heaven', who prides himself on his common-sense and who shrinks from Methodism as the fanaticism of perhaps well-intentioned but certainly dangerously deluded men.)

(1) The Gospel of Salvation by Faith does not abolish strict morality, because this sort of Faith is obviously the mainspring of all good works. (2) St. Paul himself had to meet this gross misunderstanding of the true Gospel. (3) The objection is made that this Gospel will lead men into sinful spiritual pride (i.e. those who try to *earn* acceptance with God by their good works know they have not yet attained. These will be modest. Those who know that they are already saved by simple trust in the work of Christ feel that they *have* attained. These are certain to be inflated with conceit!) Wesley agrees that there is a danger here, but those who keep it clearly in mind that their salvation is

entirely undeserved, and that all they deserve is damnation, will be kept from this danger. (4) The Gospel of free forgiveness may indeed make spiritually insensitive men think that God condones sin, but God can keep the sincere in a state of penitence. (5) An objection: 'If you tell men they can earn their own salvation there is something they can do about it. If you tell them they cannot you will plunge them into despair.' Answer: Man *ought* to despair of his own works, but not of God. (6) (By 'uncomfortable' is meant that all this talk of depths of penitence and heights of divine rapture digs men out of their familiar common-sense religion of 'duty to God and the King', and is 'all very disturbing'. This was the key objection to Methodism.) Wesley declares that in the true sense this is a very comfortable Gospel. (7) Objection: 'Salvation by Faith may be true in theory, but is absolutely certain to be misunderstood in these various ways to their own ruin by those who are uninstructed in theology. The Methodist preacher ought to exercise more reserve!' Answer: Indignant rejection of this plea. (8, 9) This doctrine, so misrepresented by many, is actually the corner-stone of the Protestant Reformation (and so of the Church to which the objector himself presumably belongs).

TEST QUESTIONS

1. Why is the study of Theology so important to the preacher?
2. In what ways has God revealed His nature and purpose to His creatures?
3. 'Be of sin the double cure,
   Cleanse me from its guilt and power.'

How does God in Jesus Christ do this, according to Wesley?

STUDY TWO

God's Self-Revelation through Nature

THE Christian Gospel in its fullness rests on the special revelation given through Jesus Christ. We have claimed, however, that God has given a more general revelation of Himself through the world of nature, and to this we now turn.

Many theologians dismiss the insight granted through this channel because, they contend, it gives no knowledge of God's work of redemption. Even though this may be true, it can be replied that: (i) The world of nature, in the light of our growing knowledge, gives us an enlarged conception of God, an additional revelation of His greatness, and ultimately of His nature and character. We see more clearly that He is a God of order, and obtain some insight into His ways of working. We realize, too, the significance of man, and see how the nature of man himself can point to the nature of his Creator. (ii) Some—good-living people amongst them—cannot accept the Christian's belief that Jesus is the Eternal Son of God Incarnate, and that Jesus' own faith in God justifies *our* faith in God. They may sincerely honour Jesus as a man and a teacher of morals. They are unwilling, however, to accept belief in God, arguing that we can never know whether or not God exists—or what He is like if He does exist. If we can produce to these 'agnostics' some evidence from the world of nature that God *is* there behind it all, perhaps we can lead them a little way towards a fuller acceptance of God as we know Him in Christ. (iii) Some people reject all belief in God on the ground that the world of nature denies that He can exist, or that it renders belief in Him unnecessary. The Christian cannot ignore this challenge from the 'atheist'. He must show that the universe does *not* deny the existence of God, but rather affirms it; and so try to remove an intellectual stumbling-block to belief in God and acceptance of the Christian Faith.

One point must be made before we go further. So often, when we speak of 'nature', *we exclude man* and set nature over against him. Mankind, however, is part of nature, and in all our consideration of the issues we must remember that 'nature' includes man with all his powers of thought, feeling and will.

At this point, the strictly logical procedure would be to consider those converging lines of evidence which seem to justify belief in the existence of God. The inherent difficulties of the subject have led us to deal with it in an Appendix (*see* pp. 236f). On your first reading, therefore, you will omit this section, but in your further study you should make yourself familiar with it.

A. THE NATURE OF GOD

Can we learn more from Nature than that God exists? Some would say 'No', and would sweep on one side all that we have been discussing as irrelevant—on the ground that, even if our evidence completely demonstrated the fact that God does exist, it could not give us any knowledge of His character. Is this true?

1. *God is Personal*

The highest point of the creative processes has been reached in the emergence of human personality. This personality is self-conscious. It is endowed with intelligence and will. It can appreciate and make sacrifices for moral issues. It can respond to, seek for, and love truth, beauty and goodness. It can bow in reverence and awe, and know deep rapture and deep sorrow. Where does such a personality come from? Can the Creator be less than what has been created? Is not the very existence of human personality a pointer—and a sure one, too—to the fact that God is *personal*? Otherwise, He could not have created what He did create when He made man.

When we say that God is personal, we do not limit God's nature to those qualities which characterise *human* nature. Divine personality must be infinitely more complex than human personality, and infinitely richer. All the same, our own selves— self-conscious, intelligent, emotional, purposive, ethical selves— are evidence of the nature of the God who created them. This conviction underlies the Old Testament doctrine that we are made in the image of God (Gen. 1[27]), as you will see in later Studies.

To appreciate the fuller conceptions of God's personality which the Christian holds, you must go forward from the world of nature, into that world of insight revealed in the New Testament. There you will begin to understand what the Christian means when he says that, in the mystery of the one Godhead, there are *three* 'persons', Father, Son and Holy Spirit.

2. *The Orderliness of God*

Everything we do in daily life takes for granted the orderliness and dependability of nature. Every day we take this orderliness for granted in countless ways, without giving it a stray thought. We assume that day and night will follow uninterruptedly; that season will follow season, as has always been the case. We assume that foods which we have found wholesome will remain wholesome, and that poison-berries will continue to be poisonous. What would happen, if nature were so capricious that we could not depend on the common metals retaining their properties? If the properties of iron, for example, could not be depended upon, the work of office, factory, school, farm and home would become impossible; transport would disappear, and water could no longer be brought from distant springs and reservoirs. What would happen if the force of gravity ceased to operate, if only for a few seconds? It is obvious that life as we know it depends utterly upon the orderliness and dependability of nature's materials and processes. But orderliness is never the result of caprice or chance; they can only create chaos.

The theist believes that this orderliness and dependability are there because they are part of the character of the Creator of the Universe, God.

Some people would go further, and say that, although God did create the world, the very orderliness He has stamped upon it prevents Him from interfering with the processes of nature. They would hold that the 'laws of nature' are so rigid that He cannot set them aside. Further, they would add, any prayer which begs God to set natural laws on one side is presumptuous and useless.

We need no reminder that many of our prayers cannot be granted, just because they contradict what others are asking God to do. H. E. Fosdick, in *The Meaning of Prayer*, has quoted a parable of the Rabbis which illustrates this. 'A mother had two sons, one a gardener and the other a potter. Said the gardener, "O mother, pray God for rain to water my plants". Said the potter, "O mother, pray God for sunshine to dry my pots". Now the mother loved them equally. Shall she pray for rain or sun?' We have no right to expect God to satisfy every whim or fancy of ours, or to meet our passing needs, irrespective of the needs of others or of His own purposes. If we are Christians, we

22 AN APPROACH TO CHRISTIAN DOCTRINE

must learn to say as Jesus said, 'Not as I will, but as thou wilt' (Mt 26^{39}).

But to argue further and say that God *cannot* use processes which He has created, in order to further His purposes, is surely to ignore the way in which we ourselves use them for our own purposes. A simple illustration will show one use we make of 'natural laws' for our ends. Many features of our English landscape are due to natural agencies; others are due to human agencies. *Natural* agencies have set a formidable hill-barrier down the length of Northern England, the Pennine Chain. Here and there, natural agencies have carved out passes between the blocks of moorlands, as at Stainmore, Skipton and Todmorden. These alone, however, would be quite insufficient to allow modern life to develop as it has done in the great industrial areas which flank the Southern Pennines. Such life is possible because *human* agencies have 'interfered' with the work of nature. Engineers have driven a series of great tunnels beneath the moors at Walsden, Standedge, Woodhead and Dore. They have cut fine roads over what were almost trackless spaces. Our present day life is possible, just because human agencies have supplemented and interfered with the work of nature, and in part have subdued nature to human needs. Or again, natural agencies would leave the Fenlands covered with water, human agencies have transformed them into the richest farm-lands in Britain. Thus, natural forces and agencies do not have uncontrolled sway over our destinies. They are being brought in ever greater measure under human control. Civilised life, indeed, depends upon our growing 'interference' with, and control of natural forces. Now such interference and control are *possible* because 'natural laws' exist and can be depended upon. Such laws are largely descriptions of the behaviour of the many materials which nature gives to us. We cannot use them in defiance of their properties; but once we know these properties, we can use them with confidence and make them our servants. It is because we can depend upon natural laws that the vast fabric of our technical civilisation has been built, and we can use its achievements for our profit, our pleasure, our harm if we are evil, and, be it also said, for the propagation of our religious faith.

If nature's processes are the tools of human wills, how much more must they be the tools of the God who created them! God is not capricious, and will not interfere with nature's processes at the whim of any suppliant. In His wisdom and knowledge, He

GOD'S SELF-REVELATION THROUGH NATURE

is not only able to use them, but He is always so doing. With our limited knowledge, we cannot know more than a very tiny fraction of the forces under His sway, but just as we constantly control and use those we know, so He must always be using the processes of nature which He has created. We cannot be so arrogant as to make our limited knowledge of nature the bounds within which God must work.

B. MIRACLE

God's power to use the natural processes He has created has an important bearing upon our understanding of Miracle. It is sometimes said that 'Miracles can't happen', just because it is assumed that not even God can intervene in the processes of nature and its seemingly unbreakable laws.

Incidentally, if we make this assumption, we are making a veiled and completely unjustifiable one; the assumption that we know all the laws of nature, and can therefore say what can or cannot happen. Of course, that is absurd.

This should lead us to a truer view of what 'natural laws' really are. They are descriptions of what we see happening around us. We can say two things about such descriptions. (i) We can never know finally what the laws of nature really are. Each law the scientist discovers to hold good is one step nearer to the truth, but not necessarily the final truth itself. (ii) The laws are never complete. Our experience is always growing, and with it our discovery of the 'laws of nature', our descriptions of how nature behaves. This means that we can never say that any event is contrary to the laws of nature, however abnormal we may think it to be. It may well be that, as our knowledge widens, much that we have thought to be impossible and abnormal will be taken into it, and be seen to be completely in accordance with the orderly processes of nature.

One further point we must make about natural laws. They do not exist apart from God. They are descriptions of the way He works. They express some part of His Being. God does not come into the world of events only in miracles, in unusual events. He is always there. The devout spirit will not therefore look for God in the strange and unusual happenings, but in the normal events of life. These can be, in the truest sense, miraculous.

It follows that, when we come to the record of some event which is claimed to be miraculous, we do not immediately deny that it could have happened. On the other hand, we do not claim that this could be the only channel through which God was working out His purpose. We take the record and try to assess the reliability of the witnesses. If their trustworthiness seems assured, we are compelled to take seriously the belief that God has used natural processes which are known to us and *unknown*, to shape events to His will (*see ANT, para.* 120).

As we try to assess the reliability of the reports, we have to take into account that bias towards the marvellous which many people have, because of which they tend to exaggerate the marvellous elements in even ordinary happenings. There are 'gospels' which were never admitted by the Church into its Canon of Scripture. They show a very marked tendency to exaggerate the wonderful things which Jesus did. By their standards, the four Canonical Gospels are sober works indeed! The same tendency *may* have affected some of the records of Biblical miracles.

More important, however, is the fact that *unique* events have taken place in the past, which have convinced those who witnessed them that God had intervened on their behalf, when human foresight could not have expected what came to pass. The Jew points to the deliverance of the Hebrews from the bondage of Egypt, and especially the salvation of the Hebrew hosts at the crossing of the Red Sea, as the greatest of such unique events. The Christian points to the Incarnation of the Son of God, and to the resurrection of Jesus from the dead.

Now for such unique events, we depend for our knowledge, first upon the eye-witnesses, and then upon the records of those who subsequently wrote down and transmitted the claims of the eye-witnesses. We cannot, with our limited knowledge, assume what could or could not have happened and then judge the records by our assumptions. We must accept and carefully examine the reports we have received.

The most important aspect of any event believed to be miraculous is, however, not that it happens. It is that the devout soul who experiences it believes that in it God has acted in such a way as to meet his immediate need, especially when the suppliant has cried for help in some deep distress. To the perceptive soul, such an event becomes a 'sign', filling him with adoration and awe.

This awareness, that God has acted immediately towards us, transforms what might seem to be only fortunate coincidences into miracles. The fact that such coincidences occur, and that the reverent soul finds God meeting his deepest needs through them, is sufficient token to him that the events are miraculous. Miracles, then, are not forbidden by stringent, overriding natural laws which God cannot 'break'. Nature lies under the hand of God, its Creator, who is always working in and through it. We cannot set limits to the ways in which He can use the powers He has created.

Further, common events can truly be miraculous, even though we have lost the sense of wonder at them, because they are so common. The birth of a child is a miracle for the devout parent. The renewal of life at spring-time is a yearly miracle for the sincere worshipper of God. The mystery of renewing life lies beyond our understanding, but, under God, it ministers to our needs and possibilities and responsibilities. It ought to be 'miraculous' to us, arousing our awe and reverent gratitude.

C. THE PROVIDENCE OF GOD

When we speak of God's Providence, we mean His direction of the worlds of nature and men to the ends He has purposed. More loosely, and quite unjustifiably, we often think of Providence in relation to our desires and prayers, and whether or not these are granted. A true doctrine of Providence must be expressed in terms of God's purposes, and not our own. Anticipating what will be said in *Study Twelve* on the Last Things, we can here say that God's supreme purpose for each of us is that we should grow in spiritual stature, through good event and ill, until we enter into unbroken communion with Him in Christ. Beyond the purpose God has for the individual, we believe that He also has a purpose for society; that all men and women should be bound to each other in Christian love, even as they are bound to God in Christ.

When, therefore, we consider God's Providence, we are really facing the question whether God can and does control the life of the world in such a way as to accomplish the ends He desires. Particularly, we face the problem of the physical evils which He allows to exist. These evils will be considered more fully in the next section. At the moment, we must affirm certain principles.

a. *God's purposes for us are spiritual and moral.* 'All things work together for *good* to them that love God'—not 'goods'. Christianity asserts that good can never be wholly defined in terms of material prosperity or physical well-being. This is not to say that we should not thank God for such gifts.

b. *God is working in and through the world* of natural processes and events, even where we cannot perceive His working. As we have shown, these processes are His, and so far from shutting out the possibility of His action, they are His ways of working. He has the power to control nature, whether in answer to human prayers or not. Yet human prayers and desires must always be subject to His supreme purposes.

c. *The world of nature is one in which our moral and spiritual growth is possible.* Men and women could not grow in moral stature if they had to make no effort, if they had no difficulties to surmount, if their endurance was never challenged. Because they live in a world where they have to co-operate with and use nature's processes to satisfy daily needs, where there are difficulties to surmount and demands to be met, they find in nature a fit setting for the development of moral and spiritual strength.

d. *In the interplay of human life, it is possible for one to influence another*; by precept, by example, by deed, by friendship. In slight measure, we each exercise such influence—some slight degree of sovereignty—over others. What limits, then, can we set to the influence which God can bring to bear upon us? There is mystery here, as indeed there always is in the influence of one soul upon another, but the fact remains; God can and does influence men and women, and thus direct their efforts, stumbling and wayward though they often are, to His ends.

Once more, we must affirm that the final purposes of God are spiritual. They may at times demand from us the sacrifice of material well-being and many of the things which we call 'good'. At such moments of renunciation, especially, we can only apprehend God's spiritual purposes when we love Him, as trustful children love their parents.

D. PHYSICAL EVILS

We cannot leave the consideration of what nature may teach us concerning God, without facing the fact that it contains evil things which seem to many to deny either that God exists, or that He can be good, or that He can be a God of power.

First, however, we must recognize that evils can be divided into two kinds. Some arise from our own motives and actions; they are 'active' or 'moral' evils. The Christian answer to the problems set by this kind of evil will be considered when we turn

GOD'S SELF-REVELATION THROUGH NATURE

to consider sin and grace. Other evils press upon us from outside, and it is these, the 'passive' or 'physical' evils, which present the gravest problems. Can they be reconciled with the goodness of God, or His providential care over His children? Some of the most important and pressing of these problems must now be considered.

a. *The moral neutrality of Nature* is held by some (earnest Christians amongst them) to be an evil thing. The natural world, they say, is indifferent to human deserts, and therefore is evil. But (i) Jesus saw in this fact a token of God's beneficence (Mt 5^{45}). (ii) If natural processes were not the same for everybody, whatever their moral character, they would cease to be dependable. Our normal existence would become impossible. The moral neutrality of nature, the fact that God does not vary natural processes in order to punish the sinner or reward the saint, is not a bad thing, but a good. (iii) God would only receive 'cupboard love', if He measured out rewards or punishments through natural agencies. (iv) Virtue would cease to be virtue, and would become a matter of mere prudent calculation of what it would best pay a man to be and do. (v) Who, in God's sight, would be fully deserving? What jealousies and resentments would be roused, even among the faithful, if each only received the due reward of his own deeds! (vi) The solidarity of the human race must always be remembered. Saints and sinners are so mixed up cheek by jowl in ordinary life, that it is absurd to expect God to reward or punish each individual through the working of natural forces. We conclude that the moral neutrality of nature is the only possible background for daily existence.

b. *Human suffering* presents a much more serious problem. With it we must link in thought the closely related problem of *disease*.

(i) In part, suffering and disease are due to human *ignorance*. But before we assert that this is evil in itself, we must bear certain facts in mind. First, knowledge alone is not necessarily good, nor does it of necessity remove suffering or disease. The horrors of war, in particular, show us that we seek for knowledge partly to inflict suffering upon others. We know, too, that people often persist in sinning, even though they know that thereby they are likely to contract disease or experience suffering. The moral problem is not therefore settled by saying that ignorance is evil and knowledge is good. Again, the only logical alternative to a world in which there is ignorance would seem to be one in which everybody has complete and infallible knowledge. God, however, has given us the ability to search for knowledge, rather than knowledge itself, and thus has made possible our continuous growth in mental and spiritual stature.

(ii) Suffering and disease are inevitable because, in the wisdom of God, we live in *closest fellowship* with one another. In our common Christian speech, we are members one of another. We often resent this fact, and ask 'Why should the innocent suffer from the actions of the guilty?' Put in this form, the question is unfair in that it takes into account only half the facts. It ignores another question of equal importance: 'Why should the undeserving benefit from the deeds of the good?' Every day our lives are enriched by the labours of countless other people, in all parts of the world and in all occupations and stations. Why should this be? Let us be honest and realistic. If we complain because we suffer from the evil deeds of others, but are eager to lose none of the benefits which come to us through the activity of others, we can hardly be said to be adopting a moral attitude. If we want to share the blessings of our common life, we must be prepared to share its sorrows. If we clearly realize the communal nature of our lives, we shall find in it a challenge to moral responsibility. We shall try to help the young and aged, and to support the weak; we shall keep our social conscience alert, and quicken it in others; we shall discipline ourselves, and influence others to accept such self-discipline—so that the sum of suffering is not increased, but rather the common good is made greater.

(iii) Suffering and disease come, too, when we *break the laws* of nature and the moral law, by our own sinful and foolish actions. We cannot condemn nature or its Creator for this. The good life is only possible if evil consequences follow the breaking of such laws, however long retribution may be in coming (*see* Ps. 73).

(iv) What we have said does not remove our conviction that suffering and disease are evil; but we must make one further point. What happens to us is not so important as is *our attitude* to what happens. Suffering matters; what matters more is how we bear it. Our courage, our selfless regard for others who are also in distress, our strength of faith in the face of suffering, our refusal to allow the happiness of others to be overshadowed by our sorrows, can bring a moral good out of evil circumstances. How often the story of disaster, on a small or large scale, is also the story of the selfless heroism of men and women.

Yet all this falls far short of the Christian answer to the problem of suffering. For that we must look forward, from what we find in the realm of nature to what is given us in the realm of grace.

c. *The fact of Death* is regarded by many as the greatest of evils. There are many reasons for such a judgement. Death comes prematurely; it separates loved ones; it leaves so many weak ones helpless in the face of adversity; it underlines the seeming wastefulness of nature's processes, in that she creates only to destroy; it thrusts us into a future which is dreaded because it is unknown; it threatens us with personal extinction.

Can nature give us any confidence in the face of the grim spectre of Death? We have seen reason to believe that the Creator has not only made moral and rational creatures, but that He Himself must also be moral and rational; that He is a dependable God, in whom we can put our trust. Now He has given us strong aspirations after communion with Himself. Are these aspirations, so imperfectly satisfied in this life, to have no fuller satisfaction in a life beyond death? Whatever purpose God had in mind for us when He created us, is it reasonable to suppose that that purpose will be realized at the end of our three score years and ten? May we not hope that this life is only a preparation for a life which lies beyond the hampering restrictions of our transcience and mortality?

But here again we must admit that that revelation of Himself and of His purposes which God has given us through the world of nature is quite inadequate to answer our questions. Death will still have its sting, and the grave its victory, until we can sing,

> *Jesus lives! thy terrors now*
> *Can, O death, no more appal us;*
> *Jesus lives! by this we know*
> *Thou, O grave, canst not enthral us.*
> *Hallelujah!* (*MHB* 216)

CONCLUSION

In this Study, we have considered God's self-revelation through nature, and have examined some of the problems which nature presents to faith. We have barely entered the porch of Christian Theology, for that is chiefly based upon the revelation given in the history of the Old and New Israel, as interpreted by prophets and apostles, and recorded for us in Scripture. In the world of nature, we have found evidence that God exists; evidence, too, as to His nature, though the knowledge we have gained from this source is only fragmentary. We have discussed the meaning and possibility of Miracle, and of God's Providence, and have given some consideration to the problem of physical evil.

Now we shall move forward to that special revelation of Himself which God has given in His Mighty Acts in history, as recorded in Scripture. Belief in God becomes not merely a judgement of the mind, but the constant self-committal of the devout soul. Our knowledge of God's nature becomes transformed when we see Him through the eyes of prophets and apostles, and especially when we see Him in the person of Jesus Christ. We come face to face with the supreme Miracle of history; the life, death and resurrection of Jesus. In Him, too, we seek and find the answer of the Christian Faith to the challenge of both moral and physical evil.

SERMON II. 'THE ALMOST CHRISTIAN'

Theme of the Sermon. The Christian religion is a complete change of heart worked by God in Christ, and not merely a system of morals. This is enforced from Wesley's own experience.

EXPLANATORY OUTLINE OF THE SERMON

I. *A Portrait of the 'Almost Christian'* (i.e., of the very good man whose goodness does not spring straight out of a conscious experience of 'the heart strangely warmed'). (1) The 'Almost Christian' is honest and just, as is the virtuous non-Christian. (2) Similarly, he is truthful, and (3) 'helps lame dogs over stiles'. (4) He lives a life of earnest personal morality. (5) He is sober and peaceable. (6) He puts himself to considerable trouble and self-sacrifice in his good deeds, and to these adds earnest Christian work. (7) He is a regular and attentive Churchgoer, a penitent and serious communicant. (8) He practises family religion. (9) The 'Almost Christian' is sincere in all this. He does not pursue good merely to avoid punishment or disgrace. (The Latin poet quoted is Horace, upon whom Wesley is unduly severe.) (10) He is moved by a sincere desire to be of use to God. (11) (Wesley now acknowledges that his audience is by this time gasping!) Is it possible for so good a man to be anything less than an excellent Christian? (12,13) Wesley discloses that his 'Almost Christian' is a portrait of himself as he was before the experience of 'the heart strangely warmed'. (Consider the tremendous power and moving human appeal of this climax. Many in the Oxford Congregation would remember the Wesley of a few years before, with his strict and zealous companions in 'The Holy Club'.)

II. *The Religion of the Heart.* (1) The 'Altogether Christian' has his heart filled with the love of God, so that his chief delight is in communion with God. (2) As he loves God, so he loves his neighbour, that is, all mankind, including evil men and his enemies. (3) The root whence this love springs is faith. (4) The Anglican Homily *On the Salvation of Man* is quoted to show that saving faith is not merely acceptance of Christian truth ('the faith of a devil'), but is also a movement of the heart and will to repentance, love and good works. (5) Continuation, to show that faith is a trust in the saving work of Christ. (Note that Wesley speaks as one still within the Church of England. Here, and elsewhere in the Sermons, 'our own Church' is the Church of England.) (6) Those who have this faith, which purifies the character, and impels to all manner of heroic service, are 'Altogether Christians'. (7) The challenge: Are the hearers even 'Almost Christians'? Are they outwardly righteous? (8) They have never sincerely intended even this. (9) But even the best of intentions to be a Christian are nothing worth without the gift of 'the faith that works by love'. (10) The summons to self-realization, and to prayer for this gift.

TEST QUESTIONS

1. What would you reply to the man who says, 'Prove to me that there *is* a God, and I'll listen to your Gospel about a divine Jesus'?

2. Can we accept the Orderliness of Nature, and at the same time believe in Miracle and Providence?

3. Outline the character of the 'Almost Christian'.

STUDY THREE

God in the Old Testament

A. THE RULING CONCEPTION OF GOD

THE Old Testament tells us how, generation by generation, God revealed Himself to the Chosen Race, and through Israel to the world (on Revelation *see* pp. 6-9). On a casual reading of the Old Testament, the value of this self-revelation in the early days is not easy to grasp. We do not feel helped, for instance, by the conception of a God who made a murderous attack on Moses and was only appeased when his wife circumcised their son (Exod. 4^{24-6}), or by the custom of 'devotion' whereby all the inhabitants of an enemy city were slain because they were dedicated to God (*see* Deut. 2^{34} and 1 Sam. 15); and there are similar primitive ideas implied in other stories quite late into Old Testament times. The matter would be more easily dealt with if we could arrange the literature in its chronological order, and then find that all the primitive ideas occur at the beginning of the time-sequence, and that all the lofty conceptions were universally acknowledged by the end—but this is not so. Parts of the books which relate to the earliest times are (in their present form) among the latest Old Testament productions, but retain much primitive material; and some of the finest ideas emerge very early on, and then give way to others of a less worthy nature. Or again, a prophet may be far in advance of his times in one aspect of his thinking, and lag well behind it in another. We must not think of a uniform progression, nor must we forget that regression often took place as well. But generally it is true to say that, as the generations passed, the grosser and more primitive ideas were driven out by loftier conceptions of God and of His purposes in history.

God revealed Himself to Abraham and the patriarchs as a God of Covenant and of Promise, but the Old Testament always emphasizes that God revealed Himself most significantly in His great act of redemption at the Exodus. Then it was that Moses knew Him to be Living and Redemptive (Exod. 3^{13-17}). This revelation of His character was constantly renewed in fresh

GOD IN THE OLD TESTAMENT

redeeming acts; yet it had to struggle to hold its place in men's minds alongside older and quite incompatible beliefs. Because, however, the Hebrews were constantly being pointed back to the Exodus, the knowledge of God as Living and Redemptive was characteristic of their ideas of God from the time of Moses onwards, and in time it transformed all their thinking. We are to notice seven profound convictions which are basic to the thought of the Old Testament, which were endorsed and deepened by Jesus, and are part of our Christian understanding of God to this day.

1. *God is Personal*

We all recognize the profound difference between 'people' and 'things'. People are able to think, feel, plan, and carry out their purposes; things have no such powers. We have this difference in mind when we use the adjective 'personal', and it will help us to understand what is meant when we refer to God as 'personal'. We mean that He possesses the qualities and powers that belong to 'people' rather than to 'things'; but, of course, in an infinite degree. (What you have already read in *Study Two*, and what you will learn from later Studies, will show you that, when we say that God is 'personal', we do not mean that He is a *person*, with the definite limitations of a person; God is much more than a person. For the time being, however, as you turn to the picture of God in the Old Testament, you need only remember what we *do* mean when we say that God is 'personal'.)

The Hebrew people believed in a living, personal God. Their faith is reflected in the special name by which they knew Him (*see AOT* on *Exodus*). This was probably pronounced YAHWEH (or JAHVEH). In the years after the Exile, the name was regarded as being altogether too sacred to be spoken by the lips of mortal man, and a more ordinary word was substituted for it. When it came to writing, the Hebrews had no vowels and simply used the consonants of the divine name (YHWH or JHVH). In course of time, in the sixth to seventh century A.D., when vowels were added to the text of the Old Testament, the scribes combined the vowels of the *ordinary* name for God with the consonants of the *sacred* name, and gave us the hybrid word JEHOVAH, which is used in our Old Testament. In this book, and like most modern writers, we shall use the word YAHWEH. But what is important is the meaning which the word had for the Hebrews. When Yahweh revealed Himself to Moses at the

Burning Bush, He gave His name as 'I am what I am'; or, more correctly, 'I will be what I will be'. By this He meant that, as one person slowly reveals his character to another through the ordinary intercourse of life, so He would show more and more fully to successive generations what He really was, and what He could do.

Thus the Old Testament tells of the relationship between a personal God and His people. In the early days, according to the stories enshrined in *Genesis*, men thought of God as little more than a glorified human being. He walked in the Garden of Eden in the cool of the evening, and suspected Adam and his wife of disobedience because they hid from Him (Gen. 3[8]). He repented of having created man and took measures to destroy him (Gen. 6[13]). He came down to see the tower which men in their presumption had built at Babel (Gen. 11[5]). He paid a personal visit to Abraham as if He were a fellow sheikh (Gen. 18[1]). The tendency to picture God on a purely human level is referred to as *anthropomorphism*. This early stage was soon left behind. When we come to the prophets, we find them insisting that Yahweh was far more than merely man. 'I am God and not man' (Hos. 11[9]). 'To whom then will ye liken God?' cries Isaiah of Babylon, and the answer is that there is no adequate likeness of God whatsoever (Isa. 40[18]). At the same time, the prophetic emphasis is upon God's *personal* qualities. So Hosea writes, 'When Israel was a child, then I loved him, and called my son out of Egypt. As I called them, so they went away from me. . . . Yet I taught Ephraim to walk; I took them on my arms; but they knew not that I healed them. I drew them with cords of a man, with bands of love; and I was to them as they that take off the yoke on their jaws, and I laid meat before them' (Hos. 11[1-4]). Only a personal God could have an intelligible purpose for His world. Only a personal God could move to redeem men from the bondage of evil into which they had got entangled. The personal nature of God lies at the very heart of Old Testament religion, as of Christianity.

2. *God is Holy*

When we speak of 'holiness', we think at once of moral purity, but this was not the original meaning of the word. A thing was described as 'holy' when men felt there was some mysterious quality about it, some unknown power in the presence of which they were wise to walk warily. In this sense, the God of the

Israelites was from the beginning thought to be 'holy'. He was separated from ordinary men and women, remote from the ordinary levels of humanity, inaccessible, and possessed of power that was beyond their understanding. Those who did not walk circumspectly in His presence were liable to suffer some evil. It was not fitting that they should come near Him when defiled by their ordinary pursuits, or His 'holiness' might be offended. Hence the various regulations as to what constituted 'cleanness', and as to how those who were 'unclean' could be made fit to approach their God. As the Israelites came to see the righteousness and love of God, they did not lose the fear of His holiness. Indeed they came to believe that it was the infinite and mysterious quality of His righteousness and love that separated Him from mortal men. Isaiah of Jerusalem repeatedly emphasises the 'holiness' of God. He is high and lifted up, and may not be approached without a wholesome sense of awe and reverence. The record of the prophet's call in Isa. 6 stresses this aspect of God's character. The worshipper cannot realize that he is in the divine presence without a profound humility and conviction of his own unworthiness. He must be cleansed before he can become God's messenger.

The result of the Exile was to increase the emphasis upon the divine Holiness. As we have noticed, 'Yahweh' became too sacred a name to be used by men. A name was regarded as being very closely related to its bearer, and the name of a deity possessed something of His power and character. Because the God of Israel was so holy, no human lips were pure enough to utter His special name. In another way, we see the heightened sense of the holiness of God in the days after the Exile. It increased the sense of distance between God and man. Dwelling in the heaven of heavens, He was too remote, too far off, to have intimate and immediate dealings with His subjects. There was need, therefore, for various intermediaries, through whom He could establish relations with men, and we get frequent mention of Angels, Wisdom, the Spirit of Yahweh, and the Word of God —agents through whom God could approach the earth. At the same time, the position of the priest grew in importance, since it was through him that ordinary people could hope to approach the divine Holiness.

Though we have come to think of God as the Father of our Lord Jesus Christ, a healthy religion should preserve this sense of awe and respect in the presence of God.

3. *God is Righteous*

From the time of Moses, the Israelites had at least a rudimentary idea that theirs was a God of righteousness. He made moral demands upon them. The Covenant between Yahweh and themselves committed them to a loyalty to His will, and if part of this obligation was simply the maintenance of correct ritual and ceremony, it did also include the necessity of behaving towards each other in a morally right way. The second half of the Ten Commandments are plainly ethical in character. God made moral demands because He was a God of righteousness. We can trace this element in the revelation of the divine character, as it grows stronger in the course of time. When Nathan the prophet rebuked David for a moral fault (2 Sam. 12[1-15]; *see AOT*), it was in the name of Yahweh. On the same authority, Elijah waxed indignant over the affair of Naboth's vineyard (1 Kgs 21[1-16]; *see AOT*). The great writing prophets sought to bring home in the most compelling way the truth of the divine righteousness. Amos, in particular, hammered away at the certainty of God's justice. No amount of ceremonial worship could excuse a people who failed to live as God desired, and that meant embodying in their conduct the principles of brotherhood and social rightness. No position of privilege in the divine scheme of things could avert the punishment that would fall upon a nation that allowed unethical practices to flourish in their midst, and persisted in inhumanity and oppression. After Amos, all the prophetic voices of Israel took his message for granted, as something beyond question. Because He Himself was a righteous God, Yahweh would not accept offerings from His subjects, unless they were accompanied by moral living and sincere repentance. (For another aspect of the Righteousness of God—His saving activity—*see ANT, para.* 450, and N. H. Snaith's *Distinctive Ideas of the Old Testament*, p. 70f.)

4. *God is Love*

The Hebrews were the Chosen People of God, and therefore it was natural for them to believe that He had a special care for them. Provided that they carried out their part of the Covenant agreement, He would look after them, and bring them prosperity and success. Beginning with this idea of a contract, we see God slowly disclosing the richer qualities of His love. Hosea, through the experience of his broken marriage, was taught to see his unchanging love for his erring wife as a reflection of the divine love for sinful Israel. God cared for His children, even when they were disloyal to their side of the Covenant. 'How can I give thee up, Ephraim?' (Hos. 11^8). As Hosea himself had to find a way of restoring his wife, and, by some form of discipline, of winning her from her waywardness, so the love of God could not be satisfied until it had found a way of redeeming Israel. A favourite Old Testament word is the 'lovingkindness' of God. It indicates His continued faithfulness to His covenant-people, and His steadfast determination never entirely to let them go. 'I will betroth thee unto me for ever; yea, I will betroth thee unto me in righteousness and in judgment, and in lovingkindness, and in mercies' (Hos. 2^{19}).

This love of God is not a contradiction of the divine righteousness. The two qualities belong together. It is right that God should express His grace and forgiveness towards Israel, because He is a God of love. On the other hand, since He is righteous, His love never degenerates into a soft indulgence. His concern is always to win His children back to right ways of living. Amos and Hosea, in fact, preach the same message, though each emphasises his own particular aspect of the vision of the divine character.

5. *There is only One God*

When, under Moses' leadership, the Hebrews were delivered from the bondage of Egypt, they accepted Yahweh as their national god, but this did not preclude the idea that other nations might worship other gods. Rather, it was taken for granted that it would be so. Melkart, for instance, was accepted as the god of Tyre, Chemosh as the god of Moab, and the Baalim as the gods of the Canaanite tribes of Palestine. This worship of one God out of many was known as 'monolatry'. In the first centuries of the settlement in Canaan (*see AOT* on *Judges*), a long and stiff battle had to be fought to prevent the Israelites from combining Baal worship with the worship of Yahweh, and so losing the distinctiveness of the revelation which was being given to them.

In theory, the way for Yahweh to demonstrate His supremacy over other gods was to lead His people to victory over the people of His rivals. But, in point of fact, Israel was defeated again and again. Onlookers might interpret this as the defeat of Yahweh, the sign of His impotence. Nevertheless, at the time of Israel's greatest disasters, when all her finest people had been carried off into exile in Babylon, and Jerusalem lay a heap of rubble, her great prophets were led to see that, far from being vanquished, Yahweh was greater even than the most powerful of His rivals. Indeed, that He was the *Only God*. He, and He alone, was the Sovereign of all the earth. We owe the recognition of this tremendous truth especially to the unknown prophet whom we refer to as Isaiah of Babylon. 'Before me there was no God formed, neither shall there be after me' (Isa. 43^{10}; *see AOT*). In Christian doctrine, we sometimes describe this conviction as the Unity or the Solitariness of God, or as Monotheism.

6. *God is the Creator of all things*

The Old Testament has a very simple picture of the world, but it proclaims the conviction that it was created by God. The opening chapters declare this faith. The two accounts of the Creation (*see AOT*) differ from each other in style and spirit, but they are one in their belief that the world, and everything in it, was made by Yahweh. Whilst the oldest strand in the Pentateuch, the 'J' tradition, in its story of the Garden of Eden, says that Yahweh made earth and heaven, and formed man of the dust of the ground (Gen. 2$^{4, 7}$), it would seem that the conception of God as the Creator of all things did not come into prominence, or have much practical significance, until a late stage of Hebrew history. The idea lay, as it were, dormant until the period of the Exile. Then the preaching of Deutero-Isaiah made it one of the cardinal beliefs of Hebrew religion. Indeed, it was the logical outcome of his monotheism. The vision of the One God of all mankind carried with it the clear thought of Him as the Creator of all things (*see* Isa. 40$^{12-26}$, 41$^{18-20}$, 45^{7}).

We owe to the Priests, who were influenced by the teaching of Deutero-Isaiah, the second account of the Creation of the world (Gen. 1–2^{3}). No doubt, during their captivity, they had listened to Babylonian accounts of how things had come into being. Amongst them was the story which told how Marduk, one of the many gods of Babylon, overcame the goddess Tiamat, who represented the primeval chaos, and so created the world and man. Possibly this very story stimulated the Hebrew priests to give their own version of the Creation, and to proclaim their confident belief that it was all the work of the one true God, whom they worshipped as their fathers had. They saw a transcendent God, standing above and beyond nature, fashioning it stage by stage, according to His plan, and finally creating man as the crown of His activity. 'In the beginning God created' (Gen. 1^{1}).

Similar thoughts of God as the Creator are found in the Psalms (e.g. 8, 19, 24). We Christians share this faith that our world, indeed the whole universe, is a mighty Act of God.

7. *God is the God of all Nations*

This conviction in its fulness springs from the belief in the Unity or Solitariness of God. If there is only one God, He must needs be the God of all nations. This truth was only slowly revealed to the Israelites. To begin with, they thought of Him as their tribal God, who, provided they were obedient to Him, would protect them, guide their adventures, and give them victory in war. After their settlement in Palestine, a religious crisis arose. Ought they to offer worship to the Baals of the land, in order to secure fertility for their crops? They thought they could do this, whilst retaining their worship of Yahweh. The issue was solved by their recognition that such mixed worship was unnecessary, because Yahweh did in fact possess all the powers and attributes of the local gods. Israel's sin was that she attributed to the Baalim what had in fact been part of Yahweh's gift to His people. 'She did not know that I gave her the corn, and the wine, and the oil, and multiplied unto her silver and gold which they used for Baal. Therefore will I take back my corn in the time thereof, and my wine in the season thereof, and will pluck away my wool and my flax which should have covered her nakedness' (Hos. 2[8, 9]).

Yahweh was the God of the Canaanites as well as of the Hebrews. A prophet like Amos represented Yahweh as ruling the surrounding nations. This is implicit in his condemnation of them for their sins (Amos 1, 2) and in 9[7] ('Are ye not as the children of the Ethiopians unto me?'). Isaiah of Jerusalem treated the growing power of Assyria as an instrument which Yahweh would use for the discipline of His own people. 'Ho Assyria, the rod of mine anger' (Isa. 10[5]).

The Exile raised the question of the relationship of Yahweh to other nations more acutely. Under prophetic guidance, the Hebrews came to see that He was the God of the whole world. His will was operative for all peoples. He would use Cyrus the Persian as His agent, both for the defeat of Babylon and the rescue of Israel. 'Thus saith Yahweh to his anointed, to Cyrus. . . . I will give thee the treasures of darkness, and hidden riches of secret places (i.e. the wealth of Babylon). . . . For Jacob my servant's sake, and Israel my chosen, I have called thee by thy name' (in order to make possible the Return to Jerusalem. Isa. 45[1-4]).

With this belief came a sense of Israel's evangelical mission. Israel had received the revelation of a universal religion, and with it a call to be the agent of the universal God and His purpose of redeeming all mankind. 'I will give thee for a light to the Gentiles, that thou mayest be my salvation unto the ends of the earth' (Isa. 49[6]). Israel did not, as we do today, send missionaries throughout the world, to convert men from all nations to the true faith. Rather, her leaders believed it to be their task to maintain at Jerusalem religion at its highest degree of purity and strength. In time, people of every nation and race would turn to the Holy City, seeking for knowledge of the One True God. 'The Lord shall arise upon thee, and his glory shall be seen upon thee. And nations shall come to thy light, and kings to the brightness of thy rising' (Isa. 60[2, 3]).

B. THE SEARCH FOR REDEMPTION

The Old Testament has more to tell us than its record of God's gradual self-disclosure to men. From the beginning, human disobedience and sin created an estrangement between God and His people. The central problem of Hebrew religion was, 'How can what has gone wrong be put right?' Sensitive men were only too painfully aware of the necessity of *redemption*, and they looked to their religion to show them how it could be accomplished.

The meaning of 'redemption' will be more fully discussed in later *Studies*. Here we need only say that, in Old Testament times, the word 'redeem' was used to indicate the payment of a price to secure some sort of release. A man might buy back a kinsman from slavery (Lev. 25[48]), or make a suitable compensation for a broken taboo (Exod. 21[30]), or retain for his own use a firstling which belonged to God (Exod. 34[20]). The emphasis was not so much upon the price paid, the method of redemption, as upon the release secured. The Hebrews recognized that, because of their sinfulness, their disobedience to the will of God, they were as those in bondage. They had to suffer the material hardships and disasters which were the results of their rebellion; and as time went on, they became increasingly conscious of their guilt and spiritual impoverishment. How could they get release? They could not liberate themselves; therefore they must look to God.

In the Old Testament, we see God gradually revealing to men the way of redemption. The full answer to the problem of human sinfulness came, of course, in Christ. But to the Hebrew people were given glimpses and premonitions of what God was to do for mankind in Jesus Christ.

1. *Redemption by the provision of a Better Covenant*

a. Abraham, Isaac, Jacob, and those descended from them, were bound to God by a simple covenant. Yahweh undertook to look after the Patriarchs if they acted according to His direction. The initiative in the making of this covenant came from God, and may even be regarded as a command. In Gen. 15^{18} we find the terms of the Covenant as recorded in the J document: 'In that day the Lord made a covenant with Abram, saying, Unto thy seed have I given this land, from the river of Egypt unto the great river, the river Euphrates'. It seems that this covenant was sealed by passing between divided animals. P's account is in Gen. 17$^{7-9}$: 'I will establish my covenant between me and thee and thy seed after thee. . . . As for thee, thou shalt keep my covenant, thou, and thy seed after thee throughout their generations'. The practice of circumcision was instituted as a token of the obedience pledged by Abraham in this covenant. *Genesis* makes it clear that both sides fulfilled the terms of the agreement. Yahweh's guidance and protection were given to the Fathers of Israel, and none of the Patriarchs is reported to have disobeyed God. Their loyal obedience is typified in Abraham's willingness to sacrifice Isaac at the divine command. Therefore the relationship between Yahweh and them is regarded as unimpaired. (We must remember, of course, that we are here dealing with an idealised account of the nation's ancestors, who are seen in the rosiest light.)

b. Moses entered, or re-entered, into the covenant relationship with God on behalf of the children of Israel at Sinai. 'And he took the book of the covenant, and read in the audience of the people: and they said, All that the Lord hath spoken will we do, and be obedient' (Exod. 24^7). Blood was sprinkled, partly on the altar, partly on the people, in ratification of their promise. The Ten Commandments, which were both ritual and moral in character, were a statement of the demands made upon the people by Yahweh. Later they were expanded into the Book of the Covenant (Exod. 20^{22}–23^{33}), and still later revised and developed as the Code of Deuteronomy, and the Holiness Code of Lev. 17-26. *Deuteronomy* explicitly brings out both sides of the Covenant. 'Thou hast avouched (acknowledged) Yahweh this day to be thy God, and that thou shouldest walk in his ways. . . . And Yahweh hath avouched thee this day to be a peculiar people unto himself, as he hath promised thee' (Deut. 26[17, 18]). From this time onwards, there is no doubt about the continued disobedience of the people of God. In spite of the recall to obedience in the message of all their prophets, the nation persistently failed to keep both the moral and the ritual regulations of the Covenant.

c. It was given to Jeremiah to conceive the idea of a New Covenant between Yahweh and His people. Probably after witnessing the failure of Josiah's reformation, he was driven to conclude that, human nature being what it was, men and women needed a change of heart before they would be loyal to God. Therefore he outlined a New Covenant, made, not between Yahweh and the nation as a whole, but with individuals. The stress was not on an outward conformity to moral and ritual laws, but on the necessity for God to dwell in men's hearts to give them moral and spiritual insight, and to create in them a love of the divine will and an eagerness to obey it. 'Behold the days come, saith Yahweh, that I will make a new covenant with the house of Israel, and with the house of Judah; not according to the covenant that I made with their fathers in the day that I took them by the hand to bring them out of the land of Egypt; which my covenant they brake, although I was an husband unto them, saith Yahweh. But this is the covenant that I will make . . . I will put my law in their inward parts, and in their heart will I write it; and I will be their God, and they shall be my people' (Jer. 31[31-33]).

This New Covenant of the heart does point the way whereby redemption is possible, but Jesus Christ had to come to make such a spiritual change a reality for men.

2. *Redemption by Reconciliation effected between God and man.*

Because of his sinfulness, man needed help in order to effect a reconciliation with the God he had disobeyed, to make him 'at-one' with Yahweh.

a. In Israel, the business of *the priest* was to give this help. He was the holy person who approached God on behalf of men. He stood in contrast to the prophet, who approached men on behalf of God. When Israel first settled in Palestine, each village had its own shrine, at which the priest carried out the ritual of religion. In *Judges*, for instance, we are told that Micah, an Ephraimite, consecrated one of his own sons to act as priest to the family (17^5). In course of time, however, the priesthood came to be confined to those who were descended from Levi. The priest's first function was to enquire the will of Yahweh on behalf of the people, which was usually done by using the 'ephod' (1 Sam. $23^{6\text{-}12}$). Their business was also to offer the sacrifices on behalf of the people. This side of their work became more and more predominant. After the reformation of Josiah, the priesthood was centred at Jerusalem, and the village priests became subordinate helpers in the service of the Temple. The Exile resulted in a much more elaborate ritual in Hebrew religion, and the priest thus became still more important. The priesthood was regarded as 'holy', that is to say, 'set apart', according to the ceremonial laws, in order to represent men before God, and it found its fullest expression in the person of the High Priest.

b. *The system of Sacrifices* arose from the desire to please God and establish a good relationship with Him. In the early days, it was thought that, when they were burnt upon the altar, the gifts of the people actually ascended to Yahweh in the form of smoke. 'Yahweh smelled the sweet savour; and Yahweh said in his heart, I will not again curse the ground' (Gen. 8^{21}). These sacrifices were occasions for rejoicing. In the '*peace-offering*', only the blood and portions of the fat were reserved for the deity; the rest was eaten by the priests and the people in a mood of festivity. There is a record of this procedure in 1 Sam. 2^{15}: 'Before they burnt the fat, the priest's servant came, and said to the man that sacrificed, Give flesh to roast for the priest; for he will not have sodden flesh of thee, but raw'. The '*burnt-offering*' differed in that the whole of the sacrifice was consumed by fire upon the altar, and no part of it was eaten by priest or worshippers. The occasions on which it was to be offered are listed on Exod. $29^{38\text{-}42}$.

The painful experience of exile gave to later sacrifices the note of humiliation, rather than of joy. The nation came to God with a sorrowful heart. The '*sin-offering*' was intended to remove the estrangement from Yahweh caused by sins committed in ignorance, and by conditions of ceremonial uncleanness, such as childbirth or leprosy. (*See* Lev. 4–5^{13} for the prescribed ritual, beginning 'If any one shall sin unwittingly in any of the things which

Yahweh hath commanded not to be done. . . .') The *'guilt-offering'* (Lev. 5^{14}–6^7) seems designed for those who were in a position to make restitution to God or man for their sins. 'If any one sin, and commit a trespass against Yahweh, and deal falsely with his neighbour . . . then he shall restore . . . and add the fifth part more thereto' (Lev. 6$^{1-5}$). Both these sacrifices carry with them the idea that sin must be confessed and removed before reconciliation could be effected.

We must remember, however, that the average Israelite did not apparently realize that the way to restore right relations with Yahweh was through spiritual repentance and faith, and not merely through the correct performance of the ritual prescribed for sacrifice. If he did what was required of him in this respect, he was sure that he would come once more into the divine favour.

c. As opposed to the priests, *the prophets* seem, at first sight, to have scorned the value of the sacrificial system. 'Though ye offer me your burnt-offerings and meal-offerings, I will not accept them: neither will I regard the peace-offerings of your fat beasts' (Amos 5^{22}). 'I desire mercy, and not sacrifice; and the knowledge of God more than burnt-offerings' (Hos. 6^6). In point of fact, the probability is that they denounced the practice of sacrifice only when it was divorced from righteousness. Given the right attitude of mind and good conduct when the sacrifices commanded by God were offered in the prescribed way, the Israelites did make a real, if limited, approach to God. The sacrifices were acts of obedience, not without their costliness, and as such had their value. The trouble was that, in all too many cases, the attempt to get near to God was not sufficiently prompted by a spiritual and moral motive. Yet both the priesthood and the sacrificial system emphasise the truth that man needs some sort of help to bring him back into a proper relationship with God. Thus the way was prepared for the New Testament doctrine that, by His sacrifice, Christ was able, and He alone, to effect on man's behalf the perfect reconciliation with God.

3. *Redemption by an Act of Divine Deliverance*

There arose in Israel the tremendous hope that God would intervene in history to effect their redemption. There would be a mighty act of deliverance, comparable to the manifestation of power and glory when Yahweh rescued His Chosen People from the tyranny of Egypt. This hope sustained the nation even in the darkest days. The nature of this intervention took many forms in the minds of Israel. To us, some of the predictions of deliverance seem crudely materialistic. Israel was to achieve political glory, earthly prosperity, and national prestige. Amos found many in his time who were looking to a 'Day of Yahweh' which would raise the nation to a great height of political power and prestige, and he was forced to remind them that it was likely to be a day of darkness for them, not of light (Amos 5^{20}). During the Exile, it was natural for the captives to dream of a divine intervention, which would lead to the restoration of Jerusalem and the increase of its former glories. In the difficult days after the Return, when both city and temple remained only shadows of their ancient splendour, the hope still persisted. Israel would be exalted in the earth, and her fellow nations would be compelled to act as her servants. 'Strangers shall stand and feed your flocks, and aliens shall be your plowmen and your vinedressers ... Ye shall eat the wealth of the nations, and in their glory shall ye boast yourselves' (Isa. 61$^{5-6}$). 'Thy gates also shall be open continually ... that men may bring unto thee the wealth of the nations, and their kings led with them. For that nation and kingdom that will not serve thee shall perish' (Isa. 60$^{11-12}$).

Nevertheless, there was a finer element in Israel's hope. It was concerned with the furtherance of the divine purpose, and the perfecting of the nation as the instrument of that purpose. The more sensitive spirits in the nation came to feel that their hope was not entirely concerned with material things, and that it was the intention of God to create a spiritually purified people, who would realize their mission as His agents. This finer conception of deliverance is at the heart of the message of Isaiah of Babylon. Yahweh will certainly restore His people, for a mighty evangelical task awaits them. Israel is the Servant of God, with a world-wide mission. 'Yea, he saith, It is too light a thing that thou shouldest be my servant to raise up the tribes of Jacob, and to restore the preserved of Israel: I will also give thee for a light to the Gentiles, that thou mayest be my salvation unto the end of the earth' (Isa. 49^6). Thus, during the long centuries, this hope of divine intervention kept men expectant, and so helped to prepare the way for God to effect His mighty deliverance of mankind in Jesus Christ.

Let us consider four of the forms of this hope, four means whereby it was surmised that God might bring about deliverance for His People.

a. *The Saving Remnant.* As it became evident that the nation as a whole was unfitted to accomplish God's purposes, hope began to centre upon a loyal core within the nation that could be used by God. After the crisis with the prophets of Baal, Elijah was shown that there was left to Yahweh a nucleus of Israelites who had not compromised their loyalty, and upon whom He could depend for the future. 'Yet will I leave me seven thousand in Israel, all the knees which have not bowed unto Baal, and every mouth which hath not kissed him' (1 Kgs 19^{18}). In the teaching of Isaiah of Jerusalem, this conception of a Remnant became much more explicit. 'I will turn my hand upon thee, and thoroughly purge away thy dross, and will take away all thy tin' (Isa. 1^{25}). The pure gold that is left will consist of the loyal few, whom Yahweh can use. 'In that day shall the branch of Yahweh be beautiful and glorious, and the fruit of the land shall be excellent and comely for them that are escaped of Israel. And it shall come to pass, that he that is left in Zion, and he that remaineth in Jerusalem, shall be called holy, even every one that is written among the living in Jerusalem' (Isa. 4$^{2, 3}$). This remnant came to be regarded, not only as *saved* from the disasters which are to befall Judah, but also as a *saving* remnant, with a divine mission to fulfil. The course of Hebrew history was calculated to determine who were worthy to be counted in this remnant. Only a minority of the Jews were, in fact, carried into the Babylonian Exile, and a still smaller number returned to restore the little city-state of Jerusalem. The idea persisted that, by means of these loyalists, God would accomplish His purpose, and institute a divine Community.

b. *The Kingdom of a Messiah.* Many of the hopes of Israel centred in the coming of a great leader, who would set up a kingdom in which God's will would be done. Because the Jews looked back to David as their ideal king, it was anticipated that this leader would spring from the house of David. 'For unto us a child is born, unto us a son is given; and the government shall be upon his shoulder: and his name shall be called Wonderful, Counsellor, Mighty God, Everlasting Father, Prince of Peace. Of the increase of his government and of peace there shall be no end, upon the throne of David' (Isa. 9$^{6, 7}$). 'And there shall come forth a shoot out of the stock of Jesse, and a branch out of his roots shall bear fruit' (Isa. 11^{1}). 'Rejoice greatly, O daughter of Zion; shout, O daughter of Jerusalem: behold, thy king cometh unto thee: he is just, and having salvation; lowly, and riding upon an ass, even upon a colt the foal of an ass' (Zech. 9⁹). There were many varied conceptions of the Kingdom, and the Messiah who would inaugurate it. In the main, it was 'a good time coming' for the Jews. Yahweh's judgement would be manifested against the Gentiles, though it might be followed by their conversion. Unworthy members would be purged from Israel, and the righteous remainder would enjoy the fullness of divine blessing. Beneath some of the rather crude predictions of material prosperity, we can see the faith that, if God is omnipotent, He must be able to set up His Kingdom on earth, and it will be a righteous Kingdom, because He is righteous. His people will be perfected under a perfect king.

c. *The Suffering Servant.* We cannot decide, beyond dispute, the identity of the Servant of God in the four poems in the writings of Isaiah of Babylon (*see AOT* on Isa. 40–55). The picture in Isa. 52¹³–53¹² is the highest point reached in Old Testament revelation. A great sufferer, who knows that his sufferings are undeserved, comes to realize that they can be used by God to redeem others. It does not matter much whether the poet had in mind an individual sufferer (Moses, Jeremiah, Zerubbabel have been suggested), or a person yet to be born; or whether he was speaking of a group of people under the figure of one man (the nation of Israel, the righteous Remnant at its heart, or the Ideal Israel of the future). Nor can we be certain whether those who were saved were Israel, or the Gentiles, or both. The important thing is that the Old Testament rises to the sublime conception that salvation might be brought about for men by one who suffered undeservedly, and allowed God to make a redemptive use of his sufferings. We must notice, however, that nowhere in the Old Testament is the Suffering Servant identified with the figure of the Messiah.

d. *The Son of Man.* In Dan. 7¹³, we have yet another forecast of a righteous and glorified Israel. 'I saw in the night visions, and, behold, there came with the clouds of heaven one like unto a son of man, and he came even to the ancient of days, and they brought him near before him.' After the successive domination of four world empires described in the preceding verses (Babylon, Media, Persia, and Greece), depicted as four beasts (the lion, the bear, the leopard, the ten-horned monster), Daniel looks to the coming of a Kingdom of Humanity. All four empires are regarded as being under Yahweh's control, and as having served His purpose. But the Kingdom of Humanity is of a different quality. It cannot be symbolised as a beast. It is to be both humane and everlasting. Daniel, therefore, sees it inaugurated by one 'like unto a son of man' (i.e. truly human). This 'one like unto a son of man' represents the 'people of the saints of the Most High', mentioned in *vv.* 18, 22, 25 and 27 of the chapter. In later apocalyptic writings (e.g. the book of Enoch), the son of man was identified with the Messiah, and, indeed, regarded as a celestial being (but *see ANT*, para. 74).

Thus, in the Old Testament, the full and perfect way of salvation is still unrevealed. But glimpses and premonitions are there, to be fulfilled, in a richer way than men could ever have anticipated, in the coming of Jesus. We close the Old Testament, waiting, with unsatisfied longings and unanswered needs in our hearts, for the opening of the New. Our answer is there.

Sermon XLIV. The Use of Money

Theme of the Sermon. Christian Stewardship in business and property. Here Wesley descends from the more general principles of practical Christian ethics to deal specifically with one particular point. This is a plain-spoken and hard-hitting exhortation, yet quite free from impracticability and extremism. As always when he does this, Wesley displays an admirable balance of English moderation and eighteenth-century common-sense with the burning zeal of 'Christianity in earnest'.)

EXPLANATORY OUTLINE OF THE SERMON

Introduction. Importance of the Subject. (1) Exposition of the text (a very difficult one, and not closely connected with the subject of the sermon). (2) Poets and moralists have commonly railed at money as a corrupter, yet it is a gift which can be used for good or ill, and is to be used by the Christian for good. ('It is true, were man in a state of innocence . . .', etc. Wesley here accepted the tradition that there was no private property before the Fall; that God ordained property, and the social distinctions which flow from it, as a result of the Fall, because sinful men will only care for what is their own; and that only regenerate men can presume to set up the ideal communal form of society. Here is a matter of some current interest!) (3) Three plain rules of stewardship.

I. '*Gain all you can.*' (1) The Christian is to pursue his business, but not in any manner hurtful to his bodily health, or (2) his morals. (Note (*i*) the characteristic ban on smuggling, against which Wesley had to fight a constant battle: (*ii*) the interesting testimony in the latter part of the paragraph. A *Deist* was one who admitted the existence of God, but denied that He was active in providence and supernatural redemption. Wesley apparently felt that the study of mathematics was detrimental to the sense of the supernatural, as some today fear that science is destructive of religious faith.) (3) The Christian is not to seek gain at his neighbours' loss by extortion, sharp practice, cut-throat competition, or gambling, nor (4) by distilling spirits. (We observe that the idea of *total* abstinence was not then known, but Wesley's eloquent paragraph gives the modern advocate his cue!) (5) The low standard of honour among some doctors is denounced. (6) The Christian is not to make a business of catering for worldly vanity. (7) This said, the Christian is then to apply himself to his daily business with unremitting diligence, and (8) progressive enterprise. (And did not Wesley come to write of his own commercial venture, his Book-room, 'I unawares became rich'? We can well believe it! But he kept his own rule and gave this income away.)

II. '*Save all you can.*' (1) None of this precious talent is to be wasted (2) upon gluttony, either of the coarse or refined variety, or (3, 4) upon fashionable living. ('Costly books', i.e., library editions, costly for their sumptuous bindings. Wesley was far too good a scholar to grudge money in the pursuit of true learning. 'Elegant gardens': all over the country the gentry were then lavishing their wealth upon the construction of those parks and ornamental gardens which are now our admiration when we visit beauty spots. It need not be supposed that Wesley would have the Methodist grow only vegetables!) (5) The Christian is not, by gratifying worldly desires, to increase them in himself, or (6, 7), in his children. (8) In leaving money to his children he is to discriminate between the spiritually wise and the unwise (though how often does affection blind a parent's eye?)

III. '*Give all you can.*' (1) This last step is essential. (2) God, the creator and sole possessor of all things, has appointed man to be a steward of what is not his own, not a proprietor. The Christian is to recognize this, and bring his goods to God as a part of his sacrifice of obedience. (3) The Christian is first to provide modest food and clothing for himself and his household, and then to give to the Church and the Christian poor, and after that, if there be still an overplus, he is to exercise charity to mankind in general. (4) He is seriously to examine any expense on self and family in the light of his stewardship, the word of Scripture, and the prospect of Judgement to come, and (5) in the spirit of prayer. (6) The sacrifice God requires is not a tithe, but the spirit of stewardship extending to all possessions. (7) The Christian is not to go by what is customary in the world, but to live out the Christian calling.

TEST QUESTIONS

1. What ideas of permanent value about God can we learn from the Old Testament?
2. How did the Covenant in Old Testament times bring home to men their sinfulness, and by what means did they seek to achieve a reconciliation with God?
3. Wesley told his preachers, 'You have nothing to do but to save souls' (*Twelve Rules of a Helper*). Is he therefore inconsistent in preaching on 'The Use of Money'?

STUDY FOUR

Man, Sin and Grace

A. THE INCOMPLETENESS OF THE OLD TESTAMENT REVELATION

IN spite of all its greatness, the Old Testament is not a finished product. It is a book of promise, of expectation, of preparation, not of fulfilment. The prophets proclaimed the will of God for their generation, and demanded of men that they should do justly and love mercy; but they could not offer the divine grace by which the good deeds and splendid achievements which they expected of men could be accomplished; in fact, they sometimes seem to suggest that man has only to muster his own moral resources to fulfil the moral law and win the favour of God. Prophet and lawgiver alike had a deep insight into the nature, the seriousness and the frightful consequences of sin, but they could offer no radical remedy; the whole intricate system of legal enactment, and the whole elaborate pattern of Temple sacrifice, did not reach the heart of the matter, though they foreshadowed the righteousness of the Kingdom of God and the perfect sacrifice which was to come. The hope of Israel remained only a hope when the last sentence of the Old Testament was written; a hope which, deferred, made the heart sick; a hope which, unfulfilled for so long, was twisted into the expectation of triumphant revenge and the setting up of a Jewish world-empire.

Dr Emil Brunner has compared the Bible as a whole to a long sentence in the German language, of which the meaning remains obscure until the last word is uttered. In that language, the most important part of the verb has often to be left to the end. You may not say, 'I have written the letter', but 'I have the letter written'. This applies however long and complicated the sentence may be, and you may have to wait for several seconds, or for several lines in a book, before you know what the sentence is really going to say. 'I have the dog with the long tail, which was the property of the soldier who used to live in the cottage at the end of the lane leading to the top of the hill, and which was last seen. . . .'—and you still do not know whether I have seen, or found, or shot, or sold, or what I have done to the animal, and you will not know until I reach the end of the sentence. So it is with the Bible. Right through the Old Testament, God is revealing Himself, but the sentence is not complete. 'God has His people and all mankind . . .', and then follow the history, the hopes and fears, the successes and failures, the virtues and the sins, the discipline and the disobedience, of God's People, in relation to God, to their own members, to other nations; and still at the end of the Old Testament we do not know God's final purpose towards it, though we have inklings and clues and foreshadowings. Then the final word is spoken in Christ, and we know. The sentence is complete, the purpose is disclosed (*see AOT, Study One;* and *Study Three* above).

B. THE RIDDLE OF MAN'S NATURE, AND HIS RELATIONSHIP TO GOD

Thus it is from the whole Bible, with the New Testament completing the Old, that we learn the Christian view of the nature, fall and destiny of man. The problem of man is the burning problem of our century. In the fifth and fourth centuries B.C., the thinkers of the time disputed deeply about the nature of matter and the physical universe. From the third to the fifth centuries of the Christian era, the great debate was about the Person of Christ. Then, at the Renaissance in the fifteenth and sixteenth centuries, the emphasis shifted to man, and since then the great thinkers inside and outside the Church have been occupied with investigating the creativity, the origin, and the hidden depths of human nature. In our time, these questions have gone deeper and deeper, until now we are face to face with the absolutely fundamental question, *What is man for?* What purpose, if any, does he serve in the total scheme of things? Not, of course, that the older questions are dead; they are very much alive, and always will be. But the question of man's nature is the one which divides the men of our time into opposite camps.

1. *The materialistic view of Man*

Underlying the 'materialistic' view is the notion that man is essentially and solely a part of nature. Thrown up, perhaps by chance, perhaps by some necessity inherent in physical matter, during the inevitable course of the evolutionary process, he is fundamentally physical. His brain works in response to the stimuli provided by his physical experiences, by the operations of his glands, and by his physical environment. The Communists tend to say that all man's thoughts and wishes are the product of economic forces—hunger, thirst, and the need for physical security. Some psychologists vary this a little by saying that the compulsions which operate in a man are mostly internal; that all conduct is really 'behaviour', in the sense of a necessary response to the things that are happening in our brains and senses. But the difference is chiefly one of emphasis. In either case, man is an animal, neither more nor less, living and acting and thinking according to the rigid laws of animal life. He is, in fact, an animated machine, which can be kept alive and manipulated by those who know the laws of his being, so long as the vital forces within him are not exhausted, or destroyed by incurable disease. On this view, of course, man has no freedom of choice; he does not decide what he will do or what he will think—these things are determined and decided by forces outside his control, and largely outside his knowledge. He has only the comforting illusion of freedom, with nothing corresponding to it in the world of reality.

On this kind of view, knowledge of God and of the unseen world is an impossibility, and the claim to it an absurdity. But this does not apply only to religion. It applies to all 'spiritual' values; truth and beauty and goodness disappear into thin air. It may be pleasing to us to admire what we call the beautiful—it gives us comfortable feelings and passes the time. We may enjoy discussing knotty points, if we are made that way. We may say that one course of action is better than another, and think that we choose it for unselfish reasons. But the admiration of beauty is just a private feeling that we have; we can never arrive at truth in any discussion, but only at thinking something which happens to satisfy our instincts; there is no such thing as virtue or goodness, but only a selfish satisfaction in doing what we like doing. In other words, conscience, artistic genius, philosophical or theological thought do not bring us anywhere in the direction of reality; they are simply by-products which appear in the process of evolution, just as coal tar is a by-product of the manufacture of gas.

2. *The Christian view of Man*

What view of man does the Christian oppose to this? He does not, of course, repudiate the findings of modern science about the origin of man and his physical and psychological structure. He is free to accept the theory that man emerged at a certain stage in the evolutionary process, having developed in some way out of the lower forms of life (*see* p. 237). He knows, of course, that the theory of evolution is as yet only a theory, though it is a very well-attested one; he knows, also, that the theory takes a large variety of forms, and he leaves the decision between them to those whose business it is to investigate these matters. In other words, he sees no inconsistency between the theory of evolution and the Christian faith. The truth of the first two chapters of *Genesis* is not concerned with the details of man's creation, but with the fundamental assertion that the universe and everything in it, and man himself, were created by God (*see* p. 38f). The details belong to two of the many ancient stories about the creation of the world; the fundamental truth is independent of the passing of time or the findings of the natural sciences. Up to this point, then, the Christian agrees with the materialists that man is a part of nature, and he welcomes the flood of light that has been shed in recent years on the structure and functions and healing of the human body, and on its close connection with the non-bodily aspects of man.

He will go further still with the materialists. Without accepting the latest theories of the latest school of psychologists, he is fully prepared, if he regards the scientific evidence as sufficient, to acknowledge that human conduct is often directed, not by the motives which we consciously recognize, but by forces within us which lie deeper than consciousness, and over which we can exercise little, if any, control; that often our so-called 'reasons' for action are really rationalizations, excuses invented afterwards, often unconsciously, for the things which we do for much less respectable reasons. That is to say that we are not so free in the exercise of will as we usually like to think. All of us are 'determined' (to use the technical term) by economic or psychological forces for a great deal of our time. It is improbable that we *freely* choose to eat the food that we eat, to wear the clothes that we wear, to obey the social conventions that we do obey; our response to many situations, of danger, of attack, of praise, of boredom, and many others, are frequently not the result of responsible choice, but part of a pattern of behaviour which we have received ready-made.

So far we are prepared to go with the materialists. But there are certain other elements in human nature, which we assert, and which the materialists either deny or dismiss with a shrug of the shoulders as being of no importance.

a. We observe, for instance, that *man is conscious of himself in a way in which no mere animal is conscious of himself*; he is conscious of being separate and distinct from his material environment, and of being separate and distinct from other people. From one point of view, the life history of each one of us is the history of the growing consciousness of separateness. As far as we can tell, a new-born baby is not aware of being separate from his mother or the world around him; then the awareness comes gradually—his mother, his father, other people become distinct entities with which he is in a relation of friendliness, or possibly the reverse. Then to the adolescent comes the full realization of separateness, causing in many cases bitter and painful experiences, while he adjusts himself to the unpleasant fact of which he is now fully aware.

b. Then again, as no mere animal is, *man is conscious of himself as persisting through time*; he knows that he is the same person as he was yesterday, and responsible for yesterday's acts; he expects to be the same person tomorrow, responsible for today's acts. In addition, he has the uncanny power of detaching himself from himself, and looking at himself from the outside, weighing up his character and abilities and experiences. He can even enter into the experiences of another, and temporarily see things from that other's point of view, remaining himself, but at the same time identifying himself with another by the tremendous power of sympathetic imagination.

c. *He has also the power of abstract thought.* That is, he can talk and think, not only about five potatoes and four thousand balloons, but also about 'five' and about 'four thousand' as abstract terms, and build an immense mathematical system upon a few simple principles and presuppositions. He can talk and think, not only about good actions and good men, and bad actions and bad men, but about goodness and badness as abstract qualities, and about beauty and courage and pride and humility. He can argue about the existence of God and the Devil, he can debate the nature of eternal life. And all this abstract thinking, though it may start, and perhaps always should start, with the evidence provided by his five senses, goes far beyond anything for which the senses could provide the evidence, into the world of eternal things, the world of what is called philosophy and theology.

d. *And he can create*; not in the absolute sense in which God creates the universe out of nothing, but in the secondary sense, according to which he arranges the things and ideas and experiences which are given by God into patterns and forms no one on earth has ever before conceived. Man—not his glands, not a system of economic urges or conditioned reflexes, but man—has created the Venus of Milo, the Parthenon in Athens, *Hamlet*, the fifth symphony of Beethoven and the jet-propelled aeroplane. No doubt he could have done none of these things, if God had not given him the raw materials, and the wit to arrange them and adapt them and transform them in the way required. But a mere animal would have been incapable of all of them, with all the help in the universe.

e. *And man is free*. He is not free, as we have seen, in an absolute and unlimited sense, so that he can choose any course of action at any moment and carry it out; the burden of such freedom would be too great for the human spirit to bear. But he is free in the main issues of life. He has the power to distinguish between good and evil, and to choose either good or evil. He is responsible for his 'moral' and 'immoral' actions, for his identification with good or evil causes, for his choice of a good or evil manner of life. If we deny this, as many do in the interests of a theory that everything in the universe, including human conduct, follows rigid laws and could be completely foretold if we only had the necessary knowledge, we are flouting the accumulated wisdom of the ages. Certain branches of science may seem to demand that everything in the universe should follow pre-determined laws, but the rest of human knowledge and judgement demand that the will of man should be free; and it is foolish, though understandable in a scientific age like our own, to repudiate the latter and give our unqualified support to the former. There must surely be truth in both contentions and in both arguments, and it is the part of wisdom both to admit that the human will is to a large extent determined, and to claim that it is in essentials free.

f. *But the noblest power of man is the power of personal relationship.* Like the rest of the animal world, human beings are drawn to each other by the ties of common blood, by parenthood, by the sexual urge. But they can also transcend all merely physical or merely emotional relationships, and reach a level where they treat each other as persons; not simply, sometimes not at all, as objects of desire or of animal magnetism. In such a relationship each retains his freedom, his individuality, his distinctive characteristics, his personal rights, and yet is identified with and committed to the other in an unbreakable bond. And that does not happen only between one human being and another, or within groups of human beings closely bound to each other by friendship and loyalty, but also between human beings and God Himself, so that God becomes no longer a distant potentate, or a benevolent administrator of the universe, but a close and dear friend, to whom we can come as a child comes to a father or mother in whom he completely trusts. Man, just in virtue of being man, has this marvellous and unique power of personal relationship with the Sovereign of the Universe.

All this—man's self-consciousness, reasoning ability, creativeness, freedom and capacity for friendship with God and man—is included in the Christian understanding of Gen. 1^{27}: 'And God created man in his own image, in the image of God created he him'. *The image of God* in man means that in all these respects man is like God, however far removed he may be from the power and goodness and wisdom of God, and that God created man to be like Himself in all these respects. Another way of describing man as he was created by God is by saying that he possessed *original righteousness*, and this was the phrase much beloved by the great Reformers, Luther and Calvin. They did not mean by this that man is virtuous by nature, or that some degree of irremovable goodness is ingrained in him, but that God created him in the right relationship with Himself, for 'righteousness' in the Bible always refers to such a relationship; and because man as originally created is in the right relationship with God, he also possesses perfect harmony and health within himself, and perfect affinity with his fellow-creatures. Such is man as he left the hands of his Creator.

C. THE FAILURE OF MAN; ORIGINAL AND ACTUAL SIN

But no one could say that the description of man, as we have so far given it, corresponds to man as we see him about the world today. Take a look at the faces of a group of city workers huddled together in an underground train on their way home from work, and you will not think that there is very much to be said for the Psalmist's assertion, 'Thou hast made him but little lower than God, and crownest him with glory and honour' (Ps. 8⁵)—if that is meant to be a description of man as we meet him every day. But it is not. There are still some people in the world—not so many as there were—who think that man as he was created is the same as man as he actually is. They talk, perhaps, of a 'divine spark' in man (for which there is no evidence in Scripture; the idea comes from pre-Christian Stoic philosophy), and suppose that, if only the right scheme for ordering society were produced, everyone would fall in with it, and carry it out, and live happily ever after. But a Christian does not look at himself and his fellow-man through rose-coloured spectacles; like the Bible writers, he is starkly and severely realistic. He knows that man, for all his enormous and impressive gifts and powers, is in fact a failure. He never really does what he sets out to do; still less has he realized his vast potentialities and established on earth a society of people living at peace with themselves, each other and God. Civilized man is rather like the son of a good family, now approaching middle age, with a good education behind him, still with an air of good manners and culture about him, still with hopes of making good, but plainly a failure and a ne'er-do-well, dragged down by his passions and his lower nature. We must always make a very sharp distinction between man as he was created by God, and man as he is found today, and we must do so even in the presence of those rare people whose characters show a victory over temptations which seems to be beyond our power.

1. *The nature of Sin*

So we come to the question of Sin (*see CAT* 24, 25). Here we are concerned chiefly, not with sins, though they are serious enough in all conscience, but with Sin. Sin is the disease; the sins of thought, word and deed which we commit are the symptoms of the disease. If that statement seems a little doubtful, make a list of your own sins, at least of those known to you. Plan to stamp them out, one by one, giving a fortnight to laziness, a month to pride, and so on. Suppose you succeed, by a great effort, in conquering laziness, getting up an hour earlier every day and cutting out all your times of idleness, and then go on to deal with your next vice. You will almost certainly find that another one will have sprung up unawares in the place of the one that you have overcome—bad temper, or self-righteousness, or something else. In other words, you have not dealt with the root of your trouble. The root of your trouble, my trouble, of man's trouble, is Sin. Read the classic passages on this subject, Ps. 51 and Rom. 7[14-24], and you will have no further doubt about the matter. 'Everyone that committeth sin is the bondservant of sin' (Jn 8[34]).

There is a great variety of words in the Bible to describe sins and the state of Sin, and each of them gives an insight into the nature of Sin. In the Old Testament, we have words which originally mean 'missing the mark', 'distortion of what is right', 'rebellion against a superior', 'unfaithfulness to a covenant', 'folly', 'senselessness'. The commonest New Testament word is the one which means 'missing the mark'; but we also have words which mean 'transgression of the law', 'trespass', 'unrighteousness'. These words are descriptions, not definitions, of Sin. If we look carefully into them, and find what is common to them all, we shall reach a Biblical definition. This definition must contain two essential elements.

a. Firstly, it must recognize the fact that *Sin is the assertion of the self against all comers*. We are born into the community of mankind, in which all men are of equal value to God, that is, of equal real value (though not, of course, equal in ability or character), and of which God is the sole legitimate Sovereign. But each one of us, in his own way, and according to his own temperament, asserts himself as being more important than anyone else, and in effect as more important than God Himself. Not, of course, that we go about proclaiming our own supreme importance, though there have been people who have even done that; but that we act and think always on the tacit assumption that no one matters quite so much as we do. We have our moments of altruism, we may give ourselves to a cause outside ourselves, we may be 'absolutely devoted' to our family. But though we may for the time being rise above ourselves, the things or people to whom we give ourselves are for the most part extensions of ourselves. In our fundamental, essential thinking and acting, we are the centres of our own universe. We judge the world, politics, food prices and shortages, other people, everything, by their relation to us and possible effect upon us; only secondarily, if at all, by their relation to the general welfare of mankind. When the Budget proposals appear, what is the first—and often the only—question that we ask?

From this central attitude spring all our false ambitions,

jealousies, lusts, quarrels, conceits—the whole gamut of vices listed by Paul in Gal. 5:19f. as 'the works of the flesh'. For Paul does not say that the flesh, in the sense of the body and its instincts is evil; on the contrary, it is the gift of God, and good. By '*the flesh*', Paul means something quite different—the human personality operating on the spirit of selfishness and using the body as the base of its operations. It is another name for what we have described as Sin. The man who tames all his carnal passions in order to gain power over the lives of men is doing 'the works of the flesh' just as surely as the rake and the drunkard. He and they alike are the slaves of Sin. It is with these thoughts in mind that we should read Paul's terrible and realistic account of contemporary civilisation in Rom. 1:18–2:29 (*see ANT, paras.* 451–2). And if we are tempted to think that the description is of a bygone pagan civilisation, with no relevance to us, it is because we are ignorant of what goes on in large and increasing parts of our own.

b. The second thing that we must include in our definition is that *Sin is always against God, and not simply against man*. When we steal or lie as a result of our inveterate preoccupation with our own interests, it is not just that we are disturbing the balance of society and spreading insecurity and fear—though we are certainly doing that; it is also, and much more seriously, that we are rebelling against God. We have placed ourselves in the position that belongs to God alone—in the centre of our universe. We have made ourselves—or our friends, or the cause which we try to serve by our cunning and dishonest manoeuvres—the supreme end of our living; and the supreme end of life is God alone. As Mr. C. S. Lewis puts it, we have called our souls our own, and that is precisely what they are not; they belong to God, and they ought to be put solely and completely at His disposal. Unless we put them at His disposal, we are living a lie which is also a blasphemy and a treason. 'Against thee, thee only have I sinned, and done that which is evil in thy sight' (Ps. 51:4).

2. *Original and Actual Sin*

It is useful at this point to distinguish between Original Sin and Actual Sin. In many people's minds the whole notion of Original Sin is mixed up with the supposed traditional doctrine that babies, being guilty from birth, are consigned to hell if they die unbaptized. Let us therefore begin by saying that Scripture nowhere suggests that, when we are born, we are already guilty, already responsible and punishable for Sin or sins. That is *not* the meaning of Ps. 51[5]: 'Behold I was shapen in iniquity and in sin did my mother conceive me'; the Psalmist is here referring to the sinfulness of the stock from which he came, not to his own. But since everyone is born with the weakness of will which is part, as we shall see (p. 62), of Original Sin, even a new-born baby is not what God wills His children to be. We can say, if we like, that he is in that sense 'guilty', or at least unworthy of the presence of God. But it is better to distinguish Original Guilt and Original Sin, and to say that, while it is debatable whether there is such a thing as Original Guilt, there is certainly such a thing as Original Sin.

a. *Original Sin as Corporate.* Original Sin has both its corporate and its personal aspect. We all belong to the body of mankind, the corporate entity of human society. And human society is infected by Sin, through and through. No man sins in a purely private and personal capacity. The effect and infection of every man's sin spread through the whole of the community of which he forms a part, and ultimately to the whole of mankind. The Sin in me increases and develops the Sin in other people, and vice versa. Especially does my Sin infect those who belong to my family; juvenile delinquency, now generally ascribed to bad home influence, is only one example of a universal principle. The presence of evil institutions in my country facilitates and accelerates the growth of Sin in me. If there were no brothels in England, that would not mean that there was no sexual vice; but the presence of brothels increases the amount of sexual vice that there is. And the effects of Sin are equally ramified; one evil deed leads to another, one act of aggression leads to revenge, and so on and on and on. No war is ever caused by a single series of evil deeds by a single set of men in a single country; every war is the result of thousands of years of human selfishness, piled and accumulated and complicated, and though the responsibility may rest more heavily on one nation or one person than on another, the total responsibility rests ultimately on the whole of mankind up to the date in question.

Into this whole complex of Sin, its infection and its effects, I am born. Almost as soon as I am born, I am involved in the Sin of my family, of my nation and of the world. I may become the victim of my father's unemployment, or extravagance, or bad temper, or my mother's possessiveness or laziness, or of post-war conditions or of pre-war anxiety. In fact, some of these factors may begin to operate before I am born. Later on, I may even feel in a sense responsible for things in which I could not possibly have had a personal share. I may feel ashamed of what England did in 17—, or of what my school did in the matter of a football match in 19—. And all through my life I shall be constantly faced with moral choices which are not between pure good and pure evil, but between two or more courses of action which are all partly good and partly evil, and I shall often find it the right and proper thing to choose the 'lesser of two evils'; for whichever course I take, as for instance in the matter of National Service, I shall be doing some harm to somebody. I am not guilty, or punishable, or responsible, until I have myself by my own free choice identified myself with some part of the evil that is in the world; but I am surrounded all my days by influences which are drawing me into guilt. If it were not for the blessed fact that there are other influences drawing me in the opposite direction, my plight, in view of my own inner weakness, would indeed be virtually hopeless. All this is the corporate aspect of Original Sin.

b. *Original Sin as Personal.* We have already approached the personal aspect of it. I am surrounded by evil influences, but there is also a weakness within myself which makes me particularly susceptible to them. For some reason which it seems difficult to determine exactly, but which must in some way be bound up with my membership of the body of mankind and the pervading infection of mankind, I find it easier on the whole to do wrong than to do right. We may put it by saying that we possess an instinct for self-preservation which is very valuable to us in early life, and that later on we find it easier to give way to it, and even to encourage it, than we do to control it and put it in its proper place. Or we may say that we are prone to work for the nearer and more obvious good, which is our own pleasure and advantage, rather than for the more remote and more arduous good, which is the glory of God and the welfare of our fellow-men. But however we put it, the fact remains that Original Sin, in this sense, is part of human nature as we know it. Presumably it was not part of human nature as God created it, or man could not be said to have possessed the divine image; therefore it must be that we have each 'inherited' it.

c. *Actual Sin.* Now that we have given an account of Original Sin, it is easy to see what is meant by Actual Sin. This takes place when we deliberately identify ourselves with evil and yield to temptation. From that point we are sinners, guilty before God. And if we do not say much more about Actual Sin here, the reasons is that we all know very fully about it from our own experience. 'Let no man say when he is tempted, I am tempted of God: for God cannot be tempted with evil, and he himself tempteth no man: but each man is tempted when he is drawn away by his own lust and enticed. Then the lust, when it hath conceived, beareth sin: and the sin, when it is full-grown, bringeth forth death' (Jas. 1$^{13, 14}$).

3. *The Fall of Man, corporate and personal*

The tragic weakness of man, in spite of his high potentialities, has always been a source of perplexity to philosophers, and of despair to would-be reformers. The Christian doctrine which explains it is the doctrine of the Fall. This can be stated in various ways, but the truth which underlies the various ways of expressing it is far more important than any form of words.

a. *The Fall of Man as corporate.* (i) Some prefer to retain the traditional account that Adam and Eve, our first parents, fell by disobedience in the Garden of Eden, and received as punishment a sinful, mortal nature. This nature they passed on to all their descendants, so that we are born with it, inheriting the weakness which we have called Original Sin. (ii) Others, recognizing the difficulty of saying that the whole human race, in its multiplied racial variety, stemmed from a single pair of man and woman, and of knowing the life story of that pair—if there was one—prefer to regard the Genesis story as a pictorial account of what happened in a different way. Mr C. S. Lewis, for instance, suggests that after a long process of evolution God created 'Paradisal man', man using all his faculties as they should be used, man living in perfect obedience to and in perfect fellowship with his Creator; that then someone or something suggested to him that he could take his life into his own hands and live according to his own will, not God's, and he decided to do so; that this act of self-will was the Fall, and that it set up an entirely different attitude of man to God which has perpetuated itself until the present day. (iii) Or perhaps we can put it more generally like this: some members of the human race at an early period of human existence, before the beginning of recorded history, perhaps at the very outset of the human stage of evolution, asserted themselves against God in some way that we cannot recall; this self-assertion, disobedience, self-will, spread like wild-fire, like an infectious disease, over the whole human race, with results with which we are only too familiar.

But, whatever the historical event, or long series of events, the inescapable fact remains that the human race as a whole is alienated from God, and was alienated, and remains alienated, by the act of human will, setting itself up against the will of God.

b. *The Fall of Man as personal.* But, however great may be the obscurity about what happened in man's early history to deflect him from his true path, there is very little obscurity about what happens to each of us as *individuals*. Each one of us repeats the Fall of Man in his own experience, and makes that general Fall his own personal Fall. Knowing that other people exist, with rights as great as ours, knowing also (in the vast majority of cases) that God exists and has supreme rights over our souls and bodies, we find that we are asserting ourselves against God and everyone else in the world, and insisting on having our own way and living our own life. That is the Fall of each one of us. And after it has happened, each evil deed becomes easier than the one before, and good deeds become harder. We begin a sort of Rake's Progress, the speed of which, thank God, is limited for most of us by the good influences in our environment; so that only comparatively few of us become utter scoundrels, while the rest settle down to a life of self-seeking respectability, taking off our hats to God on Sundays, perhaps, and giving a certain amount of attention to the welfare of others, but making quite sure that No. 1 has really the first place in our lives.

Thus the Image of God, the likeness to Himself conferred on man by God at his creation, the 'original righteousness' of which we have spoken, is disastrously impaired, and in some cases (so far as we, at least, can see) completely lost. This result is sometimes called Total Depravity. These words sound horribly grim, and can easily be misunderstood. They do not mean that every single part of the human personality is completely corrupt; that would not only be an insult to human achievement and human character, but also untrue to the facts. The meaning is rather that there is no part of us which has entirely escaped corruption. Even our power of abstract thought, which has the best chance of being immune, is tainted; when we seek to think quite disinterestedly, our thinking is distorted by the desire to prove what we should like to prove; and happy is the thinker who is conscious of his own weakness in this respect. And even our noblest achievements, which seem at the time to be entirely free from thoughts of self, reveal on later investigation slight traces of the desire for praise or for inward satisfaction. As Calvin says, 'relics of the image of God remain impressed even on our vices'—but traces of our corruption are imprinted even on our virtues. In this sense, man is 'totally depraved'.

D. THE GRACE OF GOD AND JUSTIFICATION

The answer to man's predicament is the Grace of God (*see CAT* 27, 28). All available human resources have been brought to bear on the problem of amending man's fallen condition, and they have all proved inadequate to the situation. Not that they have entirely failed; education, social reform, political progress, the administration of justice, and many other social agencies, have done a great deal to neutralize the effects of sin. An illegitimate child, or a child of drunken parents, has now in many parts of the world the chance of developing his powers to the full, like any other child. 'Backward' races are being brought to the power and opportunity of self-government. Then our education, our citizenship, our legal system, all play a great part in restraining our animal impulses and diverting our vital forces into useful channels. For all this we ought to be immensely grateful to God; without it we should be back in the jungle, or would never have left it. But in spite of it all, man without the grace of God remains a fallen creature—as any social worker or colonial administrator would have no difficulty in admitting. There is sometimes moral progress inside civilizations, though it rarely affects the whole body of the people; but it is always succeeded by degeneration and decay, and the total advance of the human race, if it exists, is so small as to be almost imperceptible. That is, apart from the work of the Holy Spirit in the Church, and through the Church in the world.

1. *By Grace*

Thus the only hope for mankind lies in the grace of God. It is easy to think or speak of it as if it were a force or an energy or an atmosphere, and we help this misunderstanding by talking too much about 'means of grace' and 'channels of grace', though such phrases have their proper place and meaning. The grace of God is not a *thing* at all. We should do better, perhaps, if we spoke rather of God who is gracious, than of the grace of God. But we cannot conveniently do that, and so long as we remember that grace is really 'love in action' and that we are all the time concerned, not with a thing which works in the void, but with a God who is actively, persistently, self-sacrificially loving us, we shall do no great harm by using the familiar phrase.

a. The grace of God is *God taking the initiative for our salvation*. He did not wait until we called on Him to come and save us, or even until we recognized our need of salvation. He did not wait until every human device had been tried, and He had to intervene to save His world from utter chaos and disaster. At exactly the right time, that is, at His time, He sent Jesus Christ to live and die and rise again for us. 'While we were yet weak, in due season Christ died for the ungodly. . . . God commendeth his own love toward us, in that, while we were yet sinners, Christ died for us' (Rom. 5[6, 8]). 'Ye know the grace of our Lord Jesus Christ, that, though he was rich, yet for your sakes he became poor, that ye through his poverty might become rich' (2 Cor. 8[9]). The initiative was His; His grace, as the theologians used to say, is 'prevenient', coming before our need and our request. One of the purposes of Infant Baptism is to remind us that God's grace does not depend on us, and does not wait for us to demand it by faith; it is there already, waiting for us to receive it.

b. *The grace of God is entirely undeserved.* Most religious thought in England is obstinately wedded to salvation by works; that is, most of us persist in thinking, however often we are warned to the contrary, that our good deeds and estimable thoughts go some way towards earning the favour of God. When a man dies, we tend to tot up in our minds his good deeds, set them against his bad ones, and hope (sometimes against hope) that on balance he will just scrape through to heaven. But this way of thinking is wholly opposed to the Gospel, whether we look for it in Jesus' parable of the Pharisee and the Publican (Lk 18[10-14]), or in Paul's majestic exposition of the doctrine of justification by faith in *Romans*. We cannot possibly deserve the grace of God. (i) As we have seen, even the good deeds on which we might have counted for merit with God are tainted with evil, and so lose much of their value. (ii) Our bad deeds and thoughts are so frequent, so habitual, that it is scarcely possible for our good deeds to off-set them. (iii) Even if they could, being what we are, we should undoubtedly fall straightway into self-righteousness, and ruin the whole effect. (iv) To talk of forgiveness as reward for merit is to bring the notions of the market-place, the prize-giving and the law-court into our dealings with God, who 'maketh his sun to rise on the evil and the good, and sendeth rain on the just and the unjust' (Mt 5^{45}). That this may never be done is laid down by Jesus, once and for all, in the parables of the Prodigal Son and the Labourers in the Vineyard. Does that mean that all the good deeds we do before we receive the grace of God are useless, and might as well not be done? Certainly not; they are the signs of a faith in goodness and rightness which may and should develop into a personal faith in Jesus Christ.

c. *The grace of God is a personal relationship* of God with men and women. That is why it is wrong and false to think of it as a thing at all. It cannot be measured, or guaranteed, or regulated, or invoked by rites and ceremonies. Personal relationships are immeasurable and incalculable, but in the last resort they are the only facts that matter in life or religion. John Oman, in *Grace and Personality*, a great book which is not nowadays read as much as it should be, goes very near to the heart of the matter when he speaks of God's dealing with us as 'a gracious personal relationship'. If we think of it in that way, we are saved from two dangerous extremes on the edge of Christian doctrine; on the one hand, from thinking with Pelagius that we can, if we try hard enough, satisfy God and enter into His favour; on the other hand, from supposing with Augustine, or at least some of his followers, and with Calvin, that God's grace descends on some men with irresistible force, making them good whether they like it or not, and passes by others entirely. God offers this relationship, this grace, to *all*, and goes to the utmost limit of self-giving love in Christ to make it available to all, and to persuade all to accept it (*see MHB* 75, 77, 144, etc.).

2. *Through Faith*

If we accept it, we are 'justified'. And so we come to the great doctrine of 'justification by faith', which was the real driving force of the Reformation, and stands squarely based on the central teaching of the New Testament. We shall do better, perhaps, to call it the doctrine of 'justification by grace through faith'; for it is the grace of God by which we are justified, and it is faith through which we accept the offer of justification. (*See Study Seven* for a full account of *justification* and *faith*.)

One of the decisive events in world history took place when Martin Luther discovered the meaning of justification by grace through faith. This is how it happened. He had been very much worried about Rom. 1¹⁷: 'For therein is revealed a righteousness of God by faith unto faith'. He took righteousness to mean 'justice'—and how could he, a weak and sinful man, possibly satisfy the justice of God? He had tried all the accredited methods of doing so by good works and ceremonial acts, even by entering a monastery and rigorously carrying out all the prescribed exercises and penances; and they had all utterly failed. Then, as he meditated and prayed day and night, it was suddenly made known to him that the 'righteousness of God' did not mean the 'justice of God' at all, but the justifying activity of a merciful God, who of His undeserved grace forgives guilty sinners. 'At this', he says, 'I felt myself to be born anew, and to enter through open gates into paradise itself. From here, the whole face of the Scriptures was altered.' Does not the same thing happen today, when a man realizes the inner meaning of justification by grace through faith?

SERMON IX. THE SPIRIT OF BONDAGE AND OF ADOPTION

Theme of the Sermon. An analysis of the different states of Christian experience connected with *Conversion*.

EXPLANATORY OUTLINE OF THE SERMON

Introduction. (1–3) Mankind is found in three states: the majority, who do not think of God; a few who obey Him for fear; and a few who love Him. (4) The hearers have passed through these three stages. (5) The first state is called 'the natural man', the second 'under the law', the third 'under grace'.

I. *The Natural Man*, '*who is not worrying about his sins*'. (1) This man is spiritually asleep, oblivious to the claims of God. (2) Because he is not aware of the awful recompense for irreligion, he deludes himself that all is well with his soul. He argues either that there is no God, or that He is a mere 'Great First Principle' remote from human affairs, or, alternatively, a God who can be trusted to condone sin. Thus he supposes that it is sufficient if he lives a respectable life. (3) He is aware that his life is not entirely satisfactory, but deludes himself that he can quite well amend it as and when he will. (4) In men of education, the devil can fortify this delusion by the employment of (reasonable and true) considerations regarding the necessity of human free will, if man is to be a responsible moral agent. (5) If things go well with him this man feels that life is giving him 'a good time', and he is well content to 'get a kick out of it'. (6) He regards himself as a very superior, emancipated, and 'modern' person, who has seen through the irrational scruples of religious people about sin, as well as their wishful thinking about salvation. (7) If he be a professing Christian he can even comfort himself by a spurious use of the Bible. (8) The unconverted, all the way up the scale from drunken, swearing, and adulterous sinners to purely formal Christians are in this condition.

II. *God's Rude Awakening.* (1) God can 'stab his spirit broad awake', either by some 'awful providence' (i.e., some calamity which gives the natural man 'furiously to think'), or by 'His word applied' (i.e., by some sermon which 'goes home to the heart'). The natural man is horrified to realize that the God he had supposed to be remote or easy-going is a holy God of terrible judgement. (2) He discovers that God requires not respectability, but inward righteousness, and the more he thinks about it the more he realizes how heinously he has sinned. (3) He is deeply convinced of the sinfulness of his heart, and (4) is sure that he merits damnation. (5) His delight in 'having a good time' vanishes. (6) He is smitten with remorse for having ruined himself, and with fear of death and of hell. (The latter part of this paragraph reflects the not uncommon occurrence in the early days of the Evangelical Revival, when those convicted of sin would often fall to the ground, groaning and crying out in anguish.) (7, 8) He tries with all his might to break with the sin he now so dreads, but finds he cannot. (9, 10) Such a one, labouring under the conviction of sin, is said to be 'under the law' (i.e. the moral law, with its threat of ruin and damnation for all who do not obey it, has thoroughly come home to the heart).

The modern reader will probably say, 'I have known not a few who have turned from religious indifference to a sincere Christian life, but I have never met anyone who has had a religious experience at all comparable to the psychological earthquake Wesley here describes'. The fact is that today the evangelist does not often succeed in reaching those completely alienated from Christianity. The long experience of the Church indicates that conversions would happen like this were God to grant to the Church a major stirring of spiritual life. Then a Gospel declared with great passion and power would take hold of some of those 'outsiders' to whom Christianity would be shatteringly new and strange. These would probably come to the experience of salvation by way of the *deep* 'conviction of sin' which Wesley here treats as the normal stage. This decisive conversion experience is common in the Church Overseas today. 'Conviction of sin' has been sufficiently usual in times of Revival, and sufficiently common in the experience of outstanding Christian leaders, that it has come to take its place in Christian theology as a part of 'the normal course of events'.

III. *God's Merciful Release.* (1) The believer is in a 'state of grace'. *Grace* is (i) the favour, the undeserved mercy, of God: (ii) the spiritual power of God at work in the heart, to carry His favour to effect. (2) God answers the prayer of the distressed penitent, and assures him of His love. (3) He sees the pledge of divine love supremely in the atoning death of Christ, and his heart is carried away at the sight. (4) He is released from the load of a guilty conscience, and no longer fears the holy God. He is released from the power of sin, and no longer fears Satan and hell. (5) He now has power decisively to conquer temptation, and (6) a transformed life witnesses to the reality of his conversion. (7) Love fills him with good works. (8) *Summary.* Three stages: the 'natural man' has the peace of apathy. His condition corresponds to that of the heathen. The man 'under the law' fights sin earnestly but unsuccessfully. His condition corresponds to that of the Old Testament. The man 'under grace' has the peace of victory. He is the *Christian.*

IV. *A Guide to Self-analysis.* (1) To divide men into 'sincere' and 'insincere' hopelessly confuses the issue, for man can be sincere in the natural and legal states as well as under grace. No man is in 'a state of grace' (i.e. on the road to salvation) unless his heart is filled with that love of God which gives him decisive victory over temptation. (2) One cause of confusion is that in actual experience a man can slip bewilderingly from one state to another. (3) Another is that it is not commonly realized that a man of attractive disposition and upright conduct can be still in the natural or legal state. (Such a one may be in fact an 'almost', not an 'altogether' Christian.) (4) Very many who pass as 'good' Christians are only in the natural state of unawakened sinful man! The work of divine grace has not started. Those in the legal state (i.e., who are trying hard in their own strength to be good men) comprise a large part of the community's most beneficial and admired citizens. Those who would be true Christians are warned not to let this obscure the issue: God has something to offer beyond all this—the indispensable and distinctively *Christian* gift of a genuine *conversion*.

TEST QUESTIONS

1. How would you describe the greatness and the weakness of man?
2. What is meant by saying that Salvation is the work of God?
3. Outline the experience of Conversion, as Wesley describes it in Sermon IX.

STUDY FIVE

The Work of Christ

A. THE FACT OF SALVATION THROUGH THE CROSS

THE question is sometimes put to us by someone who is genuinely anxious to understand the Christian faith: *How can the death of someone in the first century possibly save from sin people who live in the twentieth century?* When we attempt to answer that question we shall naturally put forward our own theory of how the Atonement takes place; but we shall not thereby convert him to Christianity, for argument alone can never do that. If he is to become a Christian, he must see for himself, and accept for himself in humble repentance and trust, the fact of Christ's death on his behalf; then, and then only, is he saved from his sins through faith in Christ.

For we are saved, not by any theories about the Cross or doctrines of the Atonement, but by Christ Himself through His death on our behalf. The *fact* of salvation through the Cross precedes and transcends any possible *theory* about it. The orthodox doctrine of the Atonement has never been laid down by the Church, it has never been prescribed by the Methodist Conference; and that omission is surely inspired by the divine wisdom, for the Work of Christ is infinitely bigger than anything that we can say about it and leaves our formulations far behind.

B. THE PREACHING OF THE CROSS

Our primary function, then, is to preach Christ crucified. By God's help, we are to bring before men's minds and hearts and imaginations and consciences, in vivid and compelling words, the fact that 'Christ died for our sins' (1 Cor. 15^3); that the crucifixion is not just an ancient story told to make us brave, or a parable or a myth or a golden legend, but a brutal, unshakable *fact*, a solid chunk of history; that Christ died, not just to give a noble example and to inspire other people to die for their faith and for the truth, but to save us from our sins, and to place us in the right relationship with God; and that if we appropriate that offer of the love of God, made to us by Christ on the Cross, forgiveness of sins is ours, the right relationship with God is ours, we are the children of God and He is our Father. And when we have done what we can to bring this home to the men and women in front of us, not in Holy Week only, but on every suitable occasion throughout every year, we are to pray the Holy Spirit to do what we cannot do, to convert sinners to God.

We shall all perform this task in our own way and according to our own gifts and powers, and under the guidance of the Holy Spirit. But if we are to be true to the Biblical revelation there are certain elements which ought to form a part of every presentation of the Cross which we offer to our congregations.

1. *The Cross of Christ is the Work of God*

We must make it unmistakeably clear that we are dealing, not with the human effort of a very brave and good man to put us right with God, but with God's initiative, God's activity, for our salvation. '*God* was in Christ, reconciling the world unto himself' (2 Cor. 5^{19}). '*God* commendeth his own love toward us, in that, while we were yet sinners, Christ died for us' (Rom. 5^8). '*God* so loved the world that he gave his only-begotten Son, that whosoever believeth on him should not perish, but have eternal life' (Jn 3^{16}). The Biblical message is not that God was persuaded to relent towards us when He saw the heroic self-sacrifice of Christ, but that He Himself set on foot the whole process of the Incarnation, Life, Death and Resurrection of Christ with the sole purpose of saving us from our sin. This is the grace of God, His free, undeserved love for us, moving towards us in the supreme desire and effort to save us (on *Grace, see* pp. 65f.).

2. *Jesus did not come to earth simply and solely to die*

We must make this equally clear. The Cross sums up and focusses the whole life and purpose of Christ; if we would see the work of Christ, we must 'survey the wondrous Cross', for there it is plainly and decisively and finally revealed and enacted. But the Cross of Christ was the historical consequence of the life of Christ, and should never be treated in isolation from it. We may put it this way. If Christ had lived and taught in another place and at another time than in Palestine in the first century, perhaps His death would have taken place by another means than crucifixion—modern states, for instance, have other ways of liquidating those whom they cannot absorb; but the life of perfect love, lived in the conditions provided by human sin, leads invariably, in all circumstances which we can possibly conceive, to the point at which ordinary human beings must either accept it for themselves or seek to destroy it. In the actual conditions of Palestine in the first century A.D., the perfect life of love, lived out to its ultimate consequences, resulted in the death by crucifixion of Jesus Christ. In other words, the life of Jesus is of one piece with His death, and the death of Jesus is of one piece with His life; He died in the way He did because He lived in the way He did, and the life and death of Jesus make one story, one closely-knit series of events. It is possible to place such exclusive emphasis on the death of Christ that His life and teaching, His courage and His compassion, His friendship and His mighty words, became merely a curtain-raiser to the crucifixion—and that is to make nonsense of the Gospels.

3. *The Cross of Jesus must not be separated from His Resurrection*

We must be even more careful not to do this. It is necessary, no doubt, to have one sermon for Good Friday, and one for Easter Sunday; but the subject of both sermons is the same, the redemption of the world through our Lord Jesus Christ, who was born, lived, died and rose again for our salvation. Sometimes we seem to suggest that the story of Jesus is a story with an intolerably unhappy ending, so unhappy that God had to do something to put things to rights, and therefore arranged the resurrection to give a happy ending after all—like 'god from the machine' in those rather strange Greek dramas, where human affairs are in such a tangle that a divine person intervenes, turns everything round and sends the audience away happy, but quite unconvinced that life is really like that. Or else we go to the other extreme, and treat the crucifixion as the end of the story of redemption, with the resurrection as an after-thought or appendix—like the last page of some of Dickens' novels, where the author tells us how the characters of the novel lived happily (or unhappily) ever after. We are not saved by the life of Jesus, we are not saved by the death of Jesus, we are not saved by the resurrection of Jesus; we are saved by the life, death and resurrection of Jesus, which is one great event, one great Saving Act of God.

Far from reversing the effect of the Cross, *the Resurrection published to the world, and set God's seal upon, what had happened on the Cross.* The Cross seemed to be the victory of evil: the Master was dead,

His followers were scattered and impotent; the movement had collapsed and was likely in a few days to be completely forgotten. It looked as if God's attempt to save mankind had failed—or rather it looked as if God had had nothing to do with the whole affair. But the reality was very different from the appearance. A conflict between good and evil is not decided by material gains and losses; the cause of justice is never defeated by the massacre of its supporters. Evil triumphs when good men become evil, not when good men are struck down and killed. If Jesus had compromised with evil—if He had run away from His pursuers, if He had hit back in word or deed at His persecutors, if He had come to hate His murderers and long for revenge upon them— then evil would have triumphed and God would have been defeated. But this did not happen, for Jesus 'when he was reviled, reviled not again; when he suffered, he threatened not' (1 Pet. 2^{23}); and on the Cross He prayed for the forgiveness of His murderers (Lk 23^{34}). He lived out the life of perfect love to the end, to the exceedingly bitter end. And so He triumphed over the worst that man could do to Him, by continuing in spite of everything to love those who hated Him and had brought Him to His death. But His triumph was concealed from His enemies and even from His friends; the verdict of failure was unanimously given by friend and foe alike.* 'And on the third day He rose again from the dead.' The true story had broken, the secret of God's victory on the Cross was revealed: God's justice and love were vindicated, and the powers of evil were eternally discomfited; for they knew that they had received a blow from which they had not recovered, and could never recover.

4. *The Blame for the Crucifixion*

We must make it plain to our hearers that the whole blame for the crucifixion of Jesus cannot be put on the shoulders of the Pharisees, the Sadducees, the Romans, and the Jewish populace of the time. The contemporaries of Jesus must, of course, share the blame; they were the historical agents of human sin. But they were acting on behalf of all of us; they did what we should have done if we had been there to do it. Especially they acted

* The Creed tells us that 'He descended into Hell'; this may mean, either that He tasted to the full the cup of death, so that nothing of what death means was withheld from Him, or that He preached during the interval between death and resurrection to the men and women who had died before His Incarnation and yet were willing to believe His Gospel when they heard it (see *CAT* 12).

as representatives of good people—of good people who pride themselves on their goodness and count on it to gain them favour with God; for it was people like that who took the major share of the work in encompassing the death of Jesus. 'Sinners', in the technical sense of the term, probably did very little towards it; for the most part they were prepared to 'live and let live', and, besides, Jesus had done many of them many a good turn. It would be pleasant to put the blame on Pontius Pilate, or Judas, or Caiaphas; but the attempt to shift the blame always breaks down in the end, and all men who clearly see the love of Jesus on the Cross are brought to acknowledge that it was *they* who crucified Him, whatever anyone else may have done towards it.

C. THE DOCTRINE OF THE ATONEMENT

We are saved, then, through the Cross, and the preaching of the Cross is the human instrument in our salvation. But when we have been thus saved, it is right and proper that we should begin to try to think out in clear and logical terms *how* this has happened; to formulate a theory which makes sense of our experience and gives us some insight into the purposes of God and His ways of working them out. Otherwise we shall be excluding one part of our personality, the mental and rational part, from our religion and disobeying the command to love God with all our mind.

Christian theologians down the ages have formulated many such theories: the very number of them is clear proof that the perfect theory has not yet been found. From each of those which have influenced the thought of the Christian Church there is much for us to learn, but the variety of ideas is so bewildering that it may be as well to suggest a few tests by which each of them should be judged.

1. *Is it true to the Biblical Revelation?*

That is the first test of any theory of the Atonement. This sounds very obvious, and is; yet it is sometimes forgotten. More than once in the history of the Church, someone has thought up an account of the way in which man may be reconciled to God, borrowing his ideas, it may be, from some non-Christian religion or philosophy; and then has painted over it a coating of Christian terms. But of Biblical foundation there is none. It does not follow that if a theory employs the name of Christ it is a Christian theory; for 'Christ' may be just a useful way of expressing our own ideas and getting them over to others. Therefore we do well to apply to all our theories the simple test of fidelity to the New Testament. This does not mean that we must not say any more than the New Testament says, for the New Testament has no fully worked-out theory of the Atonement; it does mean that no theory deserves consideration unless it starts from the New Testament's message, and always remains faithful to it.

2. *Is it wholly consistent with the nature and character of God as revealed to us by and in Jesus Christ?*

This second test is really a development of the first. Not infrequently sub-Christian ideas of God, even anti-Christian ideas, have crept into and distorted doctrines of the Atonement. Sometimes they have come from the Old Testament, taken as it stands, unconfirmed and unfulfilled by the New—whereas we have seen that the Old Testament becomes a source of Christian doctrine as it finds its confirmation and fulfilment in Christ. Sometimes they have come from legal, political and economic notions and customs current in the time of the author of the theory; much of medieval thought about the Cross was highly coloured by the conditions and conceptions of social life which we know as the Feudal System, and God appears as a feudal monarch. Of course, the customs and ideas of any age or place may be very useful in throwing light on some aspects of the work of Christ, or may serve as illustrations to drive home some vital point in the Gospel of the Cross. But this is a very different thing from allowing non-Christian notions of God to determine our doctrine of the Cross. We have seen 'the light of the knowledge of the glory of God in the face of Jesus Christ' (2 Cor. 4[6]), and we dare not permit that knowledge to be darkened by the intrusion of an alien system of thought.

3. *Does it show the Work of Christ as something done once for all?*

As something done without our knowledge and before we were born, yet available for us and for all mankind; something 'objective'? That is the third test. Christ died for all—whether anyone has faith in Him or not, whether anyone accepts God's offer of forgiveness or not. The work of Christ does not become operative for *me* until I accept it for myself in penitence and faith; but the work of Christ has been done, finished, once and for all, whether I repent and believe, or obstinately prefer my own manner of life. The reality of the Atonement does not depend on my experience of forgiveness, it is simply *there*, freely offered for me and all men to accept. When Christ died and rose again, something happened which revolutionized the whole human situation, and the world can never be the same again. I am born into a different world from that of Amos or Socrates or John the Baptist, because Christ was crucified and rose again. That is why we must reject any suggestion that the sacrifice of Calvary needs to be repeated on the altar or in my experience in order to operate fully, and must test any doctrine of the Atonement on the score of 'objectivity' and 'once-for-allness'. The Atonement has taken place—make of it what I will.

4. *Does it show the Death of Christ as available for me?*

This fourth test corrects the one-sided emphasis that would appear in our thought if we applied the third test exclusively. There is great truth on its own level in the old love-song:

> *If she be not fair to me,*
> *What care I how fair she be?*

And it leads us to a truth in the matter which we are discussing. If we speak of the Atonement too much as an event, a transaction, a victory which has taken place before we were born, and without our knowledge and consent, we are in danger of leaving the personal, individual element entirely out of the message of the Cross, and that would be a fatal thing to do. Every Christian prays to be able to echo the words of Paul: 'That life which I now live in the flesh I live in faith, the faith which is in the Son of God, who loved me, and gave himself up for me' (Gal. 2[20]). The Cross is an objective fact; but it is also a deeply personal matter. So we must apply this final test to all our theories of the Atonement: do they show how 'Christ has taken away my sins, even mine, and saved me from the law of sin and death'? Do they show how I may come before God, not in fear as a slave, not in pride as a keeper of the law, but humbly, trustfully, fearlessly as a son, justified freely by His grace, reconciled and brought near by the blood of the Cross?

D. THE HISTORIC THEORIES OF THE ATONEMENT

With these four tests in mind, we can now go on to consider the most famous and searching theories of the Atonement. We shall probably find that not one of them stands up with equal success to all four tests, but that all contain most valuable elements of truth. All of them are developed out of verses or passages from the New Testament. For our convenience in thinking of them, we shall put each of them under the heading of its leading idea; but in no case will the leading idea exhaust the significance of the whole theory.

1. *Christ our Champion against the hosts of evil*

The theory which claims pride of place—though not, of course, monopoly of the truth—in any treatment of the Atonement, must be the one that is widely known as the 'classic' theory of the work of Christ. The essence of it is that Christ, as the Champion and Representative of the whole human race, fought and defeated in the Cross and Resurrection all the evil forces that make war against the soul of man (*see* pp. 74f.). It springs ultimately from such passages in Paul as this: 'And you, being dead through your trespasses and the uncircumcision of your flesh, you, I say, did he quicken together with him . . . having put off from himself (or, better, "despoiled") the principalities and powers, he made a show of them openly, triumphing over them in it' (i.e. the Cross: Col. 2^{15}); and from the whole emphasis of the New Testament that Christ has conquered once and for all the demons, 'the world rulers of this darkness', who until His coming held the race of men in fearful bondage.

Many of the early Christian Fathers made much of this idea, and developed it in various ways. Irenaeus, for instance, who was bishop of Lyons from A.D. 180–190, puts it in this form: Man by the Fall has lost the capacity for immortality. The purpose of the Incarnation was to restore it to man. 'On account of His infinite love Christ became what we are, in order that He might make us what He Himself is.' So He recapitulated, went over again, all the experiences of Adam—with the exactly opposite result; in His birth, temptations, miracles, death, descent into hell, and resurrection He dealt a series of hammer-strokes against the Devil and all his angels, and finished them off with the final blow of the Ascension. He did all this on our behalf, and caused us to share in His victory. In order to make Irenaeus' meaning plain, and if we may compare sacred things with secular (though to English people these particular 'secular' things are almost sacred!), it is a little like a batsman, going in late in the innings when his team has collapsed, who masters one by one the bowlers who have made havoc of his predecessors, and finally makes the winning hit, giving to all his team a tremendous victory. Christ has defeated all our enemies, and we are more than conquerors in Him.

Athanasius (A.D. 296–373), the great Bishop of Alexandria, put it a little differently. Death is the penalty of sin, and man has therefore died. He requires a new principle of life which shall overpower the principle of death and corruption in man. So the Word of God became man as the representative of the human race, and in His human body conquered death and all the powers of evil. 'He became man in order that we might become divine . . . and He endured the outrage which befell Him at the hands of men in order that we might inherit immortality.'

Martin Luther embraced this idea with great enthusiasm, and it was his characteristic way of describing the Atonement. 'The true and proper office of Christ is to wrestle with the Law, with the sin and the death of the whole world, and so to wrestle that He must suffer and abide all these things; and by suffering them in Himself conquer and abolish them, and by this means deliver the faithful from . . . all evils.' Christ has joined battle with the 'tyrants' who seek to lord it over human life, and administered an absolutely final defeat. The issue of this Holy War is not in doubt, even though the fighting may continue for many years to come—the decisive battle has been fought and won on the Cross and in the Resurrection. Or, as Luther puts it in his most famous hymn:

> *With force of arms we nothing can,*
> *Full soon were we down-ridden;*
> *But for us fights the proper Man,*
> *Whom God Himself hath bidden.*
> (*MHB* 494—*see* the whole hymn.)

We may in our day be rather doubtful about the whole conception of the 'Devil and his angels'. Not all of us believe in the Devil;* fewer of us in his angels. But evil is, on any account, highly organized and exceedingly powerful, and its roots run deep into every human soul. This theory does assure us that the struggle against it, which is plainly beyond our unaided powers, has been undertaken by Christ and victoriously carried through. And if we miss the note of personal forgiveness and encounter

* On the Devil, *see* pp. 89f.

with God, we do gain from it the supremely Christian confidence that in the cosmic war against evil the victory of God is absolutely secure and that a full share in it is ours for the taking.

A famous, and rather quaint, extension of this theory is found in several early Christian writers. It is rather doubtfully based on the words of Jesus: 'The Son of man came not to be ministered unto but to minister, and to give his life a ransom for many' (*see ANT, para.* 147), and takes for granted that, being the bondslaves of the Devil, we need to be literally ransomed before we can be free. God offered Christ as a ransom to the Devil, and the Devil, thinking that he was making an excellent bargain, accepted Him, and Christ was crucified. But he was cheated of his prey, for the resurrection released Christ from his clutches, and he was left with neither his slaves nor his ransom. This notion of the 'double-crossing' of the Devil, for all its oddity and crudity, does bring home to us the shattering fact of our bondage to sin, and the stupidity of our occasional pretence that, if we only made a sufficient effort, we could set ourselves free; nothing less than the suffering and death and resurrection of Christ could ever do that.

2. *The satisfaction of God's honour and justice*

Anselm (1033–1109), one of the most notable of all the Archbishops of Canterbury, laid it down that man as a rational creature owes to God entire subjection to His will; *nothing less than this will satisfy the honour of God.* Man, by his sin, fails to pay this debt. But the debt must be paid, for God's honour must be upheld; and since man has insulted God by his disobedience, *more* than the exact amount of man's original debt to God is now owing to Him. God cannot simply forgive the sin of man, for *that* would leave His honour unsatisfied. He must have either punishment or an equivalent for what man has taken from Him. Punishment would destroy man, God's costliest creation, and such destruction is alien to God's mind. So He chooses to have equivalent compensation, or *satisfaction*. Man cannot possibly offer it on his own. Only one who is both God and man can offer it: the satisfaction required is so great that only one who is God is capable of giving it; it is owed by man, and only one who is man is in a position to pay the debt. Christ, who is both God and man, paid our enormous debt by the voluntary sacrifice of Himself; thus the necessary satisfaction was made, and God's honour was vindicated.

Probably we find this insistence on God's honour rather repugnant, and we do not like the idea that God is not satisfied until the debt we owe is paid in full; we tend to think that God, if He wills, can forgive us out of hand, and that there is every reason for thinking that He does so will—all that is needed to obtain forgiveness is our repentance. That seems to us to be the plain teaching of Jesus in the Gospels. But this way of thinking ignores what the Gospels certainly do not ignore, the fact of guilt —that we are liable to punishment for our mad rebellion against God; that God as the ruler of a moral universe cannot simply wash the slate clean; that the obliteration of the count against us cost Christ the agony of the Cross. Whatever its defects as an account of the forgiving love of God, Anselm's theory leaves us in no doubt of our status as sinners before God and of the infinite self-giving of Christ for our sake.

3. *The moral influence of the Cross*

We enter a very different, and probably much more congenial, atmosphere when we come to the thought of Anselm's younger contemporary, Abelard (1079–1142), whose speculations made him a storm-centre of medieval theology. Abelard rejected all ideas of ransom to the Devil and of satisfaction to God. He claimed that the righteousness of God is only another name for His love, and that the doctrine of the Atonement is simply and solely concerned with the love of God. God was always ready, and is always ready, to forgive us all our sins. The difficulty about forgiveness, he said, does not lie in anything that has to do with God and His requirements; the difficulty is in us, our stubbornness, our excuse-making, our self-centredness, our unrepentance. Therefore Christ died in order to win us back to God; He gave us the highest possible proof of love in order to kindle our cold hearts to love and faith. That is the whole meaning of the Atonement.

No one in modern times would deny that Abelard has put his finger on an essential part of the Gospel and brought us back from complicated argument to the understanding of the words: 'I, if I be lifted up from the earth, will draw all men unto myself' (Jn 12[32]). The defect of Abelard lies not in what he says, but in what he omits or denies. There is no trace in him of the idea of guilt, which we have seen to be a necessary part of the Gospel. And we are bound to ask of him what Christ has done for those who do not accept Him. For he seems to make the efficacy of

Christ's work entirely dependent on our response to it; and the idea of His taking away the sins of the whole world is wholly lacking.

4. *The Sacrifice once offered*

Before we can satisfactorily deal with any particular form of the sacrificial theory of the Atonement, we must clear a certain age-old misconception out of the way. It has been widely thought that when we speak of the death of Christ as a sacrifice for sin, when we quote, for instance, 1 Cor. 5^7, 'Our passover hath been sacrificed, even Christ', we imply the view that God needed to be 'propitiated', that the wrath of God needed to be assuaged, by a sacrifice which involved the shedding of blood. Now it is quite true that many Christian preachers and theologians of the past have formulated a sacrificial theory of the Atonement on that presupposition—as if God's attitude to sinners needed to be changed, and could only be changed, by a blood-sacrifice. But the New Testament writers implied no such view, and modern writers who speak of Christ's death as a sacrifice for sin have no intention of suggesting that God needed to be placated and appeased before He was willing to forgive us.

The key New Testament passage in this connection is Rom. 3$^{22\text{-}25}$: 'There is no distinction; for all have sinned, and fall short of the glory of God; being justified freely by his grace through the redemption that is in Christ Jesus: whom God set forth to be a propitiation, through faith, by his blood, to shew his righteousness, because of the passing over of sins done aforetime, in the forbearance of God' (*see ANT*). The old interpretation of this was that the death of Jesus Christ propitiated God ('whom God set forth as a propitiation'). But now we know that the Bible does not speak of propitiating God, though pagan religions often do; so Paul cannot mean that here. But the Bible does often speak of 'making a propitiation', in the sense of performing an act by which guilt is removed; it would be better to call this 'making an expiation' (the word 'expiation' means such an act), since 'propitiation' is so misleading. The Old Testament prescribes various ways of doing this in particular cases—sprinkling blood, for instance; and the priest is often commanded to act on the people's behalf in such matters. But in really serious cases the most enlightened writers of the Old Testament say that only God can make the expiation, and they speak of God as doing so. That is what Paul describes God as doing in this passage; and the 'expiation', the means by which the guilt of human sin is annulled, is the death of Christ. Paul is so completely remote from suggesting that God needs to be propitiated that he depicts God as Himself giving up Christ, His only-begotten Son, to death in order that the guilt of man may be expiated, obliterated. Our guilt is annulled by the death of Christ, which is in this sense a sacrifice for sin, the divinely appointed means of our forgiveness.

We ought to understand in the same way the other New Testament passages in which Christ is described as the 'propitiation for our sins': for instance, 1 Jn 2²: 'If any man sin, we have an advocate with the Father, Jesus Christ the righteous: and he is the propitiation for our sins'—His death is the means by which our guilt is annulled. 'The blood of Jesus his Son cleanseth us from all sin' (1 Jn 1⁷).

With all this in mind, let us study the form of the sacrificial theory of the Atonement which is most likely to appeal to modern minds. This is undoubtedly the one expounded in recent years by Dr Vincent Taylor. The real nature of sacrifice, he says, according to Biblical ideas, is that it is a method devised by God by which we can approach His majesty and holiness; in sacrifice the offering is slain so that its life may be set free to serve God, for 'the blood is the life' (Deut. 12²³). We were estranged from God. Christ came to reconcile us to God. We know that the New Testament writers thought of Him as a sacrifice slain for us; we know also that, in accordance with His own definite teaching, they also regarded Him as the Suffering Servant of God depicted by the Second Isaiah, who endured pain and death as the representative of His people (*see ANT, paras.* 101, 133–4). We may say, then, that He died as a representative sacrifice making a perfect offering of Himself on our behalf and to represent us. His perfect offering was threefold in its nature: (i) it was an act of perfect obedience to the will of the Father; (ii) it was an act of perfect submission to God's judgement on sin; (iii) it was an act of perfect penitence for the sins of men. Thus it was perfectly pleasing to God.

But where do *we* stand in the matter? Christ has acted as our representative, but until we turn to Him, we have not appointed Him or recognised Him as such. To reconcile us to Himself, God has triumphantly disclosed His love for us in the self-giving of Christ, so that we may know that He receives repentant sinners; and He has expressed that love so powerfully in the same act of Christ that we are moved to respond in repentance and trust. When we respond in this way, we identify ourselves with the offering which Christ has made on our behalf, and His offering becomes our offering. Thus the sacrifice of Christ and our response combine to complete our reconciliation to God.

It is no good blinking our eyes to the fact that the idea of sacrifice, in the Biblical sense of the word, plays little part in the life and experience of the average modern man and woman—or, it must frankly be added, of the average Christian. We are bound to ask ourselves whether we can really describe our relations with God in such words. It is hard for us to enter into the minds of people like the New Testament writers, who thought of sacrifice as an obvious and necessary element in man's approach to God; and much harder still to commend that attitude to our hearers. But if we are willing to make and sustain the effort required, we shall find that a whole area of the Christian religion is lighted up for us which before had been wrapped in darkness. God is infinitely holy; we are sinners, putting ourselves in the place which belongs to God. Our self-centredness cannot be brought close to the holiness of God by a mere stroke of the pen, or even by an act of the will. Only the most complete and absolute self-giving, the perfect offering of ourselves, can bring us close to God. But of this we are quite incapable. Christ therefore undertakes it and carries it through as our representative; we have but to turn from our selfishness in even the most imperfect spirit of repentance, and so appropriate that self-offering of Christ; and in Christ the perfect offering of ourselves is made.

5. *The completion of our Penitence*

Christians have always understood that God has mercy on us and forgives us, if we truly and sincerely repent. But this is not so simple as it sounds, for true repentance is not so easy as it sounds. All too often our 'repentance' is mixed up with all sorts of other things—remorse, fear of punishment and other unpleasant consequences, fear of losing favour with those whom we love, shame at loss of prestige, and so on; and too often diluted by the lurking, unconfessed knowledge that when the same temptation comes again we may fall again, and even want to fall again. Above all, the taint of selfishness comes in to mar even our most sincere feelings and acts of repentance. It was with this in mind that two 19th-century theologians, J. McLeod Campbell in Scotland and R. C. Moberly in England, worked out in different ways the theory that the Cross was an act of '*vicarious penitence*'. (Turn back to p. 84 for Vincent Taylor's use of the idea.)

Moberly states the theory in this way. Penitence is the most distinctive feature of Christianity, and it is only possible to a human person, as one who has a capacity for righteousness, has sinned and become wretched because of his sin. Penitence is the expression and the relief of love. If penitence were to do its perfect work, it would so change a man that he would be absolutely one with the spirit of holiness. God forgives those who are perfectly penitent. But perfect penitence is far beyond us, as we have seen, and if it is to come within our reach a Mediator is needed. If such a Mediator is to succeed in his task, he must act voluntarily and out of pure love; he must be so closely related to the guilty one that he can be his representative; and he must by his endurance on behalf of the guilty be able to produce the beginnings of repentance in the guilty. Christ has satisfied all these conditions, for He is Man, the Perfect Man, and humankind is summed up in Him. In His death He perfectly repented for the sins of the whole world, and both judged and conquered sin, setting it under the judgement of God's eternal righteousness. By His patient endurance of the suffering which He did not deserve, He stirred in us the beginnings of repentance; but our repentance was very feeble. Christ identified Himself with it, completed it by Himself, repenting perfectly on our behalf, and offered it to God. Thus God received perfect penitence from us—for Christ is our representative—forgave us and made us His children.

The idea of vicarious penitence may give us pause. For how can anyone, even Christ, repent for the sins of others? Yet when Christ was baptised in the Jordan with the baptism of John (*see ANT, para.* 101), when He 'was made to be sin on our behalf' (2 Cor. 5^{21}), must it not be true in some profound way that He identified Himself with our weak aspirations after goodness, our imperfect sorrow for sin, and perfected them and presented them to God? Even so, a father might 'complete the penitence' of his erring son.

6. *We deserve Punishment, but we receive Forgiveness*

One of the ideas that has appeared from time to time in our discussion of the Cross is that of the punishment of sinners. We do not like that idea very much nowadays. We are not at all sure that God is the sort of person who punishes sinners; and we are certainly not going to believe that Christ took upon Himself the punishment that was due to us—for that would be monstrously unjust. The New Testament certainly says nothing about vicarious punishment; but the idea of punishment in itself is not disposed of so easily. Dr Leonard Hodgson, in one of the most recent studies of the Atonement, has shown that the repudiation of the idea of divine punishment springs from a confusion between the way in which we as individuals ought to treat our fellowmen, and the way in which communities and higher authorities ought to treat those subject to them. No doubt it is true that we as private persons are not entitled by any moral law to avenge ourselves on those who offend us. But the case of a community and its members is very different. It must disown wrong acts done by its members, lest its good name and its welfare be damaged; that is, it must punish criminals. And God also must punish sinners. Our whole life comes to us from Him. We are free to use it as we will, but if we use it in a manner contrary to His purposes, He must disown us and punish us, lest He be found to condone and encourage sin. This is the meaning to be attached to the 'wrath of God', and Dr Hodgson does not want us to omit from the *Venite* the final clause: 'unto whom I sware in my wrath that they should not enter into my rest'.

But God has no desire to punish us; His whole will is to forgive us. In Christ He *has* forgiven us; we have only to accept that forgiveness for ourselves. And He has forgiven us in this way. In our human relationships, when we are injured, we 'react', we hit back, we take revenge—and the evil already done is continued and multiplied. If a boy in a boarding school steals a collar stud from his neighbour, the victim of the theft will, perhaps, steal one from his neighbour, and he from his, and so on and on. If that were all, the whole matter would be regrettable, but not very serious; the last person left studless would no doubt borrow from someone else who was lucky enough to own two studs. But that is *not* all. Human sin does not work out so simply as that. For each new theft brings ill-feeling, bad temper and a host of other evils in its train, and the resultant evil at the end of the story is entirely out of proportion to the trivial misdoing which started the whole process. So it is always with human sin, and that is one reason why the evil in the world is so widespread and so deeply rooted. Each of us is a 'conductor' of evil in a small, or not so small, way. But Christ on the Cross 'when he was reviled, reviled not again, when he suffered, threatened not' (1 Pet. 2^{23}). That is, He refused to 'conduct' evil any further; He took the sin of the world, which had brought Him to His death, into Himself, and made it the opportunity for goodness and mercy. That is the nature of the divine forgiveness, expressed in the passion and death of His Son.

Clearly we have not here a full exposition of the universal scope and power of the Atonement; but we do gain a further insight into the grace of God, 'whose property is always to have mercy' and forgive.

What shall we do with all these theories of the Atonement? Commit them to memory in order to satisfy the examiners? There is no harm in doing that. But there is something much more important to do—study them with care and prayer; add to them everything else of value that we can find on the subject; welcome into our thinking everything that throws light on human need and divine forgiveness; discard what needs to be discarded (and if we think maturely, we shall find that there is not very much discarding to do); and mould our own doctrine of the Atonement in accordance with the teaching of the New Testament. But there is one thing that we may not do—claim at any point that we have a complete and perfect theory of 'the love which passeth knowledge'. If any theory seems to explain everything, it is condemned by that very fact; for God's grace and the work of Christ are infinitely beyond our theories. And all our theorizing is only valuable, or excusable, insofar as it helps us to lay a firmer hold on the promises of God.

E. THE PROBLEM OF SUFFERING

We have spoken much of the evil in the world, but we have so far limited our discussion of it to that part of it which comes under the heading of sin. But sin is not the only part of evil, though it is the part which has the most disastrous and far-reaching consequences. There is also the human suffering caused by sin, partly in the life of the sinner, usually still more in the lives of innocent people; there is human suffering—including most forms of disease—which is not caused by sin; there are natural disasters, uncaused by sin, which apart from causing human suffering seem to us to be evil in themselves; and there is the pain in the animal world. For those who believe in the goodness of God, these things constitute a real and pressing problem. It has been handled in *Study Two*, and for a full treatment of it we have to turn to books on 'the philosophy of religion'.

But the Christian has a message about suffering which is primarily practical rather than theoretical. It is, firstly, that Christ on the Cross entered into the deepest depths of human suffering, and took the whole of human suffering into Himself; which means that God shares all our pain, and that we may share all our pain with God. And, secondly, the Resurrection shows that the last word about human life does not rest with pain and death, but with joy and life. Christ's conquest of death is also His conquest of pain; and as we are invited to share His conquest of the one, we are also invited to share His conquest of the other. This does not mean that we have privileges in the matter of avoiding pain and material disaster; if we have a privilege as Christians at all, it is largely in the direction of having more material disadvantages to contend with. It does mean that, however shattering and decisive and destructive any particular experience may seem to be, however desperate our earthly situation, there is nothing in life or death which can separate us from the love of God which is in Christ Jesus our Lord.

F. THE HOPE OF GLORY

The subject of heaven belongs properly to the *Study* on the Last Things. But it needs to be mentioned here, lest it be thought that the Christian hope of a future life is something tacked on as a kind of extra to the Christian faith. There have been teachers who have suggested that life after death, though real, is somewhat irrelevant at present. 'At the moment we are concerned with this present life. We can turn our attention to the next when the time comes.' But actually the Christian hope of eternal life springs from the Christian assurance of the grace of God in this life by an inevitable logic, just as the resurrection of Jesus Christ followed inevitably upon His crucifixion. If we are bound by faith to Christ, we are 'in Christ', as Paul is never tired of saying and implying. This is, He takes us up into His life, His sufferings and death, His resurrection in glory, His eternal life with God the Father, so that we share all these things with Him.

> *Made like Him, like Him we rise;*
> *Ours the Cross, the grave, the skies:*
> *Hallelujah!*

NOTE ON 'THE DEVIL'

In the preceding pages, we have neither affirmed nor denied the existence of the Devil. The great majority of Christians, all through the centuries, have believed most firmly in his reality, and there is a very strong case for this belief. Is it really possible that all the moral evil in the world has been caused by the sole agency of man, and is it not perhaps the sign of man's overweening pride that he should think himself able to produce such vast results? And what shall we say of the evil in nature, the evil which manifests itself in earthquakes and diseases and disasters? (*See* pp. 26f.). To answer these questions, Christians have asserted the existence of an Enemy of God, at work in God's world, with the power and will to tempt mankind and bring evil on the created order. Such a being is not, of course, another God. He is a created being, perhaps a fallen angel, with strictly limited powers; and his efforts to frustrate the will of God are doomed to final failure.

It is quite clear that Jesus and the apostles believed in the existence of Satan, this Enemy of God (Mt $4^{1\text{-}11}$, Lk 22^{31}, 1 Cor. 7^5, Acts 5^3, etc.), and the New Testament is full of examples of his malign power.

Some Christians, however, find it hard to believe in such a person. They ask whether God would have allowed one of His creatures to have such power to pervert His creation, and are afraid that such a belief limits the sovereignty of God. Also, they feel that to ascribe temptation to the Devil tends to give man an excuse for his evil-doing.

We may take warning from these doubts. When we assert the existence and power of Satan, we must be careful to bear two things in mind: (i) When the Devil tempts us and we fall, the sin is *ours*, and we may not shift any part of the blame. (ii) Satan has been finally defeated in the Cross and the Resurrection (*see* pp. 79f.). Before His passion, Jesus in a vision saw 'Satan fallen as lightning from heaven' (Lk 10^{18}). He saw His coming victory before it happened, and by His passion the victory was won. Satan is defeated, though he does not yet acknowledge his defeat, and fights on with scarcely diminished force.

> *And let the Prince of ill*
> *Look grim as e'er he will,*
> *He harms us not a whit;*
> *For why? his doom is writ,*
> *A word shall quickly slay him.*
> *(MHB 494)*

THE WORK OF CHRIST

SERMON VIII. THE FIRST-FRUITS OF THE SPIRIT

Theme of the Sermon. The degree of Sanctification which follows immediately from Justification.

EXPLANATORY OUTLINE OF THE SERMON

Introduction. (1-3) Those who have been justified by their faith in Christ have no condemnation resting on them (i.e., they know they are 'right with God').

I. *The Life 'In Christ' and 'In the Spirit'.* (1) Paul teaches that those who believe are 'in Christ'. (This great Pauline phrase is explained in *Study Seven*, p. 121, and should be contrasted with another Pauline phrase, 'in Adam'. Look forward to p. 154 where, in a note on Sermon V, the meaning of 'in Adam' is discussed.) Sinful men who disobey, by their disobedience 'stand in with' Adam in his sin and in his death. In effect they say 'I take him as my type'. These are 'in Adam'. By contrast, those who open their hearts to trustful and obedient faith in Christ 'stand in with' Christ, both in His Cross-bearing (i.e., His sacrificial life of sinless obedience to the Father) and in His Resurrection victory. Man can say 'I take Christ as my type' by taking Christ's name, living by faith in Him, obeying Him, pledging allegiance to the community of His people, and by 'taking up the Cross', i.e., by facing the claims and troubles and wrongs of life in the spirit of Christ. These are 'in Christ'. The morally victorious Christ is now in possession of their lives. (2) Those who are 'in Christ' are not 'in the flesh'. (What Paul means by '*the flesh*' has already been explained. Turn back to *Study Four*, p. 60. See also *ANT* on Gal. 5$^{16\text{-}26}$.) (3) Those who are 'in Christ' find that the rebellious 'flesh' is being put to death. However, this is a gradual process, for temptation ('the root of bitterness') still comes with power. Nevertheless, the believer has secure power to overcome temptation, so that each attack works a lesson of good. (4) The believer is also 'in the Spirit' (a Pauline phrase not easy to distinguish from the point of view of practical Christian experience from 'in Christ'). (5, 6) Those who are 'in the Spirit' show a progressive sanctification of life.

II. *The Good Conscience of the Christian before God.* (In this important section, and with great insight, Wesley sets out, on the one hand, the irremovable human limitations which are consistent with love to God, and, on the other, that *voluntary* dallying with temptation which is inconsistent with it.)

(1) The Christian is not condemned (is 'right with God') on the score of past sins, which are forgiven. (2) He enjoys the Witness of the Spirit, giving him an assurance of salvation. (3) Nevertheless, he may have temporary lapses from true faith. (4) He is not condemned for present sin, for Christ gives him secure victory over temptation. (5) The sincere believer need not be separated from God by a guilty conscience on the ground that he is painfully aware that in him there is still that bias (which is what Wesley means by 'inward sin') which makes evil easier to do than good; (6) that his heart is deceitful and a constant battle-ground with sore temptation; or (7) that he cannot give to God that ideally perfect service which is offered in heaven, either in moral obedience or in devout worship. (8) Thus the Christian is not guilty because of these *infirmities*, as set out above. (Wesley does right to call in question the description of these as 'sins of infirmity'. That they are there is a mark that man is a fallen creature. The Christian rightly feels humiliation before God on their account. But they are not sins for which he is *responsible*.) (9) There is no guilt attaching to what the believer genuinely cannot help, though (10) he may rightly feel grief over it. (11) The most difficult case of 'infirmity' to estimate is that element of surprise, or of inexperience of life, which may hurry the believer into a false choice without being fully aware of it. If the 'surprise' is genuine there is no true guilt. (12) However, the 'surprise' may be the result of past spiritual slumbers. For this condition the believer is guilty. (13) If he is surprised into wrong the sincere believer will rightly feel grieved and ashamed, but need not have a troubled conscience (provided that he learns his lesson from experience).

(Sin, as Wesley here describes it, is 'a wilful thought or action for which God can hold the individual *personally* responsible'. This definition is sound so long as it is clearly in mind that the question of *personal* guilt is being discussed. However, the religious consciousness does tend to think of 'sin' as *everything* in human life by which man falls short of the ideal moral and spiritual perfection of God. The above notion of sin is narrower than this. If it has a failing it is that it is purely individual, and has no place for the corporate corruption of the race. Those who work from the broader view of sin naturally tend to say that complete sanctification is not possible this side of heaven.)

THE WORK OF CHRIST

III. *The Subject Applied to the Enquiring Hearer.* (1) The believer is invited to rejoice in his confidence in God. (2) If he is conscious that he has fallen into sin since his conversion he is not to despair of his faith, but is to take courage that he can start again in penitent faith. (3) But, on the other hand, if he is aware that sin still has power over him, he is certainly not to trust that he is *now* acceptable to God on account of the reality of his *past* experience. (4) The awakened believer is not to repine because he is so painfully aware that he is still a frail man, very far from the perfection of God. It is a part of the Christian experience to become increasingly aware of just this pain, so that the believer may be led by the Spirit to a deeper, more sensitive, and humbler penitence. This is the path to growth in grace, and Perfection. (5) When the believer is confronted with his own human infirmities he is not to despair of the Christian life, but is to recollect anew that his sole sufficiency is in divine grace. (6) If he is entrapped into a fault by surprise or inexperience it is to be the occasion of sincere penitence, but is not to be allowed to destroy the believer's childlike joy and confidence in God.

TEST QUESTIONS

1. How would you set about constructing a theory of the Atonement?

2. In what sense was Christ's death a Sacrifice?

3. Describe the Christian's victory over sin, its full scope, and its limitations, as portrayed in *Sermon* VIII.

STUDY SIX

The Person of Christ

CHRISTIAN doctrine may be likened to a seamless robe from which no piece can be taken without the whole being marred. For the purposes of discussion it is necessary to divide the material into subjects; yet, as the writer of each *Study* in this book must have recognised, all that is said about any one theme is incomplete, and to some degree distorted, unless all the rest of the Faith is remembered. This is particularly true of the doctrine which we are now to examine, the doctrine of the Person of Christ, or 'Christology'. If we say that the Person of Christ is central in Christian doctrine, we do not imply that this is the only doctrine; we mean that everything that the Christian believes—about God and man, about this world and the next, about the Christian Church and Christian Ethics—depends upon what he believes about Jesus. And the Christological doctrine is central in our theology because Jesus Himself is at the centre of all Christian life. That fact is abundantly clear in the New Testament itself.

John's Gospel says, 'These (signs) are written that ye may believe that Jesus is the Christ, the Son of God; and that believing ye may have life in his name' (Jn 20^{31}). The professed purpose of that Gospel is to convince the readers of the full deity of Christ, in order that, through that faith, they may enter into 'life'. We shall not now pause to examine the meaning of the words deity, faith, life. Whatever their meaning may be, the same purpose lies behind every book of the New Testament. No page of that volume could have been written by anybody who did not hold this belief that Jesus is the Christ, the Son of God; who did not wish to bring others to this faith; who did not know that this faith was the entrance gate to a new kind of life. (By the way, James is not an exception, as is sometimes wrongly suggested. See 1^1, 2^1.) It is not merely that each writer affirms, in his own language, the unique relationship of Jesus with the Father—

although that is most significantly true.* It is even more important that the whole New Testament glows with faith in Jesus. Mark well that preposition *in*. It is not sufficient to say that Christians hold the faith *of* Jesus; as Dr Denney wrote years ago, 'Christianity as it is represented in the New Testament, is a life of faith in Jesus Christ. It is a life in which faith is directed to Him as its object, and in which everything depends upon the fact that the believer can be sure of his Lord' (*Jesus and the Gospel*). That is the faith which we are now to consider; but first we must recall how that faith began to be held.

A. THE SAVIOUR KNOWN THROUGH HIS WORK

One of the traditional divisions in the study of Christian theology, to which reference was made above, is the division between the *Person* and the *Work* of Christ. Under the first heading we consider *Who* Jesus was (and is); under the latter we ask *What* He did (and does and will do). It is of the utmost importance to bear in mind that this distinction is an artificial, even if a necessary one; the answer to neither question can be found if the other is ignored. What Jesus did was due to Who He was; Who He was can only be recognised by knowing What He did. In the more strictly logical order we should discuss His Person first, for the work of Christ was work that only He could do. But in the order of human experience, that is, of the way in which men come to faith, it is through what He does that they come to know who He is. That is why in this book, unlike most similar books, we have discussed the Work of Christ first. You must never forget that all that is said here finds its strongest support in what was written in *Study Five*, and in the parts of *Study Four* which have special reference to the Second Person of the Trinity. When we come to preach the message about Jesus, we must always recall that the Saviour is known through His works.

1. *The Apostolic Preaching*

The fact that Christ's Nature was made known to men and women through His deeds is most clearly shown in the New Testament itself, and our first approach to that evidence may be

---

* In *Jesus the Son of God*, I have tried to summarize the evidence for this statement. There is not space to repeat that summary here, but any reader, if he will, can satisfy himself that no New Testament writing offers us what is sometimes called 'a merely human' Jesus.

a brief survey of the earliest Christian preaching. In a book that has had a very great influence since it was published in 1936, Dr C. H. Dodd made a study of the Apostolic Preaching (*The Apostolic Preaching and its Developments*). At the end of the book there is a fascinating chart in which the teaching of the following passages is set out in parallel columns: Acts $2^{14\text{-}39}$, $3^{13\text{-}36}$, $4^{10\text{-}12}$, $5^{30\text{-}32}$, $10^{36\text{-}43}$, $13^{17\text{-}41}$; 1 Cor. $15^{1\text{-}7}$; Rom. $1^{1\text{-}4}$, 2^{16}, 8^{34}, $10^{8\text{-}9}$. (There are also a few passages from *Galatians* and *1 Thessalonians*.) If you cannot secure a copy of that chart, at least spend a little time reading those references. You will be struck by the similarity between them. It would take us too far from our present subject to mention all the similarities, important as they are. But the outstanding fact is that all these records of what the first Christians preached centre upon the work of God in and through Jesus Christ Himself. There is the clearest proof here that, so far from the first preachers being content to advocate 'Christian principles', or to call men to follow the example and share the beliefs of Jesus, they *preached Christ*. They declared repeatedly that in the birth, life, ministry, death, resurrection and ascension of Jesus a way had been provided for the remission of sins. They called men and women to believe in this Jesus and to be baptized in His name. And everything they taught about what it means to live as a Christian depended on that proclamation and that invitation.

Of course there is more evidence than this. Notice, for example, how each of the four Gospels concentrates attention upon the Person and Work of Jesus. Dr Gordon Rupp, in a striking illustration, has compared reading the Gospel narratives with the experience of travelling in an express train as the brakes are applied and the train slows down, until, at last, it screeches to silence. So, Dr Rupp points out, the Gospels fasten our attention on a single life, then on thirty years of that life (very rapidly), then on two or three years . . . a few months . . . a week . . . two days 'which are evidently conceived to be of such importance that they are described to us hour by hour. So history slows down in the Gospels until at last all history moves from action to passion and jerks to a halt before the three hours of silence of Jesus on His Cross' (*Principalities and Powers*, p. 32). That is finely said. We must. of course, add to it (as Dr Rupp would) that after this halt at the Cross, the story in the New Testament suddenly gathers new momentum with the Risen Lord, and from that point a new History begins that spreads ever more widely.

But the death of Jesus is central as well as crucial; everything the Christian believes depends upon what he believes about this Jesus, and the focal point of that belief is the death of the Son of God. The Saviour is known through His works.

2. *Jesus reveals and reconciles*

Illustrations have now been given—and they are only illustrations—of the fact that the whole of the New Testament points a finger, as it were, to Jesus Himself. We may see a little more clearly why this was inevitable by considering the fact that Jesus is portrayed as both Revealer and Reconciler. He is both the One who makes God known and the One who brings God to men and men to God.

The obvious way to establish that fact is to look up in a Concordance the words 'reveal' and 'reconcile', with the nouns derived from them. (I leave you to do that for yourself, as a reminder that it is impossible to study Christian theology without a good Concordance.) Highly significant passages will be discovered, but they will not be very numerous, for these words do not occur very often. If, however, you look at all the terms which suggest 'revealing' and 'reconciling', you will find a vast amount of material, and, incidentally, discover a fact of great importance; namely, that different New Testament writers teach the same truth in a different language. You would have to notice, not only explicit references to our Lord revealing and reconciling, but every word and phrase and incident which imply, either that through Jesus people have come to know God as never before, or that through Him they have been brought into a new relationship with God—a relationship which has all kinds of consequences. It is impossible briefly to illustrate that study without reducing it to a fragment. If you will have that search in mind during your reading of the New Testament in the next few months, then, even if you are familiar with the Bible, you may be surprised to discover how saturated with this awareness of the work of Christ as Revealer and Reconciler the pages of the New Testament are. When we remember that most of these pages were written by men who had previously been devout Jews, firmly believing in One God, it becomes truly startling that they should ascribe to Jesus both their knowledge of God's character and their experience of God's greatest gifts. Yet so they did. This was the primary reason why the Church very quickly ascribed to our Lord divine titles, and, before very long, summarised this truth about Him by saying that He was Truly God. We must now consider the origin of that term in more detail.

B. TRULY GOD

The Christian Faith holds that our Lord Jesus Christ is Truly God, Truly Man. As we shall see, the essential point is that those two descriptions should be held together. It is, however, inevitable that we should discuss them separately, and so we ask, firstly, why He is called Truly God.

The first part of the answer to that question has already been given; it is because He did and does for mankind what only God can do. It is necessary, however, that we should inquire a little more deeply. The Christian reader of this book will have no doubt that his Lord is Truly God; it may be that nothing said here can, or should, increase that conviction. It is also true that Christian faith involves much more than acceptance of statements made about Jesus. But this all-important matter is one that calls for our most careful thought; it is no little thing to say that God became Man. Most important of all is the answer to the question, 'Is this faith in Christ simply something that men invented, or did this Christ really live?'

Now, as I have said, the sources for our knowledge of Jesus all come from believers in Him. Some people therefore say, 'Ah! they were all prejudiced. The actual Jesus of history was a very different person from the Christ of Christian belief'. The brief answer to that statement (so often made today) is that the only Jesus of whom we have any record whatsoever is the Jesus of whom we are compelled to say, either, 'Truly God', or, 'This man was an imposter'. So far as we can do so in a few paragraphs, we shall now see the reasons for that answer.

1. *Jesus' words about Himself*

Jesus spoke about Himself and His own work in a way which implied His unique relationship to God the Father. This is sometimes expressed by referring to the 'claims of Jesus'. I do not like that term; it suggests that our Lord debated or argued the facts about Himself. On the contrary, the striking truth is that He seems to have taken for granted these, to us, amazing facts about Himself. It is not that on a few occasions He claimed some special privilege for Himself; it is that always He spoke as no other man, not even a prophet, has spoken. His enemies were sometimes quicker to realize this than were His friends. Fully to prove the truth of what has just been said, it would be necessary to go through the whole of the four Gospels. Here are just a few of the facts.

(a) The clear statements recorded in the Fourth Gospel (e.g. Jn $5^{19ff.}$, 6^{46}, $10^{30ff.}$, $14^{6ff.}$, etc.) are supported by the *very earliest records* of His teaching that we possess. I mention this because the foolish statement is still often made that in *John* we find a 'divine' Jesus and in the Synoptic Gospels a 'human' Jesus. Note carefully these words:

> All things have been delivered unto me of my Father and no one knoweth the Son, save the Father; neither doth any know the Father, save the Son, and he to whomsover the Son willeth to reveal him (Mt 11^{27}; Lk 10^{22}).

These words are recognized as coming from the earliest of all the sources of the New Testament writings, yet they sound exactly as though they had been written by John. They imply that Jesus was in a unique relationship with God the Father; and that, whereas He Himself needed no introduction to the Father, it was His unique function to introduce others to the Father. What a preposterous statement this is, unless it is true!

(b) In many other ways, also, Jesus consistently speaks of God as Father in a manner which distinguishes *His own relationship with God* from that into which all of us may come through Christ Himself. For example, a most careful study of all the uses of the word 'Father' (applied to God) by Jesus shows that 'Jesus drew a clear distinction between the sense in which God is Father to Him personally and to the disciples corporately'.* This fact not only helps us to understand why the whole of the New Testament, unlike much modern teaching, stresses that we may become children of God only through Adoption and Grace, but it also provides the most convincing evidence of the fact that Jesus always spoke about Himself in the unique manner that we are describing. We dare to believe that we are interpreting our Lord's own thought about Himself when we say, 'In His nature and being He is eternally one with God the Father' (*CAT* 8).

(c) The name for Himself which Jesus seems often to have used—*Son of Man*—implies, at least, a unique understanding of

* In *Jesus, Master and Lord*, H. E. W. Turner sets out the evidence for this statement. *See* also *TWB*, p. 78b.

His own Person and Work. This is a difficult bit of New Testament study to which you have already been introduced (*ANT, paras.* 107-9, 134). It must be sufficient to add here that, so far from 'Son of Man' implying that Jesus was just an ordinary man, the reverse is the case. This Son of Man is a mysterious Figure who is to come in glory and to judge the world. Moreover, this Son of Man sets Himself before men as One who has the kind of authority which those who believe in God can only ascribe to God Himself, and who exercises powers that only God can exercise (e.g. Mk 2^{10}, 2^{28}, 8^{38}; Mt 13^{41}; Lk 18^8; Jn 5^{27}, etc.).

The word 'unique' has been used several times in this section, and it is used in its proper sense for that of which there is no other example. Thus Dr J. S. Whale, employing this word carefully, sums up the 'claims' of Jesus by writing,

'The language of Jesus about Himself implies a unique oneness with God, a unique moral authority over men, a unique salvation toward them, and a unique mastery over the powers of evil' (*Christian Doctrine*).

You would do well to convince yourself of the many instances of those four facts.

2. *Jesus' other teaching*

Not only do we find in the recorded words of Jesus about Himself these clear indications of His deity, but His teaching about all subjects implies the same unique character of His own Person and Work.

(a) *The Sermon on the Mount* is sometimes alleged to be an example of moral teaching that does not demand the full faith in Christ Himself. But see how Jesus sets Himself above even the accepted understanding of the Law (Mt $5^{24, 28, 34, 38}$); how He asserts that men's destiny depends upon how they receive His teaching (Mt $7^{24\text{ff.}}$).

(b) It seems hardly necessary to say that the *Miracles* of Jesus were stated by Himself to provide evidence that God's reign was being manifested. 'If I by the Spirit (Lk 'finger') of God cast out devils, then is the Kingdom of God come upon you' (Mt 12^{28}). Christ refused to perform miracles as a method of compelling men and women to believe in Him, but He made it abundantly clear that through His works God the Father Himself was acting in the world. He expected people to recognize this, and He responded to their faith when they did so.

(c) If we read the *parables* of Jesus carefully, we discover that, far from being mere stories with a moral, most of them seek to focus attention on Jesus Himself. How often this fact is missed in sermons about the parables! To take only a few examples, how is it that we can fail to see that the parable of the Wicked Husbandmen is talking about a son, and that this son is Jesus (Mk 12[1ff.] and parallels); how can we read the parable of the Sower, without recognizing that Jesus is speaking about the word that He Himself is preaching (Mk 4[3ff.] and parallels)? Of course, those who first heard the parables also failed to understand that they pointed to the unique work of Jesus Himself; that they were, as Dr C. H. Dodd has so rightly called them, 'parables of the Kingdom'.

(d) *The Kingdom of God*, or the Kingdom of Heaven, is often thought to be nothing other than a 'new world' which men can 'build', if they accept the 'principles' of Jesus and 'apply' them. The words set in quotation marks in that sentence sum up a great deal of so-called Christian teaching in recent years; every one of them is foreign to the letter and spirit of the New Testament message about the Kingdom.

The Kingdom of God is clearly set forth as the Reign of God, introduced by Jesus Himself (e.g. Mk 1[14f.], 12[34]; Mt 4[17]; Lk 8[1, 10], 10[9]), into which men and women 'enter' as they believe in Him. It is a Kingdom which already exists; but it is also one which is 'to come', and its future depends, as does its present existence, upon Christ Himself (compare Mt 12[28] with Mk 14[25]). And so here, in this teaching about the Kingdom, we are brought to One who does the work of God as only God can do it (*see ANT, para.* 103).

3. *The Unexpected Messiah*

I have deliberately refrained from previously mentioning the term *Messiah*. This may seem a strange omission, especially when we recall that we began with John's reminder that his Gospel was written in order that we might believe that Jesus is the Christ (=Messiah) as well as the Son of God. But, for our present discussion, we cannot start from the idea of the Messiah, and say that, because Jesus set Himself forth as the Messiah, therefore He was Truly God; that would imply that this was what the term Messiah meant before He came. We know, on the contrary, that there were many different ideas about the

Messiah when Jesus came (*see ANT, paras.* 73–81), but none of them involved that unique oneness with God which Jesus in fact possessed. It was not that Jesus confirmed men's ideas of the Messiah; it was that He re-made their conception of the Messiah (*see ANT, para.* 107). That is a very large and profound truth for all who would gain a true picture of our Lord. A fascinating and rewarding study is to see how our Lord gathered together much that had previously been believed about the Messiah, the Suffering Servant, and the Son of Man, fused the three into one, and in so doing transformed them (*see ANT, paras.* 101, 134, etc.). He was the Messiah, the Suffering Servant, the Son of Man; He did fulfil all that the prophets had spoken, as the New Testament constantly affirms. But He was greater than the prophets, and greater than the prophets had ever imagined that the Messiah would be. He Himself was Son of God, Truly God.

4. *The faith of the first Christians*

I hope that we have now obtained evidence for the fact that the writers of the Synoptic Gospels clearly taught the full deity of Christ. That same faith is disclosed in the words of the Prologue to the Fourth Gospel, where we are told that Jesus was the Word made Flesh, and that the Word was not only with God, but was God (Jn 1¹). It is no less plain in such words of Paul as Rom. 1⁴ ('declared to be the Son of God with power'), or in 1 Cor. 8⁶ (where all things are said to have been created through Him—cf. Col. 1¹⁶), or in the triumphant conclusion of *1 John* (5²⁰). These are only a few illustrations.

But perhaps the faith of the early Christians in Jesus is most impressive in ways which are not quite so obvious to the modern reader. Remember, again, that most of them were Jews who believed with intensity that there is only one God. Yet they pray to Jesus, they call Him *Lord*. This title might suggest to us merely a mark of respect, but when it is recalled that in the Greek version of the Old Testament (on which many of these Christians had been brought up), *Lord* is the word used to translate the name of God (Yahweh), we can understand why Dr Turner has suggested that, when the first Christians called Jesus *Lord*, this was 'the simplest possible way of affirming that, centrally and essentially, in the depths of His Being, Jesus stood on the side of God rather than that of creatures' (*Jesus, Master and Lord*, p. 228. *See* also *CAT* 9). We may say that 'Jesus is Lord' was the first Christian

Creed (*see ANT, para.* 488). Long before the Creeds, as we know them, were written, people were thinking of Jesus as they thought of God, and—even more significantly—they were thinking of God in the way that they thought of Jesus. He re-made their idea of God. Not only were they sure that God had done many mighty works and signs *through* Christ, not only were they convinced that God had been working *in* Christ; they were already thinking of Him and worshipping Him as one who was Himself God.

They were *worshipping* the risen, ascended, exalted Christ. That is the important point. Before there were carefully framed creeds, men and women were seeing Jesus 'at the right hand of God' (Acts 2^{33-6}, 7^{57}). It must be remembered that, whilst that term 'at the right hand of God' may suggest to our minds two 'gods' standing side-by-side, it would have no such meaning for Jewish minds. All too often, in these days, we forget the message of Ascension Day. The first Christians were quite sure that for a few weeks the Risen Lord had manifested Himself to men and women; but they were equally sure that He had returned to the Father, and that He ever lived to make intercession for them (Rom. 8^{34}; Heb. 7^{25}).

And yet, never for one moment did they believe in the existence of two Gods. To use technical language, their Christology never changed their Monotheism. There were many reasons for this, but one reason was that they believed that Jesus was Truly Man as well as Truly God. Whoever He was, whom they had known and seen, He had not been a second 'God', and He had not been a 'God' pretending to be a man. Jesus was Truly Man.

C. TRULY MAN

It is probably not necessary to spend time in convincing you that Jesus was fully man; that He lived a completely human life. This is often demonstrated by saying that He grew from babyhood, suffered, and enjoyed human life, as we do, and that He died as all men die. But we must say more than that. God is Spirit and has no *physical* body; He is not confined to one place at a time. Jesus had a body; Jesus was only in one place at one moment; Jesus was not Spirit.

1. *The significance of the Humanity of Jesus*

Although these facts may appear to be obvious, it is very necessary to recognize their importance.

a. We notice, firstly, that the New Testament itself does so. Reference has already been made to the frequent allegation that John offers us a more 'divine' Christ (whatever that may mean) than do the other Evangelists (*see* p. 99, above). On the contrary, John goes to special pains to stress that the Word was made *flesh*. There are not a few indications, both in his Gospel and in his Epistles, that, even by the time that he was writing, the full and complete humanity of Jesus was being questioned by some believers. Strange as it may seem to many modern people, it is probably true that the early Church found it harder to believe in the complete humanity of Christ than they did in His deity. But the New Testament leaves us in no doubt about this matter.

b. It is also important to stress that our Lord was Truly Man because it was this that led to some of the very hard (and sometimes bitter) controversies about Christ in the first three centuries A.D. We shall not study those controversies in this book, but they are important because it was as a result of them that the Creeds (which as Methodists we acknowledge) came to be drawn up. Some of the false teachings which were rejected by the Councils which formulated the Creeds were these:

> That Jesus was a divine Being appearing to be a man.
> That Jesus was a man who was made 'divine' after His death.
> That Jesus was in fact half-God and half-man; for example that He had a human body but a divine mind or soul.

These and other notions, expressed in somewhat different words, were resolutely attacked by the main body of Christians. When you come to read the history of these discussions, you may be shocked by the bad feeling that was sometimes aroused, but you will recognize that everything that Christians treasure was at stake. Our whole faith depends upon a belief in a true Incarnation, that is, in the fully human life of God-made-Man. It is impossible to say which view is more contrary to the Christian faith: the view that Jesus was simply a very wonderful man, essentially like the rest of us; or the view that He was in fact God, and not man at all. We shall see more about that in the next section.

c. It is especially necessary to stress the full humanity of Christ in view of the present-day thought about Jesus. Some might claim that all that we need to do today is to help people to believe that Jesus was God, and that this is the only difficulty in their minds. That is not so. In previous paragraphs I have allowed myself to speak of Jesus as 'God', and this is very often done by some of those Christian writers who have most helped many in our generation; e.g. Mr C. S. Lewis and Miss Dorothy Sayers. I do not suggest that it is false so to describe Jesus, but it is important to recall that the New Testament itself prefers to call Him 'Son of God', and that the full Christian description of Him is either 'God-made-Man', or 'Truly God, Truly Man'. Just when we are seeking to bring other people to faith in Christ, we may unintentionally hinder them by leading them to think that Jesus of Nazareth was some kind of divine Being who, as it were, played the part of a human person. That way of thinking, as the early Church knew, leads to the denial of the full Christian faith. (Of course, Miss Sayers and Mr Lewis are well aware of this danger, and have done much to counteract it.)

Whilst answering questions in the open air, I was asked, 'Was Jesus Christ an ordinary man like ourselves?' The questioner was very much in earnest: how would you have answered him? If I said, 'Yes', then I might leave him believing in what is often called 'a merely human Jesus'; if I said 'No', I should even more seriously mislead him. I could not think of the perfect answer; the best that I could say was, 'Jesus was a real man, as real a man as you or I, indeed more so. He was not an ordinary man, but an extraordinary one; He was not just like us, but He was like what I want to be, and what He can help me—and you— to be'. I know that was not an adequate answer, but I hope it was on the right lines.

2. *Jesus was not 'two persons'*

One other point remains to be made about the humanity of Jesus. Some books about our Lord *seek to distinguish what was 'divine' in Him from what was 'human'*. For example, it may be said that He was divine because He worked miracles (in spite of the fact that He said 'greater works than these shall ye do . . .'); or divine because He did not sin, but human because He suffered and died. Or, again, it may be said that He was divine in that He knew all the truth about God, but human because there were other things that He did not know. I can only register my conviction (for which, I think, much support could be obtained from some scholars) that this is not a helpful approach. In the last section of this chapter, we shall recall that Jesus is named both God *and* Man, but we may notice at once that any attempt to mark out the 'divine' person in Him implies that we know what 'divine' and 'human' mean before we know the truth about Jesus. Is not the very opposite true? It is through Him alone that we know the truth about God and man. Moreover, was not our Lord 'Truly God' when He was suffering and dying? (*See MHB* 191, v. 3.) Was He not 'Truly Man' when He spoke about God, when He was tempted in all points as we are, without sinning? In short, I suggest that we cannot divide our Lord into two parts or aspects, and call them 'human' and 'divine', as though He were two 'persons' in one body. It was just this which was done by some of the thinkers whose views were condemned by the early Church, and I think that modern attempts to make the same kind of division only repeat the old heresies in new forms.

Even at the risk of making this section more difficult, I must warn you that one of the most popular Christologies in recent years has been what is known as *Kenotic* Christology. A few words about this. The word 'kenotic' comes from the Greek word translated 'emptied Himself' in Phil. 2^7 (read *vv.* 1–11, and *see ANT* on this passage). Briefly, this theory is that we best understand Christ by thinking that, during His earthly life, the Son of God gave up most of His divine attributes or characteristics, so that He might live an earthly life. Of course, the Christian teachers who hold this view also teach that He was Truly God. That is what I find hard to understand. If He gave up being fully divine, how could He be truly God?

We are touching on themes beyond our understanding, and perhaps the wisest course is to remember that that is so. 'Did the Son of God give up all His eternal work whilst the earthly life of God-made-Man was being lived, *or* did He add to all His eternal work the experience of being Man?'—if we must answer that question, then I, for one, would agree with Archbishop William Temple in preferring the second alternative. But I do not think that we need ask that question, and I am sure that we cannot fully answer it. Certainly the *Philippians* passage does not deal with this matter. *Verses* 6–11 are probably part of a Christian hymn; Paul used those words to call his readers to humility, offering them the example of Jesus who, although He possessed as a right all the privileges of being equal with God, yet humbled Himself to the life of a servant and to death on the Cross. Paul was not discussing what that meant to the Eternal Son of God Himself—who can know that? Still less was he implying that Jesus ceased to be fully Son of God. He was emphasising that the One who was on an equality with God lived a complete and lowly human life. That is the fact that matters. Some Christians like to speculate about how much Jesus knew whilst He was on earth; some even venture to surmise what all this meant in the experience of the Triune-God Himself. I can only suggest that to such questions we should not attempt to give answers. All of us can say, 'He humbled himself, becoming obedient even unto death, yea, the death of the cross' (Phil. 2^8).

> *He chose a poor and humble lot,*
> *And wept and toiled and mourned and died*
> *For love of those who loved Him not.*
> *(MHB 854)*

This, indeed, we must proclaim. He lived our life within all the conditions of human existence; that is the truth behind all the so-called kenotic theories. But what this meant to the Son of God Himself, that only He knows. That we cannot know. 'It is a thing most wonderful, almost too wonderful' to know—almost but not quite, for we can know and believe that it happened. It is, however, equally important to know that it happened to *Him*.

> *He sent no angel to our race*
> *Of higher or of lower place,*
> *But wore the robe of human frame*
> *Himself, and to this lost world came.*
> *(MHB 62)*

He came Truly Man, 'our God contracted to a span, *incomprehensibly* made man'. 'Though he was rich, yet for your sakes he became poor, that ye through his poverty might become rich' (2 Cor. 8^9).

D. TRULY GOD, TRULY MAN

We have looked at each of these terms separately, but we began by noticing that this is a dangerous method, because it suggested a separation that does not exist. In the previous section, we have rejected any attempt to divide our Lord into two parts, or persons. If anything is certain about the thought that lay behind the Creeds, it is that those who formulated them also wished to make the same denial. That fact is somewhat obscured for us today because, in the English language, we speak of Christ having 'two natures', and we speak of the Father and Son as 'two persons' of the Trinity. We must remember that we are then translating Latin words, and that words tend to change their meaning. I want to try to show now that the term 'two natures' as applied to our Lord does *not* imply that He was two different Beings living somehow in one body, and that the statement that there are three Persons in the Trinity does *not* mean that the Son and the Father and the Spirit are different Gods. The second point, however, belongs more fully to *Study Eight*, and will only be touched upon here.

1. *The Definition of Chalcedon*

Although this is not a book about the history of Christian doctrine, we cannot ignore that history. We all too often forget that we are not the first people to wrestle with the attempt to understand our Faith and to express it in words. When we read a little more about the discussions among Christians long ago, we begin to realize that there are indeed few new problems. I have heard a youth group, and even questioners in a public meeting, asking (in other words) the same questions which were asked about Jesus in the first centuries A.D., and even making the very mistakes that then were judged to be heresy.

It was at the Council of Chalcedon, in the year 451, that hundreds of years of discussion about the Person of Christ was summed up and concluded. When we say 'concluded', we do not mean that no further discussion about our Lord has taken place; countless books about His Person have been written and are still being written. But, since Chalcedon, there has been no General Council of the Church which has re-stated our belief about Him. And so, difficult as this part of our study is, we must try to understand this historic way of describing the Person of Christ.

The words that head this section—Truly God, Truly Man— are at the beginning of a very long and involved sentence in the findings of the Council. That sentence begins:

'Therefore, following the holy Fathers, we all with one accord teach men to acknowledge one and the same Son, our Lord Jesus Christ, at once complete in Godhead and complete in manhood, truly God and truly man, consisting also of a reasonable soul and body. . . .'

There is no full-stop at that point, but we shall stop there and ask what lies behind these words.

This Council affirmed (as, I have suggested, the New Testament evidence leads us also to believe) that Jesus was a real man and, at the same time, God. It is impossible to believe that He was what we now call a *divided person*. If anything is clear about Jesus, it is that He was a unified, or, as the psychologists say, an integrated person. It is unthinkable for us, as it was for those Christians long ago (although they used different words, and thought in rather a different way), that our Lord was a kind of Jekyll and Hyde, sometimes being 'God' and sometimes being 'Man'. Yet it is equally impossible for us to deny, either that He was God, or that He was Man. These were the facts that Chalcedon had to face; these are the facts that we still must accept and express in our statements about Jesus. And so it was said that He was 'complete in Godhead and complete in manhood'. In order to emphasize this *completeness*, and at the same time to assert that He was not what I have called a divided person, they used four Greek adjectives. Speaking about what they called His two 'natures'—which we may call (in manufactured words) His God-ness and His Man-ness—they said that these were *without confusion* (not mixed up), *without change* ('God' and 'Man' did not change their meaning in the case of Jesus), *without division, without separation*. The last two expressions probably meant more or less the same thing in different words, namely that the 'God-ness' and the 'Man-ness' of Jesus were not two separate, divided parts of Him. You may probably think that this was a very difficult way of expressing the truth, but when you study the difficulties that the Council members had, in view of the lack of easy words to use, you may come to think that they could hardly have been clearer. At least it must be said that they took tremendous pains to emphasise that their Lord was One Person, who was in the fullest sense divine, and in the fullest sense human. They said a good deal more, in that long sentence, than has been quoted here. Most of it emphasises the same points, but there is also one other important point in this pronouncement.

The Council also wanted to make quite clear *the relationship between the Son and the Father*. It was, as a matter of fact, about this point that the fiercest controversy had arisen in the previous generations. Cynical people have said that all the excitement was over one little Greek letter. It certainly looks like that, for the argument was summed up in the question, 'Was Jesus *homoousios* or *homoi-ousios* with the Father?' The first word means 'of the same substance'; the second means 'of like, or similar, substance'.

Was this nothing but a quarrel over a letter? By no means.

The word translated 'substance' is a very difficult one, which I shall not attempt to explain fully. It is sufficient for our purpose to notice that the question was whether Jesus, the Incarnate Son of God, was merely like the Father, or whether He was absolutely and wholly one with Him. Or, to put it rather nearer to the way in which they thought, whether the Son was completely God, or only uniquely *like* God. If we asked, 'Did Jesus share the "stuff" of which God is made?', we might be thought both crude and stupid; but, so long as we do not think that 'stuff' means anything material or physical, we shall not go very wrong. In other words, the Council wanted to say, in the clearest and most emphatic way, that when the Son is called God, the word 'God' means everything that it means when we use it about the Eternal God our Father. And, as the doctrine of the Trinity shows, when they spoke of the Father, Son and Holy Spirit as 'three persons', they did not mean separate individuals, which is what we mean by 'persons'; they affirmed One God.

2. *Why this matters*

Perhaps, one day, Christians will find an easier way to express their faith than Chalcedon found, but what they will mean will be the same. Jesus is our Saviour, but only God can save. In our anxiety to help people to become Christians, we are sometimes tempted to try to make it easier for them by merely saying that Jesus is like God, or that Jesus has for us 'the value of God' (a very famous Christian said that), or that Jesus leads us to God. But then we are in danger of making our Saviour somebody less than God; and then we are in danger of worshipping the man Jesus instead of God, or alongside God. That is why these chapters lead up to the Doctrine of the Trinity; that is why all truly and fully Christian life depends upon the work of the Triune God.

Dr Donald Baillie has said: 'The God who was incarnate in Christ dwells in us through the Holy Spirit: and that is the secret of Christian life'. Some people would be surprised if you told them that to be a Christian is thus to know the work of the divine Trinity, but if you will carefully read Eph. 2^{1-18}, and read *v.* 18 several times, you will see that Dr Baillie did not invent this description of Christian life. Indeed, do you not know in your own experience that this is true?

One more word must be said. The language of Chalcedon is not language which men and women can easily understand today. To do that, they must give as much study to the actual words used as they give, for example, to studying the words used for the parts of a motor-car—and few people are ready to work as hard as that in studying Christian beliefs. We must ask them to think, but we should not expect them to become theologians before becoming Christians. What, then, are the aspects of our belief in the *Person* of Christ which are essential for evangelism? Who is our Saviour?

Jesus of Nazareth lived a fully human life, and this is recorded in the pages of the New Testament. This human life was lived by One whom we call Son of God, by which we mean that He shared completely the life of God. Before all creation, in the eternal world, He was one with God the Father. For a short time, He added to all the other work that He had done the living of an earthly life, during which He did all the mighty works that the New Testament tells us about. Of all that He did on earth, we may say both that God the Son did these works, and that the Man Jesus did them. At length He was crucified and buried, but He rose again from the dead and, after a short time, resumed His eternal life with the Father. He still lives, the Son of God who was once made Man; so that, in the Godhead Himself, there is knowledge of our earthly life, knowledge gained by experience. At the end of this Age, He will complete His work.

That He is one with the Father and yet, somehow, distinct from Him, is part of the doctrine of the Trinity; what He has done and will do for us, is the doctrine of the Work of Christ; who He was and is, is the doctrine of the Person of Christ. These doctrines always remain beyond the full understanding of human beings, but the simplest and the wisest of men may know Him as Saviour and worship Him as the only-begotten Son of God.

NOTE ON 'THE VIRGIN BIRTH'

Nothing has been said above about the Virgin Birth of our Lord. The New Testament evidence for this has been examined (*see ANT, para.* 182). Attempts are sometimes made to discuss and decide this question on purely *theological* grounds. For example, some have argued that the belief that Jesus had no human father sprang from a false notion that the sexual relationship is evil, or is the means by which sin is 'passed down' from one generation to another. Such a notion is quite untrue, and there is no ground for saying that Matthew and Luke thought in that way. Others have suggested that it would have been impossible for God to be made man, if the birth of Jesus had taken place like other human births. Who has the knowledge for such a statement? I do not believe that such arguments are valid, or that we can decide the matter by reference to 'science'. If what we believe about Jesus is true, it is quite clear that no other baby can be compared with the Child of Bethlehem. Of Him we say, 'It was by the power of the Holy Ghost that Jesus was born of His human mother, and He was in Himself both human and divine' (*CAT* 10).

Therefore I have nothing to add to what Mr. Greville Lewis has written, except to underline his plea that we are dependent for our knowledge upon the statements—and upon the lack of other references—in the New Testament. I know no adequate reason for rejecting the traditional belief; but I do not think that it is impossible, or even difficult, to be a Christian whilst one is unable to be sure about this particular question. The student who would like to think further is recommended to read the excellent treatment of this subject in O. C. Quick's *Doctrines of the Creed*, chap. 15.

Sermon XV. the great privilege of those that are born of god

Theme of the Sermon. The New Birth, considered in relation to growth in grace, and the possibility of lapses in believers.

EXPLANATORY OUTLINE OF THE SERMON

Introduction. (1, 2) Justification and the New Birth are two names for the *initial step* in the Christian life. The distinction is not that one is before the other, but that Justification is the initial step considered from the point of view of man's standing in the sight of God. It is 'being made right with God': it is forgiveness. The New Birth, on the other hand, is the initial step considered from the point of view of the actual change in disposition and conduct which then starts. (3, 4) Confusion on this point needs to be cleared away if the Christian's victory over sin is to be understood.

I. *The New Birth Explained.* (1) It is not the same as Baptism, but is a complete change of heart worked by the Spirit of God. (Wesley, speaking as an Anglican clergyman, has in mind the teaching of the Prayer-Book Baptismal Office—which he did not reject, though he did labour to guard it against misunderstanding —namely, that the baby is 'born again' in Baptism. By this is meant, of course, not mere magic, but that the Christian life of a Christian child begins in infancy, and is marked by his first incorporation into the Church.) (2-4) Comparison of the unspiritual man to an unborn child. There is in him the possibility of knowing the reality around him, but that possibility is not yet realized. (5) When the child is born his senses start to function as the outer world presses in upon him. (6, 7) So the unspiritual man is surrounded by the world of God, but is insensible to it, until (8-10) the knowledge of God breaks in upon him, and he responds in worship and love and obedience.

II. *The Problem of Sin in Believers.* (1) In principle, those who are born of God do not sin. (2) By 'sin' in this connection is meant a known and voluntary transgression for which the sinner is personally responsible (i.e. it does not include also all those other moral and spiritual limitations whereby man is less than the perfect image of God, yet for which he is not responsible, and which will remain with even the mature believer until he gets to heaven). (3) Some have been led to reject this text (and therefore to assert that definite moral compromise is *inevitable* to the Christian), by the practical observation that some who were undoubtedly born of God undoubtedly sinned. (4) For example, even the Psalmist committed adultery and murder, while (5, 6) even under the Christian order the Apostles themselves were found at times in compromise and sharp dispute. (7) The painful discrepancy between principle and practice is due to the circumstance that believers do not 'keep themselves', as they can and ought, i.e. they are not invariably in a state of complete belief. Even a saint can commit 'negative inward sin', i.e. can fall into devotional slackness, which leads to dallying with temptation, and so in turn to loss of faith and spiritual weakness. Then there is nothing to prevent him from falling into a gross lapse. (8, 9) The process traced out in the case of David, and (10) Peter.

III. *The Process of Temptation, and its Prevention.* (1) A sincere saving faith is all-sufficient to prevent a yielding to temptation, but it does not prevent temptation itself. Therefore, if a believer be found in an outward fault it is to be presumed that an inward devotional slackness, and dallying with temptation sufficient to impair faith, have gone first. (In general we may agree with Wesley in this analysis, but his description of the preparatory secret dallying with temptation as a 'sin of omission' is open to question. The term 'sin of omission' half suggests that inward sin is less positive and heinous than the outward action, while Jesus laid the guilt firmly upon the inward sin of the heart.) (2) Those who are born again must therefore take every constant care to 'keep themselves', and to nourish the spiritual life which is in them by responding to God's action upon them, in the spirit of worship and loving obedience. (3) God indeed takes the loving initiative in drawing man to Himself, but He does not compel. Thus if man fails to make the due response the Spirit will cease to draw. (4) The believer must not be cock-sure, but be ever on guard against the onset of temptation.

TEST QUESTIONS

1. We are compelled to say about Jesus, *either* 'Truly God' *or* 'This man was an imposter'. Why is this true?

2. Jesus was not 'a divided person'; He was truly God *and* truly Man. What do we mean by this statement?

3. To what extent is it fitting to describe the first step of the Christian life as a 'new birth'?

STUDY SEVEN

The Holy Spirit

SALVATION is the work of Christ; it is also the work of the Holy Spirit, or, as He is sometimes called, the Holy Ghost, which means exactly the same. 'The Holy Ghost is God the Lord and Giver of life, who continues and fulfils the work of Christ in the life of the Church and of the believer' (*CAT* 17). This does not mean that Christ did this work up to a certain date, and that the Holy Spirit then took it over and 'continues' it in that sense; it means that what Christ did on earth and what He still does in heaven for our salvation is brought into our lives by the Holy Spirit. We shall therefore begin by considering salvation. *Study Five* has shown what Christ did; we are now to see how it works in the believer. Afterwards we shall consider what can be said about the Holy Spirit in particular.

A. SALVATION

We must consider what salvation is, how it is obtained, and what follows from it.

1. *What is Salvation?*

a. *Salvation is past, present, and future.* We have been saved (e.g. Eph. 2^8), we are being saved (e.g. 1 Cor. 1^{18}), and we shall be saved (e.g. 1 Cor. 3^{15}). Salvation is primarily a great act of deliverance like a drowning man being rescued, or a man being cured of a terrible disease; and thus the Christian naturally thinks of it as something that happened to him in the past, when he was justified and born again. But that does not end the matter. Just as a man saved from a disease by an operation might yet take a long time to recover his health, so most Christians are still 'recovering' their spiritual health, and thus in the present they are being saved. And the completion of this process lies in the future.

But what precisely is salvation? 'Salvation is deliverance from sin into a new life of righteousness that begins on earth, survives death, and is perfected with God in heaven' (*CAT* 26). All men desire to be delivered from what they regard as evil; sin, whether men realize it or not, is the greatest of all evils, and it is supremely from sin that we need to be delivered (cf. Mt 1^{21}).

b. *What does God do when He saves us?* 'By His grace He freely converts, justifies, regenerates, and sanctifies every repentant sinner who has faith in Jesus Christ crucified for us' (*CAT* 27). This sentence shows that the deliverance has various aspects known by different names. We shall consider these in turn; it would be helpful to look up the words in a Concordance and read the articles on them in *TWB*.

(i) *Conversion*. 'We are converted by God when we respond to His grace in repentance and faith' (*CAT* 29). Conversion means turning, or rather being turned, from sin to God, and thus in the Bible it is very similar to repentance, but it has come to mean that whole change in a man's character and outlook which salvation produces. Many psychologists describe it as an 'adolescent phenomenon', as if that disposed of the matter; but that is not an adequate description of it, for adults and children also can experience it, nor is it an explanation of how it is possible. The classic example of conversion is that of Paul (Acts 9$^{1-19}$), which was a sudden conversion, though some process must have gone on in his heart in preparation for it. But Christian experience has shown that conversion may also be gradual.

We now come to those words which describe *the change which God works in our relationship to Him*.

(ii) *Forgiveness*, or pardon, or remission of sins. This does not necessarily mean that the consequences of sin are removed, for the results of some sins, such as murder, can never be undone. It means the removal or cancellation of sin as a barrier to fellowship. We are so accustomed to using the word 'forgiveness' in our relations with each other that it calls for no further explanation.

(iii) *Justification*. 'We are justified when God pardons our sins and accepts us as His children' (*CAT* 32). Strictly speaking, forgiveness is the removal of a barrier, whereas justification is the positive acceptance into a new status. But they are so closely linked that the words are often used interchangeably. Justification does not mean 'making righteous', but 'acquitting', 'treating as righteous', 'putting in the right' (*see ANT*, para. 453; and Wesley's *Sermon* V and Notes on it). How it is possible for a righteous God to be a God that 'justifieth the ungodly' (Rom. 4^5), we must consider later.

THE HOLY SPIRIT

(iv) *Adoption.* In ancient times it was perhaps commoner than it is today to adopt children into a family. The use of this metaphor brings out vividly how completely God accepts us. God is the Father of all men, and all men are potentially His sons, but we are not fully so until we become so by adoption (cf. Rom. 8^{15}; Gal. 4$^{4-7}$; and *see* Wesley, *Sermon* IX).

(v) *Redemption.* A person adopted into a family in the ancient world might first have been purchased, by the payment of a 'ransom', from slavery; and thus we have another vivid metaphor. This particularly emphasizes the price that was paid on our behalf (cf. 1 Pet. 1$^{18-19}$, and *see ANT, para.* 147) and the liberty which we enjoy from sin and bondage to the law (Gal. 5^1).

(vi) *Reconciliation.* This word describes in the simplest possible way the changed relationship between God and man. It is God who by the death of Christ reconciles man to Himself (2 Cor. 5$^{18-21}$). By it we pass from a state of enmity or estrangement to one of peace with God (Eph. 2$^{14-17}$).

(vii) *Dying and Rising with Christ.* Paul is describing salvation when he speaks of being crucified (Rom. 6^6; Gal. 2^{20}), dying (Col. 2^{20}), being buried (Rom. 6^4; Col. 2^{12}), being raised from the dead (Col. 2^{12}, 3^1; Eph. 2^6), quickened, i.e. given life (Col. 2^{13}; Eph. 2^5), and set down in the heavenly places (Eph. 2^6) with Christ.

We now turn to certain other words which describe not so much a change in our relationship to God as *a change in ourselves.*

(viii) *Regeneration.* 'We are born anew when God justifies us and brings us by His Spirit into the new life of righteousness' (*CAT* 33). Regeneration, or the new birth, occurs at the same time as justification, but is distinguished from it; regeneration is the actual entry on the new life of righteousness. In our thinking, though not in actual time, justification precedes the new birth. Justification relates to 'that great work which God does *for us,* in forgiving our sins' and the new birth to 'the great work which God does *in us,* in renewing our fallen nature' (Wesley, *Sermon* XXXIX; and *see* XIV and XV). The new birth is essential for entry into the Kingdom of God (Jn 3$^{1-15}$). Wesley on the whole teaches, though he sometimes introduces qualifications, that every Christian is thus free from committing *outward* sin, that is, from deliberately doing what he knows to be contrary to the law of God. What happens to *inward* sin, we shall see later (pp. 118f.).

(ix) *Sanctification.* Fundamentally this means 'being made holy'. Holiness is primarily a characteristic, indeed we may say, *the* characteristic of God Himself (*see* pp. 34f., above). Holiness in man is a gift of God, and means that he is separated or dedicated to God. This dedication expresses itself in a certain new quality of life. At the new birth we enter on that new life; but that change, though real, is incomplete; a process of growth must follow it. Methodist theology usually refers to this process when it speaks of sanctification. 'We are made holy as we grow by the power of the Holy Spirit in the new life and in love towards God and our neighbours' (*CAT* 34). This process starts when a man is justified, and is a consequence of justification; yet it is of a different nature. Justification is being *treated* as righteous; sanctification is being actually *made* righteous (*see* Wesley, *Sermon* V). This process gradually removes inward sin, and its goal is entire sanctification.

We have now considered the main words and phrases which the Bible uses to describe salvation. They contain many vivid metaphors; the slave-market, the law-court, the family are all pressed into service. The preacher should not be perplexed by the somewhat subtle relationships of these words to each other as revealed by precise New Testament scholarship; he should rather view the variety of the terms as providential, and exult in using and explaining all these terms in his preaching. They are illustrations ready to hand. He will also make constant use of the words forgiveness, pardon, and reconciliation, which are not so much metaphors as descriptions of everyday human experiences, themselves capable of being richly illustrated from literature and from life.

We may sum up what we have said about the change which God works in our relationship to Him and the change which He works in us by comparing justification, one of the words describing the former change, with sanctification, one of the words describing the latter.

Justification	*Sanctification*
Deals with sin as guilt	Deals with sin as corruption
Is a relative change (i.e. a change in our relationships)	Is a real change
Is a change in our status	Is a change in our nature
Treats us as righteous	Makes us righteous
Confers pardon	Confers holiness
Restores us to God's favour	Restores us to God's image
Is done for us	Is done in us

All these benefits are connected with the death of Christ and are part of His work. 'What did Jesus do for us on the Cross? He atoned for our sins, that is, reconciled us to God and obtained for us all the benefits of salvation' (*CAT* 36).

2. *How is Salvation obtained?*

Anyone who clearly realizes his great need for this precious gift of salvation will naturally ask, 'What must I do to be saved?' (Acts 16^{30}). The plain answer is that we are saved by grace through faith (cf. Eph. 2^8). We have already considered these two very important words, grace and faith (*Study Four*); let us look at them again in this new setting.

a. *Grace.* 'Grace is the undeserved love of God to all' (*CAT* 28). Grace is God taking the initiative for our salvation; it is entirely undeserved, and it is a personal relationship (pp. 65f). The truth about God taking the initiative is sometimes expressed by saying that God chooses, elects, or predestinates us to salvation. This is true in the sense that salvation comes from God's decision to save men, not from any decision on man's part to be saved; our decision would be of no avail, were it not for God's decision. Nevertheless we are free to choose whether or not we accept God's offer (Deut. 30^{19}). It is also true that God chose the children of Israel (whom we sometimes call 'the Chosen People') in order that by them His salvation might be proclaimed to all the nations, in which responsibility the children of Israel largely failed. Some theologians have gone further and said that God selects some men for salvation and others for damnation, that God's grace descends on some men with irresistible force, and passes by others entirely (*see* p. 67). This is known as 'double predestination', and was held by Calvin, though modern Calvinists hardly hold it at all. We have already rejected it. Against this view that God wills that only some men shall be saved, we hold that God offers this grace to *all*: He wills *all* men to be saved; and Christ died for *all*. This is called Arminianism, after the theologian Arminius; it avoids Calvinism without falling into the opposite error of Pelagianism (*see* p. 67). But, though God wills all men to be saved, some men never hear this offer; of those who do, some accept it and some refuse it. Those who accept it, do not do so by any merit of their own, but are enabled to accept it by the Holy Spirit; but this does not mean that the help of the Holy Spirit is refused to others; for His help is included in the offer.

Thus those who, having heard it, refuse it, are themselves alone responsible for refusing it. That they are free to do so in a universe where God rules is part of God's gift to us of freedom; and that some do actually refuse it is part of the mysterious problem of evil. This Arminian view is not confined to Methodism, but it is one of our distinctive emphases, one of those doctrines which we particularly stress. It is sometimes called the Universality of Salvation, or the doctrine that all men can be saved.

b. *Faith.* 'Faith in Jesus Christ is trusting in Him alone for our salvation' (*CAT* 31). In Greek, the verb 'believe' comes from the noun 'faith'; and thus the answer to the question, 'What must I do to be saved?' is 'Believe on the Lord Jesus, and thou shalt be saved' (Acts 16$^{30\text{-}31}$). This faith is not simply an intellectual assent that this or that is true, though the acceptance of Christ does involve some intellectual convictions; it is an utter trust and reliance on Christ, in which we cast ourselves upon Him and Him alone for our salvation (*see* Wesley, *Sermon* I). We are justified through faith, not by works (cf. Gal. 2^{16}), that is, not by our own good conduct. It is not inconsistent with this to say 'Faith apart from works is dead' (Jas 2^{26}); a trust in Christ which does not result in good conduct is no true trust; yet we are not saved by our good conduct, but by the trust which is its source. We have seen what happened to Martin Luther when he grasped the meaning of 'justification by grace through faith' (*see* p. 68); and Methodism gladly adopts the same watchword. But we must not pride ourselves on our grasp of this, or think that we have achieved anything by managing to have faith. That would, as it were, make faith another 'work'. It is not our faith, viewed as a particular attitude in us, which brings salvation; salvation comes from the Christ in whom we trust.

c. *Repentance.* 'Repentance is turning to God in sorrow for our sin' (*CAT* 30). It must accompany faith. Christ's call was to repent and believe (Mk 1^{15}). Repentance is not merely remorse, nor merely to change our mind, but to change our whole attitude, to turn from sin to God, with the intention of obeying God in the future.

Thus, as salvation is by God's grace, the only conditions required on our part are repentance and faith. But they are not simply the prelude to salvation. Faith is the dominant note of the whole Christian life; and, as the new birth does not take sin out of our lives altogether, we must continue to repent also.

d. *How can God justify us?* How can God, who is holy and utterly opposed to sin, make this offer to us sinners without requiring any further qualification on our part? He is not indeed bound by any moral law which is external to Him or beyond His control; but is He not bound by the holiness of His own nature? The answer lies in the Cross, as we have seen in *Study Five*. The question now arises in this form: How is it possible for God to justify us before He sanctifies us? How can He treat us as righteous before we are in fact righteous? There seems something artificial or fictitious about this. We might reply, with a proper play on the word, that we are not bound to justify justification; it is enough for us that God thinks it right. But we can see some further light on the question. In view of the fact that Christ is our Representative (*see* pp. 79f.), God views us, in the moment of justification, not as we are in ourselves, but as we are by virtue of our faith in Christ. We are not yet like Christ, but we are 'in Christ', as Paul says. We are in fact, and by no mere fiction, in a new relationship to Christ. This relationship both gives us a new status (justification) and begins to refashion our nature (regeneration and sanctification). We are still sinners, but by God's grace we are sinners who are in Christ, and so we are acceptable to God in His beloved Son, who made a perfect offering of Himself to the Father.

e. *What is the status of those who cannot make even this simple response of repentance and faith?* In Old Testament times men could believe in God, but they could not, consciously at any rate, believe in Jesus Christ; yet some of them enjoyed salvation in this life (e.g. Rom. 4[3]). Some theologians wish to extend this to some others who, as happens even in our own day, never hear the offer of salvation. Moreover children, whether or not they are brought up in Christian homes, are at first too young to repent and believe; do they not in any sense have salvation in this life? The New Testament writers do not say much about this. Paul, for instance, was so deeply influenced by his own sudden and dramatic conversion from Judaism to Christianity that he said very little about those who are born into Christian homes (*see* p. 181 on the baptism of infants). But it is not the preacher's main work to answer such questions about those who cannot respond; he is faced with those who are capable of responding, and to them he makes the definite and positive offer, 'Believe on the Lord Jesus, and thou shalt be saved'. Men come to Christ by very varied experiences, but all alike must be urged to take Christ for themselves as their personal Lord and Saviour.

3. *What follows from Salvation?*

The preacher must be able to speak also to those who have already accepted the offer of salvation. When this acceptance is gradual, it is difficult to distinguish the deliverance from the consequences which follow from it. But we must distinguish as clearly as we can in our thought certain stages which sometimes merge into each other in our experience. For this purpose, we may recall the illustration of the man saved from a disease (p. 115). First he is saved *from* sickness; and so terms like 'justification' speak of salvation *from* guilt and alienation, though some of the terms like 'adoption' also imply that we are saved *to* something, namely, life in the family of God. Afterwards there may be a long process in which a man recovers his health; this corresponds to 'sanctification', and we have already considered this when speaking of the original rescue, though there is still something to be said about the completion of it (pp. 123ff.). But we have also still to speak in general about the kind of life that the saved man can now lead, the new life of righteousness which follows from, and is the consequence of, the original deliverance.

a. *Fellowship with God* is its chief characteristic. We have a share in Christ (1 Cor. 1^9), in the sufferings of Christ (Phil. 3^{10}), in the Holy Spirit (Phil. 2^1; 2 Cor. 13^{14}), and, at the Lord's Supper, in the Body and Blood of Christ (1 Cor. 10^{16}). (The English Bible does not say 'have a share', but these passages can all be translated in this way.) We love God. We are in Christ and Christ is in us. Indeed a great wealth of expressions can be used to describe the intimate relationship in which we now stand to God. Moreover, we still have faith; if we gave up that trust by which we first accepted salvation, we should fall back into a state of estrangement from God. But if we have faith, we have this communion, and God's gift of salvation is a wonderful thing, because it not only delivers us from sin, but brings us into this life of fellowship. God's gift to us is communion with Himself.

b. This fellowship with God brings us also into *fellowship with each other*. Those who are in Christ are also members of His Body, the Church, and are bound to make use of the 'means of grace' in order that by faith they may continue to receive the grace of God. We are not saved by prayer or sacraments, but the neglect of these is perilous to those who are saved by grace through faith. Therefore *Studies Nine and Ten* will deal with the Church (*see* Wesley, *Sermon* XII).

c. The Christian life also involves *loving our neighbour*. We are not saved by our works, but good works result from faith. Our virtues do not bring salvation, but certain virtues have their place in the Christian life as 'the fruit of the Spirit' (Gal. 5^{22}). This is in no way incompatible with justification by grace through faith; it is part of the sanctification which is a consequence of it. The idea that, because we are saved, we are free to sin as we like is a deadly heresy. Therefore *Study Eleven* will deal with Christian Ethics.

There are two consequences of salvation which are reckoned among the distinctive emphases of Methodism. We have already mentioned one other such emphasis, the Universality of Salvation (p. 119). We must add to this Assurance and Christian Perfection. The three can be set out in this way:

> All men can be saved.
> All men can know that they are saved.
> All men can be saved to the uttermost.

d. *Assurance* is the certain knowledge that we are saved. 'How do we know that we are saved? By the sure Word of God, by the inner conviction of the Holy Spirit in our hearts, and by the fruit of the Spirit in our lives we know that we are saved' (*CAT* 37). The inner conviction of the Holy Spirit is thus described by Paul: 'The Spirit himself beareth witness with our spirit, that we are children of God' (Rom. 8^{16}). The doctrine is often called the Witness of the Spirit (*see* Wesley, *Sermon* X). This assurance is not essential to salvation, but is a privilege generally given to Christians.

e. *Christian Perfection* is the same as Entire Sanctification, or Scriptural Holiness. It is also sometimes called the second blessing, though that phrase is used in a variety of senses. Perhaps the best name is Perfect Love. 'We are entirely sanctified when the Holy Spirit fulfils His work in our lives and we love God and our neighbour perfectly' (*CAT* 35). As we have already seen (pp. 117f.), sanctification is a process which begins when we are justified and born again, but continues afterwards. According to Wesley, by our regeneration we are free from committing outward sin, but we are not freed from inward sin; sinful thoughts, tempers, and motives remain, and cleave to all that we do, though by reason of our justification we are not condemned even for these. Sanctification is the gradual removal of this inward sin. When it is all removed, or, as it is sometimes put, the root of sin is removed, then nothing remains but the pure love of God and our neighbour ruling our tempers, words and actions (*see* Wesley, *Sermon* XXXV). This is 'the sanctification without which no man shall see the Lord' (Heb. 12[14]). Many Protestants have taught, against the Roman doctrine of purgatory, that this entire sanctification is conferred on the saved in the moment of death. Wesley went beyond this, and taught that it could be conferred *before* death, and said that he had known many instances, though he never unambiguously claimed it himself. The doctrine has been much criticized, but it must be remembered that it is not asserted without careful qualifications. The perfect man is constantly dependent on Christ; if he loses his faith, he will lose his perfection. Moreover he is still fallible, liable through ignorance to make mistakes which may lead him to actions which are contrary to the will of God, for which he must seek God's forgiveness; and he has not reached finality, for his love of God is capable of constant increase. Thus qualified, the doctrine is of great value; it is right to stress sanctification as well as justification, love as well as faith, holiness as well as pardon. Therefore we must 'press on toward the goal' (Phil. 3[14]), and be satisfied with nothing less than perfection.

The remaining consequence of salvation is heaven, which will be dealt with in *Study Twelve*.

B. THE HOLY SPIRIT

Having thus seen the richness of the salvation which Christ works in us through the Spirit, we now approach the doctrine of the Spirit by another method, asking what the Bible says explicitly about Spirit. Two points are to be noted. First, the Bible uses the word 'spirit' to refer to evil spirits and to the spirit of man, as well as to the Spirit of God. We shall try to confine ourselves to those passages which refer to the Spirit of God. But sometimes these uses are so mixed together that it is hard to say whether a sentence refers to the spirit of man (as indwelt by the Spirit of God), or to the Spirit of God (as indwelling the spirit of man). We use a small 's' in the one case and a capital 'S' in the other; but if someone were to dictate Rom. 8 to you, you would have to think very carefully when to use capital 'S' and when not. Secondly, there are often references in the Old Testament to the spirit of God, or the spirit of the Lord, where a small 's' is used. This is because the Old Testament writers did not themselves think of the spirit of God as a distinct Person in the Trinity, for that doctrine had not been revealed at that time. Their own language did not distinguish between small and capital letters, but we use small letters in this case, in order to be faithful to their point of view; but of course we now view the 'spirit of God' in a different light because of the doctrine of the Trinity, as we shall see later (pp. 142f.).

1. *The spirit in the Old Testament*

The word for 'spirit' in Hebrew (as also the Greek word in the New Testament) means also 'wind' and 'breath'; and references to the spirit of God have usually some idea of the force and strength of a gale, or else the idea of life which we associate with breath. The spirit of God was conceived as a powerful energy working through men and enabling them to perform extraordinary feats. Thus the leadership of Gideon and the physical strength of Samson are ascribed to the spirit of the Lord (Jges. 6^{34}, 14^6). The craftsman owes his skill to the spirit of God (Exod. 31^{3-5}). Prophesying is ascribed to the spirit of the Lord, from its strange ecstatic beginnings (1 Sam. $10^{6, 10}$) to its sublimest heights (Isa. 61^1).

The Psalmist hoped that the holy spirit might not be taken away from him (Ps. 51^{11}), thus perhaps implying that it was a normal possession of the pious Israelite; but the spirit was also associated with the coming New Age (Joel 2^{28}, quoted in Acts 2^{17}) and the coming deliverer (Isa. 11^2).

The spirit of God is also said to have taken part in the work of creation (Gen. 1^2, Ps. 104^{30}). This arises from the connexion between breath and life, and is the origin of the phrase 'Creator Spirit' (cf. *MHB* 293). But, apart from a few such references, the sphere of the spirit's operations is not the world as a whole, but the lives of men.

Some of the Old Testament writers tended to think of God as remote, but their use of the term 'spirit' was their way of saying that He was also near and at work among men. They did not think of the spirit as a distinct 'Person', but their conception paved the way for the acceptance of that doctrine.

2. *The Spirit in the New Testament*

In the *Synoptic Gospels* the Holy Spirit is mentioned in various connections in the birth-stories: He is particularly connected with the conception of Jesus (Lk 1³⁵); hence the Apostles' Creed says, 'Who was conceived by the Holy Ghost'. John the Baptist spoke of the coming One who would baptize with the Holy Spirit (Mk 1⁸); and the Spirit descended on Jesus as He was baptized by John (Mk 1¹⁰). Thereafter He was 'full of the Holy Spirit' (Lk 4¹). The teaching of Jesus in these Gospels about the Spirit is very slight. No doubt He held back teaching on this doctrine, as He for long held back the secret of His Messiahship, because His hearers were not yet ready to understand it. It is a testimony to the accuracy of the Synoptic writers, writing after Pentecost, that they did not invent teaching on this point to put on the lips of Jesus.

Before His Ascension, Jesus promised the Holy Spirit to the disciples (Acts 1⁴, ⁵, ⁸; cf. Lk 24⁴⁹). Acts 2, which is in many ways the most important chapter in the Bible, describes His coming on the day of *Pentecost*, which we now celebrate as Whit Sunday (*see ANT* on Acts 2). Joel's prophecy was thus fulfilled, and the disciples perceived many signs of the power of God at work: the fire, the wind, the speaking with tongues. These signs, however, were not so important a result of the coming of the Spirit as was the preaching of the Gospel, which began then and has continued ever since. Hitherto they had waited for the fulfilment of the promise without preaching the Gospel; now we have the first Christian sermon, an example of the apostolic preaching which is the model for our preaching today. In it, Peter said that the exalted Jesus had poured forth the Holy Spirit, and that the same gift was offered to all who would repent and be baptized (Acts 2³³, ³⁸). Many responded, and the chapter closes with a description of the Christian Church. It was now fully constituted for the first time, and the speaking with tongues may be taken as a prophecy that the Gospel would be preached to the whole world.

In the rest of Acts we read of the Spirit acting in all kinds of ways. The Spirit came at the beginning of the Christian life, and this would usually be at baptism, as promised in 2³⁸; but sometimes the Spirit came before baptism (10⁴⁷), and sometimes the laying on of hands was also necessary (8¹⁴⁻¹⁷, 19¹⁻⁷). There was thus not a complete uniformity of practice about ways of entering the Church, but the possession of the Spirit was an essential part of the life of every Christian; He was not confined to a few leaders or to the spiritually mature; they had all received the Spirit. Thus when we pray, as we often do, that He may come to us, we are really praying that we may know more fully Him whom as Christians we already possess. Yet some men are specially described as full of the Spirit ($6^{3, 5}$). There are also certain special activities of the Spirit, such as guidance (15^{28}) and prophecy ($11^{27f.}$). The phrase 'gift of the Spirit' has really two meanings, and it is helpful to distinguish the gift *consisting of* the Spirit Himself, which all Christians have, from those further gifts which are *given by* the Spirit.

Paul connects the Holy Spirit with almost every aspect of the Christian life; Rom. 8 is particularly important. To have the Spirit of God, or the Spirit of Christ, is an essential part of belonging to Christ, being made free, being a son of God, walking after the spirit (Rom. 8^{1-15}). Thus the Spirit is the Agent who brings salvation to us. He also bears witness of our salvation; this is the gift of assurance (*see* p. 123). He is also connected with our entry into heaven by the idea that He is the firstfruits, a kind of first instalment; the full payment will be made later (Rom. 8^{23}). He also helps us by making intercession for us when we do not know how to pray (Rom. 8^{26}).

Elsewhere in Paul it is equally clear that having the Spirit is an essential part of being a Christian: 'no man can say, Jesus is Lord, but in the Holy Spirit' (1 Cor. 12^3). In the same passage (1 Cor. 12–14) he speaks of special gifts, such as prophecy, which, as in the Old Testament, the Spirit gives to men. This is bound up with his idea of the Church as a body in which there are various kinds of ministry; but he shows a certain fear that some of these gifts may be wrongly used in public worship, particularly speaking with tongues and prophesying; he wants everything to be done in an orderly manner, and he implies that by far the greatest gift is love. The famous description of the fruit of the Spirit (Gal. 5^{22}) shows a similiar concern for the more ethical results of receiving the Spirit. Thus the Spirit is connected with sanctification (cf. 2 Thess. 2^{13}).*

* Some people think that Paul speaks of 'the fellowship of the Holy Spirit' (2 Cor. 13^{14}; cf. Phil. 2^1), meaning 'the fellowship created by the Holy Spirit'. But the phrase is better translated 'participation in the Holy Spirit' (*see* p. 122), and thus does not indicate any special connection between fellowship and the Holy Spirit, though of course fellowship, both with God and with our fellow-Christians, is part of the work of the Holy Spirit, like everything else that flows from salvation.

The activities ascribed to the Spirit by Paul, such as revealing, indwelling, helping, witnessing, are such that he *must have thought of the Spirit as personal and as divine*. As we have seen in Rom. 8, he speaks of the Spirit of God, the Spirit of Christ and the Spirit, apparently without any difference of meaning. Thus the Spirit is very closely connected with the exalted Christ, but the two are distinct, not identical. Paul does indeed once say 'the Lord is the Spirit' (2 Cor. 3^{17}); his meaning is not entirely clear; some think that 'the Lord' should be in inverted commas, so that the sentence means that in the passage in Exod. 34 which is here under discussion, 'the phrase "the Lord" means the Spirit'. In any case Paul can hardly mean to identify them completely, for in the same verse he uses the phrase 'the Spirit of the Lord'. Nevertheless Paul nowhere states the doctrine of the Trinity which the Church afterwards found it necessary to formulate; and, though there is nothing in his writings which is inconsistent with this doctrine, yet he uses expressions which belong to an early stage of the development of Christian Doctrine. Such a verse as Eph. 2^{18} shows how he conceived the distinct functions of the Persons of the Trinity to be connected.

The Fourth Gospel and the first Epistle of John contain numerous references to the Spirit, many of which simply confirm what we have learnt elsewhere. In particular, we see that it is essential to be born of the Spirit (Jn 3^5; cf. 1 Jn 3^{24}, 4^2). There is no Christian life without the Spirit. In Jn 7^{39} we read, 'But this spake he of the Spirit, which they that believed on him were to receive; for the (Holy) Spirit was not yet (given); because Jesus was not yet glorified'. The words in brackets are not found in all the manuscripts; but even without them it is hardly meant that in the lifetime of Jesus the Holy Spirit did not exist at all, but that the disciples could not *receive* Him till after the Death of Jesus.

In the *farewell discourse* which Jesus is reported to have delivered in the upper room, certain passages about the Holy Spirit are of great importance, and should be considered with Acts 2 and Rom. 8 as major contributions to the New Testament doctrine of the Spirit. They are Jn 14$^{16-18, 26}$, 15$^{26-7}$, 16$^{7-15}$ (*see ANT* on these, especially on the word 'Paraclete'). In the first of these, Jesus says that He will pray the Father, and the Father will give *another* Paraclete; this word is used several times in this discourse, always of the Spirit; in 1 Jn 2^1 it is used of Christ. To return to Jn 14$^{16-18}$, the Paraclete is said to be the Spirit of truth. The verse, 'I will not leave you desolate: I come unto you', presumably means that Christ comes in the form of the Paraclete; the Paraclete is His Representative, a kind of second self. In the other passages the Paraclete, the Holy Spirit, is described as One who will teach them, bring to their remembrance all that Christ said, bear witness of Christ, convict the world in respect of sin and righteousness and judgement, guide the disciples into all the truth, and glorify Christ; 'for he shall take of mine, and shall declare it unto you' (Jn 16^{14}). The Spirit is clearly conceived as personal; in some places in the New Testament it is not clear in the Greek whether the Spirit is described as 'He' or 'It', but in this last passage the word is clearly and emphatically 'He'. It is equally clear from the references to 'sending', 'proceeding', and so forth, that the Spirit is distinct from both the Father and the Son. The function of the Spirit is not to operate, as it were, on His own, but to bring Christ to mind; and this harmonizes with the idea which we have already met that He is the Agent who brings salvation. The words 'God is spirit' (Jn 4^{24}, R.V. mg) refer to the whole Godhead, and not specifically to the Holy Spirit; so they do not affect the questions we have been discussing.

This Gospel contains a description of the offer of the Holy Spirit to the disciples on Easter Day (Jn 20^{22}: *see ANT* for the relation of this to Pentecost).

3. *Conclusions*

In later years, as the doctrine of the Trinity was more precisely formulated, the Church affirmed the personality, deity and distinctness of the Holy Spirit, together with His equality with the other Persons. The Apostles' Creed is brief on this subject, but the main points are well put in *the Nicene Creed*: 'I believe in the Holy Ghost, the Lord and Giver of life, who proceedeth from the Father and the Son, who with the Father and the Son together is worshipped and glorified, who spake by the Prophets'. On this, we may note the following points. 'Giver of life' refers chiefly to the work of the Spirit in giving to us spiritual life, that is, in bringing to us salvation; but it is thought by some to refer also to the work of the Spirit in creation. The clause 'and the Son' has been much disputed; it was a late insertion, and has never been accepted by the Eastern Churches; but the doctrine, which is known as the Double Procession, serves to remind us that no inspiration purporting to come from the Holy Spirit can really be ascribed to Him, unless it is in harmony with what we know of Jesus Christ. The Spirit, as we have said, does not operate 'on His own'. The clause 'who with the Father and the Son together is worshipped and glorified' is an emphatic assertion of the deity of the Holy Spirit. The 'Prophets' referred to in the last clause are probably both the Old Testament prophets and the prophets who in the early Church were regarded as exercising a kind of Christian ministry (e.g. 1 Cor. 12[28]); their work is continued in prophetic Christian preaching.

a. *Was the Holy Spirit operative among men before Pentecost?* There is no need to take Jn 7[39] (*see* p. 128, above), to mean that the Holy Spirit did not perform any functions before Pentecost. Jesus at least had received the Holy Spirit (p. 126). Moreover, some of the functions ascribed to the spirit of God in the Old Testament, though the writers did not have the conception of a separate 'Person', presumably were in fact performed by the Holy Spirit. For some of the functions in the Old Testament resemble those in the New Testament. Thus, in the New Testament, the Holy Spirit takes the things of Christ and declares them to men; He points back to Christ. But the Old Testament prophets point forward to Christ, and thus it seems reasonable to think that the spirit of God which inspired them was the Holy Spirit performing His usual function of pointing to Christ. We must not, of course, distinguish too sharply between the functions of the Persons of the Trinity, for they co-operate in all their functions in relation to the world. Nevertheless their functions are distinguishable; particular functions are properly ascribed to particular Persons within the Godhead. Thus we may with confidence ascribe to the Holy Spirit all those main tasks ascribed to Him in the Bible which relate to pointing to Christ or bringing salvation. But when the Bible ascribes to the spirit of God functions such as creation, which we normally ascribe to some other Person of the Trinity, then we must suppose that they are primarily the functions of that other Person, but that the Holy Spirit has some part in them.

b. *Is sanctification the special work of the Holy Spirit?* There does not seem any biblical ground for ascribing justification especially to Christ and sanctification especially to the Holy Spirit. Some people speak as though we could be justified by Christ without receiving the Spirit at all; such Christians (they say) ought then to seek sanctification (by which they mean entire sanctification) as a further gift, and then they will receive the Holy Spirit as a kind of finishing touch to the Christian life. Such texts as 1 Cor. 12[3], Rom. 8[14], Jn 3[5] seem sufficient to dispose of this view. We ought to urge those who are justified to seek entire sanctification, but this ought not to be put in such a way as to imply that they are complete strangers to the Holy Spirit. But even those who agree that sanctification is a process starting at the same time as justification, often ascribe justification to Christ, and sanctification to the Holy Spirit. There is no ground for this; all salvation is wrought by Christ in the Spirit.

c. *We can now summarize the work of the Holy Spirit.* The biblical references are not given, because this section summarizes what has already been drawn from the Bible. It would be a good form of revision to supply them for yourselves. One or two points not explicitly contained in the Bible have been added by inference from it.

(i) He had some part in creating the world.

(ii) He has some part in giving physical, intellectual, and similar general endowments to men.

(iii) He inspired the Old Testament prophets, who pointed forward to Christ.

(iv) He was connected with the conception, the baptism, and the whole life of Christ.

(v) His primary activity among men, which began at Pentecost, is to apply salvation, that is, to bring Christ to men. He first brings the sinner to salvation.

(vi) He is thus associated with the rite which is the outward sign of entry into salvation, namely baptism; and is sometimes associated also with the laying on of hands. Thus today we may think of Him as operative both at baptism and at the reception of new members.

(vii) He guides and teaches, and brings Christ to remembrance.

(viii) He dwells in the Christian, maintaining his justification and working towards his entire sanctification.

(ix) He bears witness of our salvation.

(x) He gives to all Christians such gifts as love, joy, peace, etc., which are His fruit, and the reception of which is part of the process of sanctification.

(xi) He gives power for the performance of the Church's work.

(xii) He gave special and extraordinary gifts such as speaking with tongues.

(xiii) He gives special gifts to those who are called to any particular office or ministry in the Church. He is therefore invoked at the ordination of Ministers (*MHB* 293, 779).

(xiv) He makes the means of grace effective and may fittingly be invoked at the Lord's Supper (*MHB* 765, 767).

(xv) He helps our prayers and makes intercession for us.

(xvi) He inspired the writing of Scripture. (This is partly an inference from His general guidance of the Church, but has some support from the word used in 2 Tim. 3[16]).

Some of these overlap, but between them they show in what a variety of ways the Holy Spirit pursues His main task of bringing to us the salvation wrought by Christ. Yet the impression probably still remains that the Holy Spirit is the Person of the Trinity whom we know least. Many people are disturbed by this, for they feel that He is the One with whom we are (or ought to be) in most contact. But it is not really surprising, for the function of the Holy Spirit is not to draw attention to Himself, but to point to Christ. He effaces Himself as He does His work. Certainly we should seek His aid, but the result will be that we know Christ better. We cannot invoke Him better than in the words of *MHB* 765, which makes this very clear, especially in the last verse:

> *Come, Thou Witness of His dying;*
> *Come, Remembrancer divine,*
> *Let us feel Thy power, applying*
> *Christ to every soul, and mine.*

Sermon X. The Witness of the Spirit

Is it possible to a man to *know* that he is accepted by God? Christian tradition has usually said 'No; the Christian ought not to doubt the faithfulness of God to His promise to save those who, through faith in Jesus Christ, use all those means of grace which God has provided as the way to come to Himself. But the believer cannot have more than a confident hope, until he gets to heaven.' At the Reformation, Protestant theology largely departed from this position. It was often argued that a man was saved or not solely on account of the sovereign choice of God. It was not to be supposed that God would change His mind. Therefore, once a believer was aware that divine grace was at work in his heart he could *know* that he was saved to all eternity. Once God had chosen to place him on the Christian path he could not fall from it, for God's grace is irresistible. One of the most significant and formative elements in distinctive Methodist theology is that Wesley departed on a third and middle course. He argued that the believer can *know* that he is possessed of the life of God in the same way that he knows that he is alive in the physical sense—by immediate experience, which indeed cannot be fully 'explained', but cannot be doubted by the reasonable man. Starting from Rom. 8^{16}, Wesley distinguished two elements in this 'experience'. First, 'the Witness of our own spirit', i.e. the common-sense argument: 'Since my conversion I have been aware that my disposition and conduct have been changed for the better, and I have a good conscience. Therefore the saving work of Christ must have started in my heart.' In the second place, God could give a confirmatory seal to this. The experience of 'the heart strangely warmed' could be so personal and distinct, the sense of joy and peace in God so overwhelming, that it was impossible for the believer to bring himself to doubt that this was the very hand of God. Wesley called this experience 'the Witness of the Spirit of God'. He regarded it as the added *privilege* of the believer, something confidently to be looked for in the Christian life, but not indispensable to salvation. Therefore the Christian should pray for this experience, but not doubt his salvation if it were not given. The two 'Witnesses' together give a *present* 'Full Assurance' of salvation. As against the 'Catholic', one can do more than *hope* that one will be saved in the end. As against the Calvinist, one must not assume that it is impossible finally to fall from the state of grace once it has been granted.

Theme of the Sermon. To distinguish the two 'Witnesses', and to show how the believer may keep himself from the danger of fanatical delusion.

EXPLANATORY OUTLINE OF THE SERMON

Introduction. (1) Many Evangelical Christians have fallen into wild delusion over this matter. (2) Many 'common-sense' Christians have flown to the other extreme. (3) The Methodist must keep a middle course.

I. *The Two 'Witnesses'.* (1) Exposition of the text (somewhat confused). (2) The general testimony of the Bible is plain enough. (3) *1 John* teaches Assurance on the basis of 'the Witness of our own spirit'. (4) The enthusiastic Evangelical, secure in his raptured experience of the warmed heart, is not to despise this more homely and common-sense argument from a change of character. (5) The Christian *ought* to be able to recognize, directly and inwardly, whether or no he does in fact love God and his neighbour, and sincerely do all good works, and whether he has a clean conscience. (6) This much is 'the Witness of our own spirit'. (7) 'The Witness of the Spirit of God' is a direct experience, mysterious, yet unmistakable, that I personally have received my share in what Christ did for all. (Compare the passage beginning 'the testimony of the Spirit is an inward . . .' with what Wesley says of his own 'experience of the heart strangely warmed': (*Journal*, May 24, 1738, para. 14). The language is so alike that it is clear that Wesley is describing 'the Witness of the Spirit' in terms of his 'heart strangely warmed'. In fact, the two are names for the same thing.) (8) Argument that 'the Witness of the Spirit' comes first of the two (though Wesley has just said it is 'superadded' to the other! The confusion is between different paths of experience. In the case of a glorious 'instantaneous conversion', such as Wesley had come to expect among his hearers, it is reasonable to suppose that the convert may have his heart unmistakably 'full of glory' before he has had time to discover whether his character is different. 'The Witness of the Spirit' has come first. Those who, like Wesley himself, come to the fullness of experience after a period of upright life and earnest search naturally find that 'the Witness of the Spirit' is 'superadded' to an existing 'Witness of their own spirit'). (9) Afterwards we are aware of our sanctification, which is (10) itself a work of the Spirit. (11) We know we have 'the Witness of our own spirit' (i.e. inward consciousness of moral and spiritual renewal) in the same way we know we are alive. It is 'there'. (12) The manner in which God's Spirit works the 'glory' is beyond our knowledge, but equally certain.

II. *How the 'Fully Assured' may guard against Fanaticism.* (This was a burning issue at the time. Any religious movement showing powerful emotion is bound to attract a 'lunatic fringe' of unspiritual men who make wonderful professions of 'divine illumination'. Wesley was troubled by such at times.) (1) How to distinguish 'Full Assurance' from religious delusions is a matter of great importance. (2) It is easy for those who have never been truly penitent for sin to 'work themselves up' into the delusion that they possess this privilege. (3) Scripture leaves us in no doubt, (4) sincere penitence must come before the assurance of pardon. (5) Those who have the genuine Assurance must be aware that God has worked a distinct moral change in them. (In other words, those who profess 'the Witness of the Spirit' *must* also be aware of 'the Witness of their own spirit'.) (6) Thus, the genuinely Assured will be found humble before God, and before those who may exhort or correct them. The deluded fanatic is typically self-opinionated. (7) Similarly the deluded will probably be found less morally strict than he was before his 'conversion'. Not so the true believer. (8, 9) Challenge to self-examination. (10, 11) We do wrong to try to press behind these practical tests to speculative matters. (12, 13) The fact of the changed life is the test for the genuineness of 'the Witness of the Spirit of God'. (14) Appeal.

TEST QUESTIONS

1. When God saves us, He works a change (i) in our relationship with Him, and (ii) within ourselves. Describe these changes.

2. What evidence do you find (i) in Paul's letters, and (ii) in John's Gospel to show that the Holy Spirit is a divine Person?

3. 'I *feel* saved, therefore I *am* saved'. Is this Methodist doctrine?

STUDY EIGHT

God the Holy Trinity

A. THE NATURE OF GOD

WE have now come to the place where we can usefully pause and draw together what we have learned about the nature of God *as He has revealed Himself* through Israel and especially through Christ. This Study is intended to form a link between (i) the account of the great central truths of the Christian Faith and of the way men came to hold them, and (ii) the presentation of those beliefs in their proper relationship to each other, and in a fashion which preserves the Faith in careful statements which are suitable for teaching and for the prevention of heresy.

1. *Christ the Revealer of God*

Just as in the Old Testament the divine significance of personal encounters with God grew upon the individual after the first impact of the events and under the influence of the Holy Spirit, and became even clearer to subsequent generations—so it was with those who encountered God Incarnate in Christ. The first believers met Jesus and He made an impression on their thoughts and feelings; they began to form beliefs about Him, as *Studies Five* and *Six* have shown. But when they tried to fit Jesus into the scheme of their beliefs about God and man, they realized that He was giving them *new knowledge* about both God and man. What Jesus taught, however, was not so utterly strange that they were repelled by it; and the character of Jesus and His obvious goodness made them willing to accept such a change in their views. But what was it about Jesus which finally made the disciples dare to call Him 'Lord', giving Him a title which they well knew had never before been used by the Jews for anyone except Yahweh Himself? To answer that question, we must go to the Gospel story; but as we do so we must remember, as the disciples themselves early learned to realize, that it was not so much a case of men discovering the nature of God in Christ, as that God revealed Himself *as* God the Son (*see* pp. 97f.).

2. *Christ accepts the Old Testament*

We shall see later how Jesus revised older ideas about God's nature; but that revision was made by a Jew within the framework of the faith of His human forefathers. He knew Himself to be the Messiah, long expected by the Jews—and that was why He was condemned to death by the Sanhedrin and under Jewish Law. When asked what was the greatest commandment (*see ANT, paras.* 156, 202), He quoted the *Shema* (that confession of faith from the Mosaic Law which was always used in the synagogue), thus reaffirming the Jewish faith in the Unity of God. The way in which He taught, and His own clear statements, show that He knew Himself to be in line with the great prophets. He said, 'Think not that I came to destroy the law or the prophets; I came not to destroy, but to fulfil'. We may say that the Jewish religion was the 'language' by which Jesus communicated His revelation, though He taught men new meanings for the old familiar words.

Not only do the Gospels bear witness to the acceptance by Jesus of the Old Testament, but the rest of the New Testament is likewise rooted and grounded in the earlier revelation. For instance, Paul's epistles are incomprehensible in many places to anyone who is not familiar with the Old Testament, so full are they of references to people and events there recorded. We might expect Paul, as the apostle to the Gentiles, to minimise the 'Jewishness', so to speak, of Jesus; but even to non-Jews he presents Jesus as the Messiah, the crown of the revelation made through the Chosen People. If Christ is *more* than Messiah of the Jews, if He is Saviour of the whole world, then Paul is confident that God has revealed this fact in the ancient Scriptures, and commissioned the Jews to proclaim that fact. So, too, the characteristic method of the author of *Hebrews* is his use of the Old Testament revelation to proclaim the New Covenant.

All this, then, bears witness to the fact that our Lord, His first followers, and the New Testament writers took over the great truths about God which were made through Israel. Our next task is to ask what additions and revisions were made by Jesus to the Hebrew conception of God's nature.

3. *The Teaching of Jesus on the Nature of God*

In our consideration of the Person of Christ (p. 101) we saw how Jesus clarified men's ideas of the Kingdom of God, and therefore of God Himself. A scholar whose knowledge of both Judaism and of the New Testament was perhaps unique, has pointed out how Jesus' command to seek and save the outcast and sinful, to constrain them to come into the Kingdom (Lk 14^{12-24}) goes beyond any thought of God's Grace held by the Hebrews. God's love goes out to seek and save the lost (Lk $15^{3\text{ff.}}$, 19^{10}). It is active, not passive. His mercy is not confined to those first chosen to be His People, but reaches out to all mankind (Lk 10^{25-37}). Thus for Jesus the active love of God is revealed as continuing and transcending the highest thoughts of the prophets and calling for new ways of expressing its fullness.

The one way of speaking of God which pre-eminently marks out Christianity from other religions is to call Him *Father*. Not that other religions have avoided using this title, but the doctrine of the Fatherhood of God has dominated Christian thought and faith, because it was predominant in Jesus' thought and speech. It has been well said, for instance, that the 'Lord's Prayer' may justly be taken as a sketch of what, in the thought of Jesus, the Father is like.* The prayer has two main divisions; one concerned with world issues, and the second with affairs of individuals (*see ANT, para.* 247). Both concerns are alike in the hands of the Father. He is seen as sovereign arbiter of the world's history. He is the object of man's complete devotion; the fullness of His Kingdom is utterly to be desired; His will stands supreme in its claim upon man's loyalty. Similarly, the Father cares for and ministers to each of His children. He is the source of their material needs; He alone can deal with the sin which destroys His image in men and dislocates His world-order; He is protector and deliverer. Now the fact that it is in a *prayer* that we find this summary of Christ's teaching about God's Fatherhood has its own significance. Jesus, of course, taught His disciples to pray in the spirit in which He Himself prayed. For Jesus, the will of the Father covers the whole life of man; the whole man may enter into communion with the Father.

Now we have seen in *Study Six* that the very earliest records of the New Testament, as well as the latest, bear witness to Jesus' consciousness of a *unique relationship* to the Father. God was not simply the Father of the faithful or of mankind; He was, in Jesus' thought and life, particularly and especially *His* Father. The experience of God as Father dominated the whole ministry

* Manson, *Teaching of Jesus*, p. 113.

of Jesus from the Baptism to the Crucifixion. This profound relationship was the supreme reality in His life. We see the effects of this experience of God as Father in His absolute trust in the Father, in His unquestioning obedience to His will, in the authority with which He spoke and the assurance with which He did all things. T. W. Manson* points out that the earlier Gospel sources (*Mark*, Q and L) show that Jesus rarely spoke to others of His unique relationship to the Father, except after Peter's confession of faith at Caesarea Philippi and then only to His closest disciples. He suggests that this reticence is positive evidence of the intense reality and deep sacredness of Jesus' experience of God as uniquely His Father; 'for every man the Holy of Holies in his life is hedged about with silence'. The fact that the authors of the later Gospels, *Matthew* and *John*, report Jesus as using the word Father much more often than the earlier Gospels shows that they were trying 'to bring into the foreground something which they perceived to be of far more vital import than would appear from such documents as *Mark* and Q'; something which was of the vital essence of the Gospel. Not only, then, did Jesus give new content to the general idea of the Fatherhood of God, but He demonstrated, in word and act, that God's Fatherhood of mankind could only be seen in its fullness by those who came to terms with the Beloved Son Himself. For Jesus, God was first and foremost 'the Father of the Son', revealed as such through our Lord's consciousness of being the Son of the Father. It follows that Jesus' *teaching* concerning the nature of the Father must yield to the revelation of the Father *in* the Son.

In all Jesus' teaching, perhaps no parable makes this clearer than that of the Wicked Husbandmen (*see* p. 101; *also ANT, para.* 153). When Jesus told this story, He had begun to show by His words that 'Be My disciple' and 'Accept the Rule of the Father' meant one and the same thing; we recall the words of Jn 10^{30}: 'I and my father are one'.

4. *Jesus, by His life, death and resurrection, shows us the character of God*

The disciples belonged to a race which believed that God had revealed His nature and purposes to men more especially in *what He had done* in and through and with their ancestors. They believed that God, in His wisdom, had chosen that method of making Himself known. When they met Jesus, and came to call

* Op. cit., pp. 99ff.

Him 'Lord', 'Truly God' (*see Study Six*) they recognized that in the acts of Christ they were seeing God *supremely* revealed. So, Paul writes of the God who 'was in Christ reconciling the world unto himself' (2 Cor. 5$^{18f.}$), and the writers of the Gospels leave us in no doubt that they were fully conscious of recording the continued revealing activity of God in the events of Jesus' birth, life, death, resurrection and ascension.

Nevertheless none of those who met and listened to our Lord would have called Him 'Master' and 'Lord' and endured criticism and hardship in order to follow Him, if they had not seen in Him goodness as they knew it, the doing of the will of God as they understood it, God-likeness as far as they knew what God was like. He 'went about doing good' (Acts 10^{38}) is the testimony of Peter. In His dealings with the unfortunate, the despised and the sinful, there was a sympathy, a patience and a self-giving *activity* of succour which made His contemporaries feel very conscious of their own shortcomings. It sharpened the criticism of the Pharisees, and caught the attention of many who would not have taken much notice of yet another wandering teacher. His works of healing and service spoke a language understood by every human heart. It was to His own *actions* that Jesus Himself drew attention in reply to the wistful enquiry of the imprisoned Baptist. To the faithful few, the later decisions and actions of Jesus were lighted up by their recollection of His life among them. Full obedience to God, enjoined by prophet and priest—what seemed to them an impossible ideal for mortal men—was unbroken throughout His life. What later believers came to call His sinlessness (which means far more than that He did no evil deed) the disciples saw as His constant communion with the Father, from which sprang the strength of purpose and love which marked Him off from all the rest of them.

Therefore, when He set His face to go to Jerusalem, some still followed Him. They were with Him in the Upper Room and caught something of the sublime meaning of His actions at the Last Supper; they had seen enough of His life to trust Him thus far; a few were near Him in Gethsemane; a few stood around the Cross and gathered in the Upper Room and went to the tomb to tend His body. Even the strangeness of His latest actions could not wholly dissipate the confidence His everyday life had aroused in them; confidence that He was revealing to them what God willed the life of man to be. Before they were able to see any triumphant meaning, any victory in the Cross, they could see in the utter love and selflessness of their Master the reflection of the nature of God.

But when, in the light of the Resurrection and Ascension, Calvary no longer seemed to be the end of their dearest hopes, the disciples realized that they had been privileged to be in close companionship with Him through whom the eternal love of God had been once and for all 'placarded' (to borrow a graphic word from Gal. 3^1) before the world; with Him who Himself had said, 'He that hath seen me hath seen the Father' (Jn 14^9).

We have now reviewed our Lord's attitude to the Old Testament; we have seen that His *teaching* takes up and adds greatly to the highest Hebrew understanding of what God is like; we have seen that the disciples saw in Christ's *life* and *death* the revelation of God's eternal nature. Not only on the Emmaus road but to all His followers, not only nor chiefly by what He taught but by His character and life and death, Christ 'opened to them the scriptures'. He 'made all things new', including their idea of what God was like.

Let us briefly look back to the seven great affirmations of the faith of Israel which are set out in *Study Three*. (i) How much more evident is the *personal* nature of the Lord of the universe when we have stood by the side of Jesus as He prayed; when we have heard Him speak of God as 'Heavenly Father'. (ii) How much more of the *holy* 'otherness' of God do we grasp as we encounter Jesus' rebuke of all sinfulness, gross or subtle, and see how His sinlessness sets Him apart from the generality of mankind; when we see His love of this God-made world and of life in it, but remember that He counted it as nothing compared with obedience to the Father's will (Mk 14^{36}). (iii) If the impression of God's *righteousness* in the Old Testament is that He demands from man an impossible virtue and ordains for sinners an overwhelming punishment, then it is in Jesus' unvarying declaration that the foundation of righteousness is love that we learn the fuller meaning. (iv) His own life of sinless obedience was the outcome of His communion in love with the Father. 'Beloved, let us love one another . . . for God is love' (1 Jn $4^{7f.}$). 'Greater love hath no man than this, that a man lay down his life for his friends', but 'the Father abiding in me doeth his works' (Jn 15^{13}, 14^{10}). (v–vii) In *Study Six* we have seen how Jesus transformed and enlarged men's thoughts of the *sovereignty*, the Kingdom of God; and we have noticed how their encounter with Jesus led them, not to a lesser, but to a greater belief in the *unity* of God than their fathers held.

5. *God in action, in the Incarnate Son and in the Holy Spirit*

We have seen (pp. 139f.) that Jesus, by His life and death, showed His contemporaries the character of God, but we have already suggested that He did more than that. He not only showed what God is *like* (i.e. like Jesus Himself); *He Himself was divine*—God Incarnate and acting in a new way as the Redeemer of mankind. At first sight it seems strange that the early Christians—Jews who believed so utterly in the *one* God—should ever have ascribed divinity to a man living among men (*see* p. 37). Their affirmation of Jesus' Lordship could never have been made unless, as a matter of personal experience, they had felt that in Jesus they had met One whose influence upon them and their fellow-believers was without parallel in human experience. They knew that they themselves were changed men, and that the divine events which had centred in the person and work of Jesus had changed the whole status and prospects of mankind. They were convinced that God had taken the initiative to save His children from sin and death, and to that end had Himself 'set on foot the whole process of the Incarnation, Life, Death and Resurrection of Christ' (p. 73); that '*God* was in Christ reconciling the world unto himself' (2 Cor. 5[19]). The God of their fathers, the God who reveals Himself (*see* pp. 139f.), had revealed Himself again, and by what He had *done* in and through Christ; for only God Incarnate could have done for them and for all what Christ had done. They could not doubt that Jesus was God, any more than they could doubt that God is One. That is the overwhelming impression left upon us by the New Testament.

But the revealing, redeeming activity of God in Jesus Christ did not end with the Ascension. The N.T. writers were also certain that the gift of the *Holy Spirit* was a part of the unending redemption which was being offered by the One God, and being wrought upon those who would accept it. In *Study Seven* we have seen how men were led by Christ to a clearer understanding of the nature and work of the Holy Spirit than had been given before. Because of the way in which our Lord spoke of Him (especially see pp. 126f.), because of Jesus' intimate association with Him in some of the critical experiences of His life, because of the experiences of Pentecost, men were compelled to believe that the Spirit who came upon them, and enlightened their minds and sanctified their lives, was not only *a* holy spirit, but *the* Holy Spirit, the One God revealing Himself to them as the Paraclete.

Now it was through the life and teaching of Jesus that the disciples had been prepared for, and enabled to interpret, the later experiences which finally brought them to recognize the Holy Spirit as God. Because they had met in the flesh One who was God, and had begun to think of God's nature as having in its unity the Father and the Son, so they were the more ready to receive that revelation through Christ which showed them that the nature of the One God was such that within the unity there were Father, Son, and Spirit. The Father of the Son is known through the Son, the Son of the Father is known through the Son, and the Holy Spirit is known through the Son. So, 'A Christian is one who believes that God has revealed Himself in Jesus Christ' (*CAT* 1).

B. GOD, THREE IN ONE

We must now attempt to understand the Christian conception of the Divine Nature in Trinity and Unity, as that conception has been expressed in the great classic statements of faith and in the preaching and teaching of the Church.

1. *The inescapable facts of experience*

To the first Christians, it was a matter of personal experience that God in Christ had come as a real man among men, and had lived a truly human life. This was something that the world had never known before, but there was no doubt about it. Jesus had been born, had lived and worked for thirty-three years, and had been executed (*see* p. 139). It was also a matter of personal experience that God was present within them, to guide and sanctify them, in the person of the Holy Spirit. God had freely chosen to come to them in this way and He was quite able to do so, even though He was the One God in whom they unshakably believed. This was the basic fact which they had learned about God's nature. No wonder they were often at a loss for words to express what they had been taught in these quite new events in human history and experience! There is no hint anywhere in the New Testament that these first believers tended to believe in two (or three) gods. When they called Jesus 'Lord', when they spoke of the Holy Spirit as 'He', they were still speaking of the *One* God. So the Fourth Gospel, one of the latest writings in the canon, records Jesus as saying, 'I and the Father are one'. They could and did speak freely about what Jesus was like, what He said and did, and of His influence upon themselves and others; they could and did speak freely of the way in which the Spirit had come to them, and of His work within them; but they could say little about *how* God could be both Father, Son and Holy Spirit. They did make many statements, some of which have been examined in this and previous *Studies*, which show that the New Testament Christians took for granted that the Christian God was to be known as Father, as Son and as Holy Spirit. There are about eighty places in the N.T. which make reference to the Three Persons in close association. The student will do well to look at the following passages: Mt. 28^{19}, 1 Cor. 6^{11}, 12^{4-6}, 2 Cor. 1^{21-2}, 13^{14}, 1 Pet. 1^2, Heb. 9^{14}, 10^{29}. Such passages convince us that the Trinitarian pattern of thinking about God was part and parcel of Christian thought very soon after the Ascension, even though there is in the N.T. no trace of fixity of wording, such as we find in the later statements of belief.

2. *The Church begins to preach the Triune God*

If the New Testament writers were unconscious of any sense of contradiction between God being One and His coming to them as Son and Holy Spirit, their immediate successors could not escape the problem. So, in the writings which came immediately after the latest New Testament books, there is abundant evidence that by that time men were trying to find words to express what the New Testament said about God, *not in separate affirmations, but in relationship to each other.*

When the second century began, the Christian Church consisted largely of people who had been brought up in Greek culture; they thought like Greeks rather than like Jews. The Greek way of thinking was much more logical than the way of thinking of the East in general, and of the Jews in particular. Moreover, the Jew 'waited upon God' to be told what He willed and what He was like; the Greek, generally speaking, reasoned out what his gods or God ought to be like, and rejected those ideas of the divine which seemed unreasonable. Now this attitude of trying to reason out what God is like clearly stands in opposition to the Hebrew idea of waiting to receive what God reveals. It is all the more wonderful, all the greater testimony to the compelling nature of the Gospel and to the power of the Holy Spirit, that so many Greek-thinking people so quickly embraced the Good News. Not that Jew and Christian did not reason *about* the revelation that came to them. If they had not done so, the Church would have shrivelled up and died, the Holy Spirit would have met with no response from men as He continued the revealing work; and, as a minor result, this book would not have been written! Christians have always believed that the Holy Spirit is constantly interpreting the revelation of Himself which God has given in history. So, when Greek-thinking people came face to face with the testimonies of those who had been eye-witnesses of the life of Jesus, and who had experienced the power of Pentecost, they began to ask *how* the One God could be 'eternal in the heavens', incarnate on earth, and indwelling in the believer; and the doctrine of the Trinity began to take shape.

3. *Avoiding the facts*

There were some who could not shake off the influence of the more 'mathematical' way of thinking, and their answer was a simple one: that *one* could not be *three*, and that *three* could not be *one*; that Jesus could not, therefore, really have been God at all, nor could the Spirit. In the second century, the Christian Gnostics said that Jesus was only a phantom, *like* a man; that the world was so wholly evil that God could never be part of it by becoming a real man. It was partly in reply to such ideas that the Gospel and First Epistle of John were written (*see* p. 104f.; also *ANT* on *John* and *1 John*).

At a later date, there were other Christian thinkers who gained a great following from among those who asked for a 'simple Gospel', even if it ignored many of the facts. These were the Arians, who were named after Arius of Alexandria; incidentally, they were great hymn-singers and this increased their popularity! They said that Jesus was neither fully man nor fully God, but a sort of intermediate being. This 'easy option', however attractive it seemed to some, could never be reconciled with the revelation of the Bible. It was to combat this heresy that, at the Council of Nicaea (in modern Turkey) in A.D. 325, an attempt was made to state fully and unmistakably what the Church believed about Jesus Christ. In *Study Six* we have seen that the discussion turned on the choice of the most suitable Greek word to describe Christ's relation to the Father (*see* p. 109). The Creed which was adopted by the Council is usually known as the Creed of Nicaea, and it contained the phrases 'We believe in One God. . . . And in

One Lord Jesus Christ . . . very God of very God, of the same substance (homo-ousios) with the Father . . . And in the Holy Spirit'. The Church thereby accepted the doctrine that there is in God a 'Threeness' or Trinity of nature. The Creed of Nicaea was later revised,* and in its final form (approved at the Council of Chalcedon: *see* p. 108) became the 'Nicene Creed', which you will find in the Order of Holy Communion and in the Order of Morning Prayer in our *Book of Offices*. The faith embodied in this Creed is today the faith of every branch of the Christian Church.

4. *The Trinity and Saving Faith*

Whenever men have been attracted by the idea of finding a 'simple Gospel' (that is, a Gospel which makes no great demand upon the mind and heart and will) the result has always been a statement of belief which was robbed of its power to save, because it was robbed of truth. This is as true today as it was in the second century. The idea that the earliest Christians had such a 'simple faith' we have seen to be false. In all probability 'Jesus is Lord' was the affirmation of faith which was expected of all who were admitted into the Early Church (*see ANT* on 1 Cor. 12^3, Phil. 2^{11}); but that affirmation had a tremendous content— it contained all the elements of the doctrine of the Trinity. Of course, we can be saved before we understand the full meaning of that doctrine—before we even know of it as a doctrine, just as the early Christians were. But we cannot progress far in Christian belief or worship before we become aware that such a doctrine is necessary to our further growth in the Christian life. The tragedy is that so many begin the course and then turn back, hoping to find satisfaction in the 'milk' of the Gospel, as Paul called it, the 'baby food', which is all we need as we begin life, but which must soon yield place to 'something we can get our teeth into'. So men discovered in the second century of our era, and they grappled with the problem of possessing the riches of God's revelation.

Many people would say that the central theme of the Gospel is not the doctrine of the Trinity, but our experience of God's salvation. Properly understood, however, our experience of salvation involves the belief in God as Three in One. *God the*

* In particular, the brief reference to the *Holy Spirit* in the Creed of Nicaea was replaced by that description of His person which we have quoted on p. 129.

Father demands from us sinful men an obedient love which of ourselves we cannot give Him. But Jesus Christ, by His life and death, perfectly meets this demand (*see* p. 84), and is able to do so because He is not only truly Man, but also *God the Son*. But that is not all. Even we are able, however imperfectly, to give obedient love to God, but we do not do this of ourselves (cf. 1 Cor. 15^{10}); it is wrought in us by the *Holy Spirit*. So, at the very heart of our experience of salvation we encounter the whole Godhead; for what the Father demands from us, the Son supplies for us, and the Holy Spirit works in us. Thus the doctrine of salvation involves, and is indeed almost identical with, the doctrine of the Trinity.

We may illustrate this further from C. S. Lewis' picture of the ordinary simple Christian as he kneels down to say his prayers. He is trying to get into touch with God the Father, but he knows that it is God the Spirit, 'inside him', who is prompting him to pray. He also knows that the God to whom he prays is the God who is revealed in Jesus Christ, and that Christ is standing beside Him, helping him to pray and praying for him. 'So that the whole threefold life of the three-personal Being is actually going on in that ordinary little bedroom where an ordinary man is saying his prayers'.*

5. *The Doctrine of the Trinity and Theology*

The attempt to describe God in His Threeness and Oneness has often been said to have arisen simply because men felt compelled to put together and to connect up the separate ideas about God which, up to that time, had been accepted by Christians. To some extent this is true; men did feel the need for joining up and tidying up their beliefs; but there would have been Creeds, and most certainly there would have been a doctrine of the Trinity, even they had not felt this need. It is also true that Christians had to try to say exactly what they believed in order to prevent people from accepting any ideas which took their fancy (such as those of the Gnostics and Arians), however far those ideas might be from fact or truth. Certainly Creeds were useful in combating the growth of false teachings, heresies which were due to ignorance of the full facts or to woolly thinking. These carefully-phrased statements of what the Church understood to be the substance of the Christian revelation were probably first formed to facilitate

* *Beyond Personality*, p. 17.

preaching and the instruction of converts who were being prepared for membership in the Church.

All these factors encouraged the clear and precise statement of beliefs, but they were only external influences on the formation of the doctrine of the Trinity.

The truth is that the doctrine is the immediate consequence of the Good News in Jesus. It is—and this way of putting it may appeal to the science student—the crystallisation of the Gospel; out of the fluidity of thought which contains all the essential elements, there comes not a mere shapeless adding-together of these elements, but a doctrine which has the characteristic form which distinguishes the Christian way of thinking abont God from all other ways; the 'thing itself', so to speak. The whole of Christian doctrine can be—must be—stated in terms of our belief in the Triune God, for Christian theology (i.e. 'knowledge of God') must be built on the knowledge of God *as He has been made known to us in Christ, through the Holy Spirit*. Hence, because the thought of God as Trinity is at the heart of the evangelical Gospel of God's redeeming love, our study of it comes at this point in the textbook; at the end of our studies of God's earlier revelation, of man's need, of the work and person of Christ and of the Holy Spirit. But we must not make the mistake of thinking that it is given at this point simply because it is a convenient summary of these other subjects. It is itself the heart of the matter, as one of the greatest Protestant thinkers of our time, Karl Barth, recognizes when he deals with the Trinity in the *preface* to his book on Christian dogmatics—before the first chapter even!

The Church was not able to set out its belief in a Triune God without much argument; we have already noticed the controversies which raged round the problems of the Person of Christ and His relationship to the Father (pp. 108f.). The Trinitarian debate was widespread, long-lasting and, unfortunately, bitter. Until the time of the Council of Chalcedon, there was a succession of attempts to settle the problems raised by Christ's revelation of the nature of God on 'commonsense' lines.

(*a*) There were some who held tenaciously to the arithmetical 'oneness' of God, and maintained that Jesus and the Spirit were different *modes* or aspects in which the One God appeared to men, rather after the fashion in which one child has to take several parts when a small Sunday School does a Nativity Play. It is still said by some that the doctrine of the Trinity is a way of saying that God has revealed Himself in three activities: as Sovereign Creator, as Redeeming Love, and as Divine Presence. Such an explanation of the Trinity, however, does not do justice to that revelation of God's nature which we find in the Bible. The Father is not only Creator but also Redeemer and Sanctifier (*Study Three*); we have noted many sayings of Christ which clearly show that He thought of His own work as being the work of the Father, and that He was conscious of the presence of the Spirit in His ministry (*Studies Five and Six*); and the epistles are full of references to the part played by the Spirit in the whole of the divine activity (*Study Seven*). Father, Son and Spirit do not stand simply for *ways* in which God showed Himself to men, or for separate divine attributes such as holiness, love and grace. The whole story of the formulation of the doctrine of the Trinity shows that the Church was determined to preserve that to which it believed the Bible testified; that 'Threeness' is a part of the very *nature* of the One God.

On the other side, there were those who felt so strongly that the evidence of the New Testament insisted on the *distinctness* of the Father, Son and Spirit that they spoke of God rather as though He were a Committee of Three; One Committee, Three People. Of course, this kind of statement also failed to do justice to the New Testament evidence, and in due course its weaknesses became clear to the great majority of Christians.

Here, then, were some grounds of controversy. If one group was anxious to use a word which emphasised the unity of God, the other side objected that the word did not sufficiently make clear the distinction between Father, Son and Spirit, and that it therefore denied the true humanity of Christ. If the second party suggested a word which safeguarded this point, or one which aimed at doing justice to the New Testament witness that the Holy Spirit is no vague feeling or working of the human mind, but really God, then it was objected by their opponents that the unity of God was being understated.

(*b*) Another difficulty arose when words had to be translated from one language into another, for some theologians wrote in Latin and others in Greek. There were no exact equivalents. This is particularly true of the Latin word *persona*, which was used to refer to each of the Three in the Godhead. The word used by the Greek-speaking theologians as their nearest equivalent to *persona* was *hypostasis*—but it did not mean exactly the same. The confusion became worse when *persona* was translated into English as *person*; and has become worse still in the last hundred years or so, during which time the study of human personality has changed the meaning of 'person' even in our own language. The result of all this is that when we speak today of 'One God in Three Persons', the idea that most of us have in mind when we say 'Persons' is one which would have deeply disturbed the Christians gathered at the Council of Chalcedon. Most certainly God is *personal*, whether He is encountered by the prophets, by the disciples in Capernaum or at Pentecost, or by you and me. But the word 'person' has come to carry for us all a suggestion of separate, *independent* existence which the 5th century theologians were anxious to avoid when they spoke of God in His Threeness.

It would really seem as though there is no better word in our language than 'person' by which we can do justice to all that we know through Christ about the Threeness in the Godhead; but we must always make it clear that, when we say 'One Divine Nature, Three Persons', we do not mean, any more than the New Testament or the Fathers meant, that God is 'three people'. This limitation of language, after all, is what we might expect. We are trying to express what is beyond human understanding—even though, by the grace of a Revealing God, He has been known in Christ to human experience, and is known in the Spirit in our experience today. Some Christian thinkers, however, believe that, while we must continue to use the word 'persons' where it is desirable to use a single word (e.g. when the expression occurs on worship), the use of the word in its current meaning has been the main cause of the widespread suspicion of the doctrine of the Trinity, and that in Christian teaching we should use a phrase of several words. Karl Barth has suggested: 'God in His three ways of being God'.

We may sum up by saying that, from the centuries of discussion and after many attempts, there emerged in the theology of the Church a form of words which was the most exact statement of the true Triunity of God which could then be attained, and it must be admitted that there has been little real improvement on that formula since the Council of Chalcedon (A.D. 451). 'There were not at the time of the development of the doctrine of the Trinity, and there are not now available, any terms which can be taken over as clearly and obviously indicative of what we wish to say about the Father, Son and Holy Spirit.'*

6. *The Communion of God*

The New Testament, which so clearly recognizes the variety within God's nature, constantly speaks of the Three in a certain order; Father, Son and Holy Spirit. This, of course, is the order in time in which men came to recognize the Three, but there is another reason for this order than that. The doctrine of the Trinity, preserving and making clear the New Testament insights, emphasises that Father, Son and Spirit are all truly God, and *equal* to each other; that there never was a time when Christ did not exist, or the Spirit did not exist; that there is no difference in importance between the Three, for they are together One God. But as the language of the New Testament shows and as the doctrine of the Trinity implies, there is a sense in which we cannot think of Christ without first thinking of the Father. So the New Testament speaks of Christ as 'coming' from the Father, and the Nicene Creed preserves this idea in the phrase 'Only-begotten Son . . . begotten of His Father before all worlds'. Again, in *Study Seven* we noticed how Paul speaks of the Holy Spirit (to mention some phrases) as 'Spirit of God', 'Spirit of Christ', 'Spirit of the Father and the Son'. Without thinking of Christ, and therefore of the Father, we cannot think of the Spirit. The Creed again puts this into words: ' . . . the Holy Ghost . . . Who proceedeth from the Father and the son. . . .' This way of expressing the dependence of the Son upon the Father, and of the Spirit upon both, is termed the *Generation* of the Son and the *Procession* of the Spirit. Among other things, it enables us to realize that there is a self-giving within the very being of God, what we may call a 'going-forth-ness' in His *nature*, and not only in His attitude to and dealings with His Creation. The love of God, which is revealed in His gracious relationships with men, in His redemption in Christ through the Spirit, is part of the very being of God. The doctrine of the Trinity, then, is an affirmation that there is communion *within* God, a perfect mutual relationship between the Three which is so simply expressed in the sublime words, 'God *is* Love'.

7. *The Mystery remains*

From the days of the Early Fathers down to our own time,

* Claude Welch, *The Trinity in Contemporary Theology*, to which the writer of this Study is deeply indebted.

theologians and preachers have sought to illumine the mystery of the Trinity by using illustrations and analogies taken from human life and experience. As preachers who proclaim the Christian faith, you may try in this way to help believers to understand more clearly the tremendous truth of the Oneness and Threeness of God; but it cannot be said too strongly that all illustrations and analogies must be imperfect, for the Triunity of God is unlike anything else known to us; and they may even be dangerous if they lead you and your congregation to think that any analogy can really and fully explain the mystery of the 'God in three Persons, blessed Trinity'.

The doctrine of the Trinity is not an unnecessary complication, substituted for simple belief by people who have lost touch with common human need. Our faith in the Triune God is grounded in the Gospel; it has come to us by divine revelation; it could never have been discovered, and it will never be completely understood, by human reason. We accept it as the truest expression of the nature of God which has ever been given to man, but in doing so we recognize that we are in a region of thought where all things go out in mystery and adoration.

8. *The Trinity and Worship*

The first believers and those who followed them, under the guidance of the Holy Spirit, began vigorously to explore the implications of their belief in the Triune God for every part of life. You will see something of the *practical consequences* of the doctrine of the Trinity in *Studies Nine* to *Twelve*. Here we only pause to stress the practical significance of the doctrine in the realm of *worship*.

We cannot ignore the connection between the *way* we worship God and the *kind* of God we know Him to be, for the one is determined by the other. If, in our worship, we forget God the Father, or God the Son, or God the Holy Spirit, our worship is impoverished. This should be the test of your own private devotions and of your conduct of public worship. Through the ages, the Church has sought to preserve in its corporate worship the fullness of the revelation of God's nature as the Holy Trinity. Moreover, the realization of God's richer, triune nature, as revealed through Christ, aroused in Christians a deeper reverence and adoration than they had known hitherto.

To illustrate this, turn to the Order of Service for the *Holy Communion* and see how the theme of the Trinity runs throughout the liturgy. First the Lord's Prayer with its petitions for material needs, for reconciliation and sanctification. Then the Collect with its mention of all three Persons of the Godhead (a feature of the Collects for the Day in the *Book of Common Prayer*). Then, a few pages later, we are called to affirm our faith by repeating the words of the Nicene Creed. See how, through the whole service, the thought moves to and fro from Him who is the Creator who calls us to Himself, to the Saviour who is the Way back, to the Spirit by whom we are enabled to accept that Way. Note how, as the climax to the prayers which follow the giving of the Sacrament, Glory is ascribed to the Three in One; and how the service ends with the Blessing of the Triune God. Here is the essence of all Christian worship.

We see, then, that it is in worship, and at its very heart, that this witness to the most Holy Trinity is made in deepest reverence and wondering adoration. The doctrine is no abstract speculation of a few philosophers or theologians. It is the reverent experience and testimony of the believing ages and of the countless, nameless faithful. 'It points us to the reality and the Godhead of the Father and of the Holy Spirit, God above us and God within us, as well as the Divinity of Jesus Christ. . . . It points us to the infinite mystery and unapproachable holiness and otherness of God . . . and to the reality of a power not ourselves that can work in us invisibly and secretly to do the will of God, as well as to 'the grace of our Lord Jesus Christ', manifest in obedience as of a Son and in willingness out of pure yet passionate love to offer His life for sinners.'*

'For of him, and through him, and unto him, are all things. To him be the glory for ever' (Rom. 11^{36}). 'Glory be to the Father, and to the Son, and to the Holy Ghost; as it was in the beginning, is now, and ever shall be, world without end. Amen.'

Sermon V. 'Justification by Faith'

Unlike most of the sermons this is a 'dummy'; not a sermon composed to be preached, but a theological essay written in the form of a sermon with a view to publication. It thus covers far too much theological ground for a sermon. This sermon gives an outline of that Reformation theology which is the general background of the distinctive Methodist preaching which is the theme

* C. W. Lowry, *The Trinity and Christian Devotion,* pp. 107f.

of most of the doctrinal sermons in the volume. The chief interest to the modern reader is: (*i*) to observe that the Gospel-substance of Wesley remains intact today, even though his intellectual background may be somewhat different, and in consequence his way of expressing certain truths not the same as we would use today: e.g. few people today would explain the sinful condition of the human race as taking its rise from a particular act of disobedience committed by one particular historical person, Adam. Nevertheless, any candid man must agree with Wesley in the practical issue that all men are without exception sinful, helpless to help themselves, and in need of a Saviour. So also we may differ from Wesley in our explanation of the Atonement, but agree with him in the *fact*, and in the necessity and sufficiency of the saving work of Christ. (*ii*) Here is a splendid example of clear and systematic exposition of doctrine.

Theme of the Sermon. Explanation of the Fall, the Atonement, Salvation by Grace, Justification by Faith, Faith and Sanctification.

EXPLANATORY OUTLINE OF THE SERMON

Introduction. (1–3) Importance of a subject which has been a matter of much confusion.

I. *Man's Need of a Saviour.* (1) God made man morally perfect, and (2) required of him perfect moral obedience. (3) The test of this obedience was the prohibition of eating from the tree. (4) Man's original state of perfect union with God. (5) His disobedience, resulting in (*i*) loss of this spiritual union with God ('death of the soul'), and (*ii*) the liability of the physical body to death. (6) This result in our first parent explains why all men are by nature spiritually dead and liable to physical disease and death. (The important passage in *Romans* to which reference is made does not quite mean that spiritual and physical death has been inherited in the same way in which an 'insane streak' or a weakness for certain diseases can be passed on. Paul's idea is more spiritually subtle and more spiritually convincing than this. As *Britannia*, for example, 'stands for' all Britons, so *Adam*, whom the Bible describes as the original man, and whose name means 'the man', appropriately 'stands for' all men. He is 'the case in point' of, the *type* of, that race which has collectively sinned, and which dies, and every individual member of which has sinned, and dies.

As Wesley says in the next paragraph, Adam is the *Representative of the race*. This is what is meant by saying that we have all sinned 'in Adam'.) (7) Christ came, and at the price of His sufferings, became a second Representative, who undoes what happened 'in Adam'. (8) On account of this Atonement God will forgive. (9) Summary. ('God is so far reconciled to all the world': note that this is *not* what 2 Cor. 5^{19}, as quoted in (8) says. Paul plainly teaches that it is man who is reconciled to God and not God to man. It is man, not God, who needs to come to another mind.)

II. *What is Justification?* (1) It is distinct from *Sanctification*, or being made actually righteous. (2, 3) Two speculative theories dismissed. (4) It is not that God chooses to regard as righteous those who in fact are not, and still less that He is in any way deceived. (The preacher is warned to be very cautious in the use of such phrases as 'imputing righteousness' to man. This language indeed has the sanction of some Scriptural passages, but it is today very liable to be misunderstood in the way Wesley points out.) (5) Justification is *forgiveness*, which is the first step of the new way of life. (The student should learn the opening definition, which conveys the heart of the matter in the simplest and least ambiguous terms. Paul's term *Justification* is 'free forgiveness' translated into 'law-court language'.)

III. *Can Man Earn Forgiveness?* (1) It is sinful men whom God forgives. (2) Some say that man must first be sanctified, i.e. made actually righteous, and by his good deeds earn his forgiveness. This is contradictory, for it presupposes that only those are forgiven who have least need to be forgiven. (3) Christ saves those who do not deserve to be forgiven (*grace*), when (4) they are convinced of sin and genuinely penitent. (5) Unconverted men can sometimes do 'good works', but these are not good in the full Christian sense, because they do not spring from a ull consciousness of the right motive. (6) Only those who have received God's grace have their hearts filled with the love of God.

IV. *The Nature of Saving Faith.* (1) Paul quoted to show that the way to forgiveness is trustful acceptance of what Christ did to open the way, and this alone. (*Propitiation*='that which wipes away whatever is offensive in the sight of God'.) It is useless to trust in obedience to the moral law to earn this forgiveness, for the unjustified cannot obey it, while forgiveness fills the heart with love and makes obedience possible. (2) Faith is a personal realization that what Christ did for all the world He did for *me*.

(3) The Anglican *Homilies* quoted for definition. (4) Faith in the atoning Christ is the only way of salvation, and (5 and 6) the all-sufficient way. (7) 'Justification by faith and not by the works of the law' exemplifies the fundamental principle that man's salvation is by *grace*, that is, the unaccountable and marvellous undeserved favour and goodness of the sovereign God. (8) That salvation should be eternally *undeserved*, and that it is to be received by the humbly penitent, destroys human pride. Pride, the desire to lift oneself up in fancied independence of God, is the root of sin. (9) The summons to penitence, and the Gospel invitation to the penitent.

TEST QUESTIONS

1. What evidence is there in the New Testament that the early Christians thought of God as Three in One? Describe how the *doctrine* of the Trinity came into being.

2. What answer would you give to the man who says that 'the central theme of the Gospel is not the doctrine of the Trinity, but our experience of God's salvation'?

3. Illustrate the doctrine of Justification by Grace through Faith from the parables of our Lord.

STUDY NINE

The Church (1)

IN this and many other countries the existence of the Church cannot easily be ignored. Some people are actively contemptuous of it; many do not heed or believe its message; a few, we may feel, ascribe to it an exaggerated significance. Yet even a superficial knowledge of the history of the modern world will make us realize how intimately it has been bound up with the story of man. Moreover, few questions have so agitated Christians among themselves as the *form* which the Church ought to take. Thus the Church has united vast numbers of men, and still does, but it also has produced some deep cleavages of opinion and loyalty. The problem is still a living one, and many books are still written about it. We are accordingly concerned, in these two *Studies* on the Church, with no mere academic question, but with an issue which vitally affects our lives as Christians, and as individuals who must take some positive attitude to the society of which we are a part. We must try to understand what place the Church holds in our Christian Faith.

Within recent years, Methodism has given considerable attention to the question, and the Conference has produced two statements—*The Nature of the Christian Church According to the Teaching of the Methodists* (1937), and *The Message and Mission of Methodism* (1946)—which are indispensable for every serious student; and what follows is in part a commentary upon them. Our first approach, however, must be through the Bible.

A. THE CHURCH IN THE BIBLE

A casual acquaintance with the Bible may lead you to conclude that there is little about the Church in its pages, but if you read the New Testament carefully, you will be surprised to discover how largely the Church figures there, although many of the references to it are hidden under various titles and metaphors. The Greek word for Church is *ecclesia* (cf. 'ecclesiastical'), which is taken over by the New Testament writers from the Greek translation of the Old Testament (the Septuagint); it means an assembly of people, called together for some purpose. The Old Testament speaks of the *Church of Yahweh*, which describes Israel as the people gathered together by God (cf. Deut. 23[2ff.]; 1 Chron. 28[8]; Neh. 13[1]; Micah 2[5]). That the *ecclesia* is the *ecclesia of God* is implied, although not always expressed, in the New Testament; the essential idea comes out in Acts 20[28] ('the church of God which he purchased with his own blood'). Hence the full meaning of *ecclesia* in the New Testament is that it is composed of all those people who belong to God, and who have been gathered together by Him. The Church is not *any* assembly of people, like a society or club, but one which is distinguished by being *God's* society, a divine community called together as something distinctive and of set purpose. In a word, the origin of the Church lies in the will and action of God.

One other important difference must be noted in the New Testament use of the word *ecclesia*. Sometimes it is used for the assembly of Christians in a particular place (Acts 5[11], 8[3]), and sometimes for the whole Church (Acts 9[31]; 1 Cor. 12[28]). Thus the *ecclesia* might be small enough to meet in one house; yet it is interesting to note that the same word is used for the whole body of Christians. We conclude that the Church is not divided into churches, nor is it formed by adding together all the little churches. Every little church is rather the local embodiment of the one universal Church. (It should be noted that the English word *church* may also refer to a building; this meaning is not found in the New Testament. *Ecclesia* always refers to an assembly of *people*. If we wished to emphasise the distinction, we might say, 'The chapel is the place in which the Church meets'.)

What is the will and purpose of God, which lies behind the origin of the Church? Briefly stated, it consists in the realization of that personal relationship with God for which man was created. You have already seen, in *Studies Four and Five*, what is involved in this; fundamental to it is the proclamation of salvation which centres in the Fact of Christ. The Gospel is Christ, the Messiah or Saviour. Our task, therefore, must be to discover whether this proclamation of the Gospel does in fact involve or imply a doctrine of the Church. By surveying briefly the various strands in the New Testament, we shall find that the message of salvation in Christ includes, as part of itself, a saved People which is called into being for a definite purpose. In other words, *a community is implied in the Gospel.*

1. *The Teaching of Jesus*

The word *ecclesia* is found only twice in the Gospels (Mt. 16[18], 18[17]), both in the First Gospel. This has led some scholars to doubt whether Jesus actually used the word (or its Aramaic equivalent): and accordingly to argue that He did not intend to found a new society—that the Church was, as it were, foisted on to the original message as a human institution. If that were so, of course, it would lose much of its authority and claim over Christians. But this is an unwarranted conclusion, since we can see that, during His ministry, Jesus had the formation of a new People of God in mind, even if He did not use the actual word *ecclesia*; i.e. the *thing* is present, if not the particular *word*. The evidence* can be summarized as follows:

a. *The Kingdom of God*, which lies at the heart of Jesus' words and works, necessarily implied a new People of God. We must not identify the Kingdom of God with the Church; rather it implies the Church. The Jews had looked forward to the manifestation of the redemptive Rule of God; Jesus proclaimed that the expected time had now come, that the decisive hour of history had struck, that God's saving sovereignty was now manifested. It was now happening in Him. But this Rule of God implied a people living under that rule. The formation of a community is involved. And since the redemptive rule of God centred in Jesus, this meant that those whom He called to follow Him formed a company living under the Rule of God. So Jesus gathered together the nucleus of the new People of God.

b. *The idea of Messiahship*, as Jesus interpreted it, implied the gathering of a community. As you have seen in *Study Six*, Jesus thought of Himself in terms of Isaiah's Servant of Yahweh in the Old Testament. This implied a community. In *Isaiah*, the 'Servant' became, through his suffering, the creator of a new People of God: so Jesus is to give His life for 'the many' (Mk 10[45]).

c. When Jesus spoke of Himself as doing the work of a *Shepherd* and of His disciples as a *flock*, He was describing His Messianic task of gathering the People of God. In the prophets, we find the idea that, in the last days when God's salvation would be manifested, the Messiah will gather and tend God's flock, i.e. the People of God (cf. Ezek. 34[12, 16, 23]; Micah 5[2-4]). In the light

* *See* A. M. Hunter, *The Unity of the New Testament*, pp. 46–59.

of this, we should understand some of the best-loved words and actions of Jesus (cf. Lk 15$^{3-6}$). Jesus is the Shepherd, sent to the lost sheep of the house of Israel, or seeking and saving the one lost sheep, while the disciples are the 'little flock' (Lk 12^{32}). A similar use of the image is found in the Fourth Gospel (Jn 10$^{4f.}$, 11^{52}, 21^{17}).

d. The preaching and teaching of Jesus were completed by His actions, which showed Him deliberately executing His Messianic task of *creating a new Israel*, the true People of God. (i) He *called* twelve disciples. Seen against the Old Testament background, this simple act takes on an added significance. It presupposes that Israel was the People of God, but that in fact not the whole of Israel had proved faithful to its calling. Therefore Israel must be re-constituted, and a remnant brought into being. In the Old Testament, Isaiah had formed an inner circle, which should be the nucleus of the new People of God (Isa. 8$^{16-18}$); when Jesus chose His disciples, He was declaring that His intention was in line with that: the number twelve was significant as being the number of the tribes of Israel. So Jesus created a new Israel, a new People of God, a New Church, although in fact it was the re-creation of the one which existed in Israel, and went back ultimately to the original purpose of God, who chose Israel as the instrument of His revelation.

(ii) Jesus *taught* His disciples. What we know as the Sermon on the Mount (Mt 5–7) is a convenient summary of that teaching, given to the disciples (not necessarily only to the Twelve) who had accepted the redemptive Rule of God which was manifested in Jesus. It is evident that a special group of people was in the mind of Jesus. The teaching is characterised by an awareness of the reality of God, in whose sight the disciples are to live, and by whom they will be judged. Along with this new teaching, which was to be the guide of the newly-constituted community, was given the assurance that the power of God was available to help in its attainment (Mt 7$^{7-11}$; Mk 10^{27}, 11$^{23-4}$). This experience is emphasised when we read about the early Church in *Acts*.

(iii) Jesus *sent forth* His disciples on a mission. This is recorded of the Twelve (Lk 9^2) and also of the Seventy (Lk 10^1). Their purpose was to preach the present and redemptive Rule of God. We are justified in believing that they made converts, and that some were added to the 'little flock' of Jesus. Once again, Jesus was intent on gathering together the People of God.

THE CHURCH (1)

(iv) At the Last Supper, Jesus *established a covenant* with His disciples. 'And he said unto them, This is my blood of the covenant, which is shed for many' (Mk 14^{24}); Paul's version is, 'This cup is the new covenant in my blood' (1 Cor. 11^{25}). A covenant implies a community with whom it is concluded, a People of God. The Israel of the Old Testament was a covenant people; now Jesus, speaking to the Twelve as representatives of the Church as a whole, establishes a new covenant with them, the new Israel of God—and yet not unrelated to the old.

This brief survey of the teaching of Jesus has led us to conclude that the creating of a community, a new People of God, was an essential purpose in His ministry. He foresaw that it would be consummated by His own death and rising again; then 'another temple, not made with hands' (Mk 14^{58}) would arise. The characteristics of this community have already been disclosed in the foregoing. It would be—

(*a*) a new People of God, the true Israel, inheriting the promises of the old Israel,

(*b*) who acknowledge the redemptive Rule of God by confession of Christ,

(*c*) who are committed to a new way of life, with the promise of power to fulfil it,

(*d*) who are sent forth to proclaim the Kingdom of God, as representatives of Christ.

Jesus comes from God; His person, His teaching and His actions are all manifestations of the saving Rule of God, now active, though still opposed by evil. In some future time, it will be openly victorious, but in the meantime those who acknowledge Christ live obediently under God's Rule, in communion with Him, actively patient and confidently awaiting its glorious consummation.

2. *The Primitive Church*

A new chapter in the history of the People of God began at Pentecost, and the Church as we know it first became an effective reality. The outstanding fact is that, when we read the story of the primitive Church in *Acts*, the same distinctive characteristics which we have found in the teaching of Jesus emerge once again. No one can fail to be impressed with the fact that the Agent at work in the story is none other than God Himself, active in the

Holy Spirit. As God had been manifest in Jesus, so now He is operative through the Spirit, working through men, gathering the Church together, and dwelling in the life of the community. To account for the apostles' ministry, or the gathering together and growth of the Church, on any merely human terms, is to run counter to all the evidence.

An examination, therefore, of the primitive Church in *Acts* leads to the following conclusions:

a. *It is recognized as being the People of God, the new Israel.* The modern reader is often impatient with the constant references to the Old Testament in the preaching as recorded in *Acts*. But the explanation of this feature is the early Church's conviction that its existence could only be understood in relation to what God had done in Israel's past, and was now doing in furtherance of His purpose in history. Peter's sermon at Pentecost was addressed to the Jews in Jerusalem, and through them to a wider number, who by responding to the Gospel separate themselves from those members of a crooked generation (Acts 2^{40}) who by disobedience forfeited their privileges in Israel. The new community is looked upon as the true Israel, which was being constituted by God out of the old Israel. It was not a party within Israel, but Israel itself, the People of God (Acts 3$^{25-6}$), and is therefore described by the same name as that given to the People of God in the Septuagint, viz. the *ecclesia*.

b. *The essential basis of the Church on its human side is the confession of the Lordship of Christ.* This is the burden of Peter's speech at Pentecost: the Jesus who died on the Cross, who was raised from the dead, who is now exalted at the right hand of God, is Lord and Christ. Many titles are ascribed to Jesus in *Acts*, but none is higher than this. 'Jesus is Lord' became one of the distinctive confessions of the early Church, from which the later creeds were expanded. Far more than the mere recital of a formula, it was both the expression of a life-allegiance and a conviction about the Person of Christ, and was associated particularly with Baptism and the Lord's Supper. So we read, in Acts 11$^{19-23}$, that the Mother Church of the Gentile mission at Antioch was brought into being by the preaching of unknown Christians from Jerusalem, who spoke to Greeks and Jews, 'preaching the good news of Jesus as Lord'. When believers expressed their allegiance to Jesus as Lord, with all that this entailed by way of repentance and trust in Him, and of baptism in His Name, they were thus brought into the Church, the sacred fellowship, and were recognized as Christians.

c. *The Church shares in the gifts and fellowship of the Spirit.* Some of the ways in which the Spirit was experienced in the primitive Church as described in *Acts* were bound to give way to different expressions as time passed; yet none can doubt that something happened which vitally affected and directed the whole company of believers. It included a new experience of God through Jesus Christ, a new emphasis on the supernatural, and a new sense of power. It was the Spirit who brought Peter's message home to their hearts and prompted their response; it was the same Spirit who brought them together in a fellowship which affected their attitude to their material possessions and the needs of others, as well as their religious experiences. The *voluntary* sharing of goods could hardly last, as the Church expanded into wider areas; yet the significant thing is that this is what happened when the Spirit of Christ possessed a group of people, and similar expressions of the Christian spirit have occurred, in one way or another, ever since. It is evident that Pentecost was a community experience, deeply personal, and yet not individualistic.

As Acts 2^{42} shows, stressing the enduring nature of the experience, 'they continued steadfastly in the apostles' teaching and fellowship, in the breaking of bread and the prayers'. This statement is obviously of great importance for our understanding of the nature of the primitive Church. The student is referred to *Study Seven* for a fuller treatment. Moffatt's version gives the sense as well as any: 'they devoted themselves to the instructions given by the apostles and to fellowship, breaking bread and praying together'. What is the precise meaning of the word *fellowship*? Considerable discussion has ranged around this question among New Testament scholars. Most likely it does not refer to the group of Christians as such, but is rather a description of their inner harmony and unity: it was the inward bond which necessarily called for outward acts in which it could be expressed. The essential factor was a common participation in the Spirit, which manifested itself in such acts as almsgiving, the sharing of property, and the breaking of bread. So the fellowship had two aspects: (i) it was fellowship in temple worship, in united prayers, in the Lord's Supper, and (ii) it was the sharing of material goods and mutual supply of material needs. 'The common experience issued in common worship, and this was expressed in the two sacraments of Baptism and the Lord's Supper, in prayer, in preaching, and in the social activities of love' (*The Nature of the Christian Church*, p. 13); and also in a spirit of praise and thanksgiving towards God (Acts 2^{46-7}). *The apostles' teaching* is also mentioned, and this must include the ethical teaching of Jesus, which was intimately bound up with the Gospel which they preached: no rigid distinction can be drawn between preaching and teaching. The apostles' teaching includes the setting forth of the Fact of Christ, and the implications of that Fact for the situation in which the Christians found themselves.

d. *The Church is a missionary Church.* Reading *Acts*, we watch the early Christians coming to a fuller consciousness that they had to spread the Gospel of salvation in Christ, at first among Jews, but also among Gentiles. Again there is the same insistence upon continuity with the People of God found in the Old Testament. God's covenant promise to Abraham had been that in his seed all the families of the earth should be blessed (Acts 3^{25}); Stephen traverses the history of Israel, beginning with Abraham (Acts 7^{2-53}): although Israel continually rejected its mission, God had sent great men, and the same thing has happened in the coming of Jesus. Those who now respond to Him are the true People of God, taking the place of the old Israel; soon the worship of the temple will be superseded, for the true People of God are not bound to any one place. Thus the Church widened its appeal beyond the Jews. The day was not far distant when it was realized that Jew and Gentile were one in the Church. It was faith in Christ which brought them into the fellowship, but not merely for their own benefit; through them the Gospel was to pass to others. Once again the purpose of God was being realized in the creation of a new people, the inheritors of the promises to the old Israel. In the pregnant phrase, the new Israel was both 'a saved and a saving community'.

3. *The Remainder of the New Testament*

The same pattern already disclosed can be traced in the remaining strands of the New Testament. In Paul's letters in particular, we come across some illuminating metaphors which stress the reality of the corporate nature of the Christian life, and enrich our understanding of the Church. The Church is called the Body of Christ, the Body of which Christ is the Head, the holy Temple in which the living God dwells, the Family of

THE CHURCH (1)

God, the Bride of Christ. Paul uses the metaphor *Body of Christ* most frequently to describe the whole community of Christians (1 Cor. 12[12ff.]; Rom. 12[5ff.]; *see ANT*). There can be only one Body of Christ, as Christ is one and not divided; Christians are baptized into this Body, and in it God gives them their appropriate places and functions. The phrase expresses the close identification between Christ and His People, and the strong spiritual bond which exists between them. It has been greatly emphasized in much recent theological writing, and a word of caution is needed against some of the conclusions which have been drawn, too confidently, about the Church as it actually exists in the world. We shall see, in the next *Study*, that the Church as an institution in the world is liable to sin. Therefore it must continually be subject to the judgement of Christ, its Head and Sovereign Lord. Nevertheless Christ uses the Church to carry out His purposes in the world. This implies the very highest possible view of the Church, since it means that Christ is really present in the Christian community. 'For where two or three are gathered together in my name, there am I in the midst of them' (Mt 18[20]; cf. also Mt 28[20]; Jn 14[16-26]). The Church exists to serve the purpose of God, i.e. through it Christ carries on *His* ministry, and the Church member shares in this Ministry of Christ.

B. THE CHURCH'S LIFE AND SERVICE

Our review of the New Testament has revealed how deeply embedded the Church is in its essential message. We now proceed to examine the nature of the Church, and then how it fulfils the purpose of God in the world. The analogy of a family will help us here. A family cannot be understood until we recognize that its true life consists in an invisible bond between a number of persons, a spiritual relationship of mutual affection which is expressed in a number of external ways. This invisible bond is the real life of the family; without it, the family does not truly function. On the other hand, we may ask why the family exists, and then we shall have to think of such things as the continuance of the race, the training and discipline of its members, and so on. Similarly, looking at the Church, we may ask (1) in what does its life consist? and (2) what is its purpose?

1. *What the Church is*

a. *A Fellowship of Believers.* The Church is 'the whole company of those who trust in Christ as Lord and Saviour and are united in the fellowship of the Holy Spirit' (*CAT* 19). The emphasis here is upon a body of people of whom the distinctive thing is that all are in a certain relationship with God through Christ. This unseen relationship can be described in many ways, as the New Testament does. Perhaps the most striking is Paul's phrase *in Christ*, which may be taken as the highest and most characteristic expression of the Christian's communion with God. The sharing of this invisible bond is the Church's true life, and from it arises the fellowship of Christians with each other. In itself, it is not a matter of organization, but is a deeply personal, though not individualistic, experience of Christ as Lord and Saviour. The person who knows nothing of the experience would find the fellowship meaningless, and could be in it only in an external way, yet not of it. On the other hand, the deeper the experience of Christ, the more real is the fellowship. Thus, while ecclesiastical order must create a body for this fellowship, it cannot create its soul. The basis of the catholic fellowship is the evangelical experience of Christ.

b. *A Fellowship which transcends death*. The Church is as wide as this fellowship 'in Christ'. Christians whose earthly life is ended have not passed beyond it, even if now, being 'with Christ', their communion with God is more perfect. This reality of the Church as a fellowship transcending death comes to what is perhaps its finest expression in Charles Wesley's great hymn (*MHB* 824):

> *One family we dwell in Him,*
>   *One Church, above, beneath,*
> *Though now divided by the stream,*
>   *The narrow stream of death:*
> *One army of the living God,*
>   *To His command we bow;*
> *Part of His host have crossed the flood,*
>   *And part are crossing now.*

These are words which repay the deepest reflection; this is the communion of saints, Christians of all ages united in Christ. Catholicism makes much of the departed saints, who by their work did more than was necessary, and so provided a treasury of merits which the Church can now distribute to the living. Protestants cannot honour saints and martyrs for any such merit available to us; even the greatest among them did no more, nay less, than they ought. But they were examples to us through their faith and obedience, their humility and patient suffering, whereby we are encouraged to have a similar trust in God. The life of the saints is a treasure, not because of merits which avail for us, but rather because there is mutual assistance among members of one body; in virtue of what they did and experienced, they help us. Neither merit nor faith can be transferred from one person to another. There can be only that mutual service by which we are assisted to have faith ourselves.

c. *A Fellowship created by the Gospel.* The testimony of the Christian faith is that this life 'in Christ', so fundamental to the Church, comes into being through God's initiative. It began with His action in Christ, and after the Ascension it was continued by the proclamation of the saving act in Christ, which we know as the Gospel. Hence we reach what must be regarded as a fundamental principle: *the Gospel creates the Church*. The Church is the Gospel-created fellowship; where the Gospel is active through the Holy Spirit, the Church is created and sustained. Therefore the Gospel is primary. Without it there could be no Church, and when it is not proclaimed or understood the real life of the Church is absent. But when the Gospel is truly proclaimed, God is active; the response of faith is called forth. Just as the Church came into being by the action of God, so now men come into the Church by faith in Christ, their response to the Gospel.

Accordingly every effort must be made to comprehend the meaning of the Gospel in all its fullness, as well as the means of making it understandable to the particular generation in which we live. Whenever the Gospel has been re-discovered in its living power, the life of the Church has been revived or cleansed. The Protestant Reformation in the 16th century was primarily a deep penetration into the meaning of the Gospel; this was the source of the reformation of the Church. It was not the founding of a new Church, but the strengthening of the one Church which had existed before. The subsequent changes in the forms of the Church were brought about in order that the Gospel might freely be proclaimed and understood, and the fellowship to which it gave rise be expressed. Similarly, the Evangelical Revival of the 18th century in England, from which Methodism sprang, did not begin because Wesley decided to form a new Church—which no human being could do. It was the fresh penetration into the meaning of the Gospel, and the response to it, which brought a new Church life into existence.

2. *The purpose of the Church's existence*

The Church is the instrument created by God for the effecting of His saving will towards mankind. From one point of view, the purpose of God in creating the Church can be regarded as directed towards the well-being of *its members*, but this must not obscure the fact that at the same time the Church, in all its activities and through all its members, exists to further the purposes of God *in the world*. A local congregation, from one point of view, can be regarded as a group of people who are being brought into the knowledge and experience of the Christian life, with all its attendant enrichments. On the other hand, the congregation is also a community of people who are meant to witness to God and His truth in the common life and affairs of their district. A Christian congregation is therefore a number of people both *in* whom and *through* whom God works. Just as faith and works must not be separated, but understood in their true relationship to each other, so Church membership is both a privilege and a responsibility, and everything in the life of the Church has a dual reference. The Church exists to nurture Christians, but also to bring new Christians into being. It is both the object of God's redeeming love, and also the instrument through which God's love is proclaimed to the world. Once this missionary and evangelistic duty is forgotten, the life of a Church is turned in on itself, and the process of stagnation and decay sets in. The purpose of the Church's existence is that it should be both a saved and a saving community (*see* p. 164, above).

The Church gives effect to the saving purpose of God (i) by the worship of God, made known in Jesus Christ, through the Holy Spirit; (ii) by the nurture of its members in Christian faith, character and experience; (iii) by witness to Christ, and the service of His Kingdom. These three aspects of the Church's service have been distinguished for the sake of illustration, but the warning must be underlined that they are not mutually exclusive. Properly conceived, worship embraces the whole of life—yet the danger in such an assertion is apparent if it seems to suggest that therefore no specific 'acts of worship' are necessary. Detailed discussion of the meaning of the Church's worship will be found in the next *Study*; suffice it to say at this point that worship is the Church's supreme activity, and man attains to his true stature as a member of God's family in the exercise of worship, for to this end was he created. Similarly, the Church provides the means whereby its members can grow in grace, in Christian character and service. But a necessary part of this activity is their training in the meaning and implications of the Christian Faith, so that they can witness for Christ and serve His Kingdom. This includes much more than what is usually, somewhat narrowly, understood by Christian witness. Through its members, in their day to day 'secular' activities, as well as in the corporate undertakings of the Christian group, the Church makes its witness for the Kingdom of God. Finally, by its evangelism the Church seeks to bring new Christians into being. Of course, it cannot 'make' new Christians. It can create the environment favourable to the growth of Christians; it can bring spiritual influences to bear on people; but in the last resort the decision by which an individual becomes a disciple of Christ and a child of God is a private and personal affair between Christ and himself. In this sense, the Church is prior to any particular member; but, apart from the individual's personal decision, Church membership cannot be an effective reality.

In these ways, the Church exists to serve the purposes of God, always as His instrument. As such, it has never to seek its own glory, since its Lord is One who came to minister and give His life a ransom for many.

C. THE CHURCH'S MINISTRY

The Church, as we said (on p. 165), carries on the ministry of Christ in the world. There is no other kind of ministry than His; it began during the days of His flesh, and it has continued to this day in and through the Church, which is His Body. Therefore *every* member of His Body shares in it. This is the fundamental principle of the Church's ministry.

But, although every member shares in this ministry, not all exercise it in the same way. The various members of a body have different functions, all of which enrich the body and together constitute its life (1 Cor. 12^{12-27}). Strictly speaking, all members of the Church are ministers, since all possess some gifts of the Spirit (Rom. 12^{4-7}; 1 Cor. 12^{4-28}; 1 Pet. 4^{10}); yet, in the New Testament description of the Church, there are some ministries which are especially noteworthy, and which are marked out for particular mention. It is obvious from *Acts* that the apostles held a special position: but we also read of the Seven (Acts 6); the Elders, who are also called overseers or bishops, because they care for the flock; and also prophets, teachers and evangelists.

We see in the New Testament the picture of a community with a rich and varied spiritual life, in which individuals exercised different functions, all of which were recognized as gifts of the Spirit. Through them all, the ministry of Christ was carried on by the Church.

But the doctrine of the ministry raises one of the most controversial points in modern theology; an issue which is at the root of one of the deepest divisions in the Church. 'Catholics' (Roman, Eastern and Anglican) hold that, even before Pentecost, the apostles existed as officers in the Christian society, appointed by Christ, to whom alone was entrusted the ministry of the Word and Sacraments; that they were a separate order from the members, and had power to govern the Church and to appoint successors. This theory claims that the true ministry of the Church has continued in unbroken succession from the apostles, by the laying on of hands, through the bishops, until the present time. It is held that this was the intention of Christ, and that without this continuous order of the ministry no Church can truly be said to exist. This is the doctrine of *Apostolic Succession*.

Although the question cannot here be discussed in detail, certain comments are relevant. Apostleship, which of course figures largely in the New Testament, is not a function which can be confined to any clearly defined group within the Church. Its essential idea comes out in the Gospels. From the company of disciples, Jesus chose some for a missionary tour and sent them out as apostles. These were not limited to the Twelve (Lk $10^{1, 17-20}$), and we know that the term 'apostle' was applied to a wider number in the early Church (*see* Rom. 16^7; 2 Cor. 8^{23}; 1 Cor. 9^1, 15^7; Acts 14^{14}). The apostles, therefore, were those who, having received the call to discipleship, were chosen and sent forth by Jesus to attack the kingdom of evil, and to proclaim the Rule of God. Having declared the message, they probably gathered together those who responded to it, and then they returned to Jesus. After the resurrection, a different situation had arisen; then we find that an essential qualification for an apostle was that he should have seen the risen Lord. Accordingly, he was able to testify to the fact of the resurrection as a foundation of the Apostolic Faith. That the apostles included others, in addition to the Twelve, seems proven by such a reference as 1 Cor. 15^7, while Paul, in virtue of the experience on the Damascus Road, did not hesitate to call himself an apostle (*see ANT, para.* 441).

Thus, numbered within the group known as apostles, were the Twelve. Because of their special relationship with Christ, it is obvious that they occupied a position of some eminence and moral authority in the Church, as we might expect; but the significant thing is that it was a position which could not be transmitted to others. Neither Paul nor anyone else claimed to be one of the Twelve, although they were apostles. When one of the Twelve died, his place was not filled; only when one, Judas, was unfaithful was another, Matthias, appointed from among those who had been with the others as companions of Jesus, and had witnessed the resurrection (Acts 1$^{21\text{-}22}$). It becomes evident, therefore, that neither the position of one of the Twelve, nor that of an apostle, could be transferred to successors, since after their death none had the necessary qualifications; i.e. none after the first generation had seen the risen Lord. The idea of an apostolic succession, in which a particular group of men within the Church succeeds to the apostolic ministry, is therefore misleading. *It is the whole Church in which the living Christ is present which succeeds to this ministry*, and the living Christ grants it in various forms to the members of the Church.

The most likely conclusion to be reached about the ministry of the Church from the New Testament is that no one pattern is to be found, such as must determine its precise form for all time. The organization of the Church's life was still fluid; the true continuity was secured by fidelity to the Gospel, i.e. to apostolic truth. In due course, the Church organized its ministry according to the pattern of bishop, presbyter or priest, and deacon. In more modern times, at the Reformation, the pattern was again altered in some of those churches which called themselves Protestant, and the separate order of bishop was abolished. In general, this was because the pure proclamation of the Gospel, and the consequent reform of the Church's life, could only be secured by freedom from episcopal control. The leaders of these churches were impressed by the fact that, when they came to examine the New Testament, they found nothing in it to persuade them that a church, to be a church, must have a separate order of bishops *of the kind they had come to know*. Although these matters gave rise to much controversy, we can now see that a doctrine of the ministry was being set forth which may justly claim to be true to the New Testament, although the actual forms it takes in practice may differ.

So far as Methodism is concerned, the conduct of public worship is entrusted to Local Preachers and the full-time ordained

Ministers. As a matter of order, the administration of the Sacraments is in general confined to the latter. Clearly the governing principle is that the 'ministry' belongs to the whole Church, which delegates certain of its functions to those with the necessary gifts and graces. When, therefore, in this section we refer to the minister and the ministry, we are speaking of the ordained Minister *and* the Local Preacher, both of whom are in the order of the Church's ministry. It should, however, be remembered that other forms of the Church's ministry are also recognized among us; e.g. the Class-Leaders.

What, then, are the essential principles of the Church's ministry? As a visible community, the Church must have an ordered life, and for this reason *the organization of a regular ministry in some form is essential*. The one abiding principle which must govern the Church is that Christ is its only Head; from Him, or from the Holy Spirit now active within His Body, the Church, the ministry in its various forms is derived. Here we are primarily concerned with that form which is most obviously derived from the pattern of the apostles' ministry; viz. the proclamation of the Gospel of reconciliation in Word and Sacrament, and the pastoral care of the Church. Jesus gave this commission first to the apostles; and, as we see from *Acts*, it was developed in the Church and is continued by the activity of the Holy Spirit. The call to this ministry comes from Christ, who alone can make a minister. Paul states the principle when he writes, 'He (Christ) gave some to be apostles; and some, prophets; and some, evangelists; and some, pastors and teachers; for the perfecting of the saints, unto the building up of the body of Christ' (Eph. $4^{11f.}$). The ministry and the ministers are therefore the gift of Christ to the Church. The very words 'minister' and 'to minister' are significant. They mean, of course, 'servant' and 'to serve'. (Nowhere in the New Testament is the term 'priest' applied to a particular body of officials within the Church.) The minister's function is to serve and magnify Christ. 'What then is Apollos? and what is Paul? Ministers through whom ye believed; and each as the Lord gave to him' (1 Cor. 3^5). The minister's virtue does not lie in himself; rather is he like a sign-post, pointing to Christ, but away from himself; he is a witness to the Gospel. 'We preach not ourselves, but Christ Jesus as Lord, and ourselves as your servants for Jesus' sake' (2 Cor. 4^5). Because the minister is primarily a servant of Christ, and because the essential ministry is that of Christ, it is Christ who chooses, calls and appoints ministers. An individual's ministry is, therefore, based first and foremost upon his personal vocation. Once this is grasped, we can understand the Church's function in the appointment of the ministry. The Church cannot make anyone a minister of Christ; it can only *recognize* him as one called of Christ, and then set him in the order of its ministry. To do this, a Church will carefully apply what tests it can. Thus any ministry within the Church rests upon a twofold basis. The living God, active through the Holy Spirit, calls men and women into His service; this personal call is essential and primary. The Church's function is then to test, as far as human judgement can, under the guidance of the Spirit, (i) the claim of a person to have been called by God to the ministry, and (ii) his qualifications of other kinds for that particular ministry. When this has been done, the individual is authorized by the whole Church, acting through its representatives, to exercise his ministry within the Church, as is done, for example, in the case of Methodist Local Preachers and Ministers.

SERMON XII. THE MEANS OF GRACE

The great principle of evangelical religion is that man cannot earn his salvation by his own efforts in Church-going and pious observances. There must be a change of heart worked by God. However, this principle can be made the occasion of error if it be divorced from other balancing truths, and taken to an extreme. Just as the excess into which the 'strong Churchman' may slip is formalism or legality, so the excess into which the warm Evangelical may slip is that of failing to give the serious enquirer after God sufficiently forthright advice that he is to wait upon God in sincere and expectant Church-going, attendance at Communion, and private prayer. In Wesley's time, some went so far as to say that the seeker after Justification should cease from divine worship and prayer, and just wait until God gave the experience to him. To continue in the means of grace was a sign that one was trusting one's diligence in them for salvation. This manifest error of unbalance was called 'Quietism' or 'Stillness'. Wesley had to fight hard against this destructive teaching, and this issue was the occasion of his separation from the Moravians who in the beginning had done so much to help him to appreciate the full significance of 'Justification by Faith'. Hence this sermon represents an important element in the historic Methodist witness. It shows

Wesley striking a sane middle course between extremes of setting too much and too little store by the ordinances of the Church.

Theme of the Sermon. There are certain divine ordinances which the seeker after God is diligently to observe in confident expectation of God's blessing; yet, while using these means of grace, he is to trust Christ alone for salvation.

EXPLANATORY OUTLINE OF THE SERMON

I. *The Use and Abuse of the Means of Grace.* (1) The Apostolic Church knew nothing whatever of the notion that to the Christian there are no *ordinances* (i.e. visible religious signs or customs) fixed by God as the means whereby He gives His grace to man. (2) As the spiritual vision of the Church became somewhat obscured with the passage of time a tendency was shown to set too much store upon the (sacramental) outward forms of religion. (3) Some wandered into the most impenetrable spiritual darkness of all, an obsession with merely formal religion. Others flew to the opposite extreme, and asserted that there were no necessary means of grace. (4) *Mystics* arose from time to time, who taught an almost purely internal and individual religion, having little contact with the life of the organized Church. These Mystics were in general genuine spiritually-minded men, who only sought to redress the balance of the external and institutional religion around them. (5) It is hardly a matter of surprise that some went too far in deprecating the means of grace and outward ordinances of the Church. (6) In more recent times some have been misled by the perhaps incautious statements of some of the great Mystics, and by their own frustration in mere formal religion. Thus they have fallen into 'Stillness'.

II. *Divine Grace and the Means of Grace.* (1) A 'means of grace' is a devotional practice ordained by God, to which God has attached the promise that those who in expectant faith do this thing will be visited by His grace. ('Preventing grace', or, to use the more usual term, 'prevenient grace', is the divine grace which *goes before* any conscious experience of salvation. It is the first drawing of grace, which makes a man begin to think of religion at all.) The three chief means of grace are prayer, Bible study and preaching, and the Lord's Supper. These are the normal paths along which God leads men to the experience of grace. (2) The means of grace are only a *means*, and not the *end*, which is the religion of the heart. Diligence in the means is not a substitute for heart religion. (3) The power is in God, not in the means apart from God. He can act without them if He chooses. (4) There is no *merit* in the means of grace (i.e. we cannot hope to earn divine favour by them). (5, 6) Many formal Christians fall into this error. (7) Practical and common-sense evangelical advice for those who would be saved by faith: 'You are to wait for God to give you His gift of justifying faith, but you are not to wait in idleness and indiscipline. You are earnestly and expectantly to use all the means of grace.' (This memorable paragraph is the focus of the whole sermon.) (8) The Bible shows us how we are to do this.

III. *A Guide to Prayer, Bible Study, and the Holy Communion.* (1) Our Lord expressly taught men to pray for grace, and (2) for the Holy Spirit (i.e. those who had not yet found Christ were certainly to pray). This is enforced in parables, (3, 4) and (5) by the promise of blessing. (6) James cited to the effect that even those who cannot pray as yet from the experience of justifying faith are to pray in confidence, that God may give them a fuller faith. (7) Christ directs us to search the Scriptures. (The objection, which Wesley hastily dismisses as 'shamelessly false', is a perfectly valid one, as Wesley would doubtless have admitted had he not been under pressure of controversy. The word in the Greek of John 5^{39} can equally well be translated 'ye search' or the imperative 'search', and most informed expositors prefer 'ye search', as more in accord with the general sense of the passage. *See* Revised Version.) (8) The Scriptures were a means of grace to Timothy. (2 Tim. 3^{16} is another text capable of being translated in two ways, and where the preferable reading destroys Wesley's point. *See* Revised Version.) (9) Reading the Old Testament is a means of grace, which (10) is profitable for those who are not yet believers. (11) Our Lord solemnly ordained the Holy Communion to be used by those who would experience an *increase* of grace. (The operative word is 'increase'. Those who have no grace are not to come, i.e. careless and impenitent sinners are not invited to the Lord's Table. Nevertheless, serious-minded seekers are to come to the Sacrament, even though they are aware they have not yet come to the full Christian experience, for God can use it to convert them.) The Holy Communion is a solemn 'showing forth of the Lord's death' both to God (i.e. it is the Church's most earnest prayer that God will do for the believer today what He did for the whole world, once and for all, in Christ on the Cross), and to man (i.e. it is the Gospel of that saving work of Christ preached not by word of mouth, but in a solemn symbol). (12) 1 Cor. 10^{16} teaches that for the believing man to eat that bread and drink that cup is the means used by God whereby he is to receive Christ's body and blood, i.e. his share of what Christ did once and for all for the world by His death.

IV. *Quietist Objections Overturned.* (Some of these arguments may today seem obscure and hairsplitting. The section shows the sort of controversy which went on at that time.) (1) It is not true to say that one cannot use the means of grace without *trusting* in them for salvation. It is an impious experiment to try leaving them off. And one *is* to trust God's faithful promise that He will make Himself known to those who use the means of grace. (2) This is not what Paul condemned as 'salvation by works'. (3) A verbal quibble exposed. (4, 5) Alleged 'proof-texts' for 'Stillness' found to be wanting. (6) Paul, rightly understood, teaches that while we are not subject to Jewish ceremonial ordinances, we are bound by the Christian ordinances.

V. *The Form of Christian Discipline.* (1, 2) The most general form of Christian experience is that the first awakening takes place by means of the public or private preaching of the Gospel. This prompts the enquirer to Bible study and prayer. He finds a natural inclination to take an increasing part in public worship, and finally in a serious and penitent frame of mind ventures to come to the Sacrament. Thus in the end God assures him of His justifying faith. (3) But in practice the varieties of experience are endless, and the seeker is not to hold back from anything good. (4) It is good to remember: First, God can act without the accustomed means. Second, there is no *merit* in the means themselves. They do not earn God's favour. There is no automatic blessing, apart from faith in Christ. Third, one is to look beyond the means to what only God can do. Fourth, one is not to congratulate onself upon one's diligence in pious observances.

TEST QUESTIONS

1. What do we learn from the New Testament about the *nature* of the Church?

2. What is the *purpose* of the Church's existence?

3. Describe Wesley's teaching on Prayer, and the Holy Communion.

STUDY TEN

The Church (2)

A. THE CHURCH'S WORSHIP

THE Christian life covers all the activities of the Christian, yet the Church engages in certain definite acts which have traditionally been known as '*the means of grace*', or 'the ordinances of religion'. All can be included under the title of the Church's worship, which ought to be regarded as the concentration of its life and faith in certain well-defined acts. Since man's true end is communion with God, which is at once both deeply personal and yet communal, Christian worship is both the expression of that communion and the means by which it is created, sustained and nourished. Christ's real and abiding presence in the Church is the supreme means of grace; but there are others, derived from this, which are modes through which God enters into immediate fellowship with man. God is not, of course, bound to these means in His approach to and dealings with man, since He is the living God; nor can we give an exhaustive description of them. Nevertheless we can summarize them under the titles of the Word of God (read, heard and meditated upon), the Sacraments, prayer, and Christian fellowship. Through these means, God approaches us according to His appointment, and for this reason they are not to be neglected or spurned by the Christian (*see* Wesley's *Sermon* XII on 'The Means of Grace').

The phrase 'means of grace' is not scriptural, and yet it may be allowed to stand as a true description of the Church's mode of worship. The reference to 'grace' serves to remind us that the primary truth about worship is that it is an activity through which God draws near to us, and acts upon us. We have a part in it, and a vital part, but it is always called forth as a *response* to God's gracious action. Rightly to understand this is to catch the wonder of Christian worship, and there is no activity so high or so important. To take part in it is to engage in man's highest end, communion with God; the very action is the acknowledgement that this is what we were made for—to live as children of our Heavenly Father. Every time the Christian 'goes to Church', he is shouting defiance at every view of man, and every philosophy of life, which would depress or distort his true nature; that is, which would treat him as other than a child of God.

1. *What worship is*

Christian worship may be described as (i) the *proclamation* of the Gospel, and (ii) the corporate *response* to the Gospel that is proclaimed, the offering of ourselves in loving obedience to God. We now proceed to see how the Church's worship conforms to this pattern in its use of the means of grace. The dual movement is essential; in so far as we speak of 'our' worship of God, we must understand that it always presupposes the *primary approach of God to us*. The very assembling of ourselves together for worship is the response to God's gracious call, through which we came into the Church in the first place. Not because we are good, or regard ourselves as better than others, do we come to Church; but essentially because we recognize that we are not worthy, and dare not come, were it not that God had bidden us, and in Christ provided the way. We claim our place only as forgiven sinners. Again, the very uplifting of our hearts to God in prayer and praise is our response to the grace of God, and is inspired by the work of His Spirit in our hearts. Furthermore, we do not come together as isolated individuals to perform a private act of devotion, but as members of the Body of Christ, a local manifestation of the whole Church, with which we join in worship.

The *proclamation* of the Gospel in the Church's worship takes various forms. It underlies the reading of the Scriptures, the preaching of the Sermon, the message of many hymns, and the celebration of the Sacraments. It is the message or Gospel of God in all of these which gives them meaning, and which justifies their use in Christian worship. Apart from the Gospel, they are merely human actions; but, viewed as means of grace, they are ways in which the truth of God in Christ is applied to us. So the key to the understanding of the Church's worship is that the Gospel is proclaimed in Word and Sacrament, to which there is a corresponding response by the members of the congregation. Vital to the understanding of worship is that it should be recognized as an 'event' in which God meets with His people, and they make their response. For this reason, worship is expressed by means of definite actions.

2. *The Bible*

The Bible is central, yet not as a mere book; as such it possesses no vitality. It tells of how God made Himself known to men in the past, in the midst of certain historic situations and by means of definite historic acts, culminating in Christ; it is the Book of the redemptive Rule of God (*see* p. 10, above). And now in Christian worship the living God, through the present activity of the Holy Spirit, speaks to the soul through its words. We have seen how the Christian Church must be understood as the re-creation of the People of God, and that the Gospel of Jesus Christ is based upon a series of definite historic acts of God, which took place within Israel. For that reason, Christian worship normally takes place within that historic framework, so that the Church enters again, as it were, into it. Therefore, the Bible is read from the Old and New Testaments, the books of the old covenant and the new.

3. *Preaching*

The Word of the living God, believingly proclaimed, must also be addressed and applied to the congregation, which lives in a different situation from that found in the Bible. Hence the *Sermon*, based upon the Bible (i.e. the historic revelation) applies its message to us *now*, and, through the words and witness of the preacher, God's Word comes to *us*. The Sermon must of necessity take many forms, but its supreme aim is the holding-up of some aspect of the truth as it is in Jesus, addressed to the minds and consciences of the congregation. For this setting-forth of Christ, the preacher must equip himself to the best of his ability, for the Gospel must be commended to the people of his generation as intellectually and emotionally satisfying. Most important of all is it that the preacher should himself become part of his Message, for he is a herald, not merely a reporter, of good news. The experience of the Church affirms that the very proclamation of the truths of the Gospel constitutes for the hearers a divine crisis, in which Christ comes creatively as Judge and Saviour.

There can be no greater task, and no higher responsibility, than that of leading a congregation in worship. In addition to the Sermon, the preacher will need to consider carefully the pattern of Christian worship and its many-sided expressions. The great danger which besets Methodist worship, just because it is largely 'free' worship, is that it may easily degenerate into a formless succession of isolated items in which nothing vital occurs. Every part of the Service is important, and has its function in the whole, in which the Sermon, truly conceived, is the climax through which Christ, the Truth and Word of God, comes to His people. Nothing can more effectively call forth that second element in worship, the individual and corporate *response* to the Gospel, the offering of ourselves in loving obedience to God. This takes place through adoration, expressed in praise and thanksgiving; through penitence and trust; and through dedication, which includes not only the offering of ourselves, but also the exercise of the priestly office of intercession on behalf of others.

The faith and experience of the Church are that, in Christian worship and the gathering-together of believers, the powers of the heavenly Kingdom are present to judge, heal, bless and strengthen. In reliance upon the Holy Spirit, the preacher must go to his high task, which is no less than the exercise of an apostolic ministry.

4. *The Sacraments*

The two factors of the *proclamation* of the Gospel, and our individual and corporate *response* to God, are found also in the Sacraments. In them, the Gospel comes to us through word *and* action, in something said and done. The Sacraments are thus the Gospel made visible, directed towards the particular persons taking part, who make their response in faith and action. In this way, God's grace is confirmed and sealed for *them*.

The Evangelical Church observes Baptism and the Lord's Supper as the two Sacraments instituted by Jesus for the whole Church (*see* Mt 28^{19}; 1 Cor. 11^{23-6}; Mt 26^{26-9}; Mk 14^{22-5}; Lk 22^{15-20}), and this should be sufficient warrant for our continued observance of them. They occupy a central place in the Church's life, because they furnish in the form of word and action a comprehensive expression of the essential meaning of the Gospel. Once we understand that they are Sacraments of the Gospel, we shall be prevented from thinking that a different kind of grace comes through them from that which comes through the Word. There is only one grace, God's giving of Himself. Therefore, the special meaning that the Sacraments hold for the Christian life lies not in the grace which is given, but in the *form* in which it is expressed.

a. *Baptism*. The simplest fact about Baptism is that it has always been regarded as a sign of entry into the Church.

THE CHURCH (2)

Most of our difficulties about it arise from the fact that it is associated in our minds with certain ideas which we feel to be untrue. It is therefore essential to grasp the truth that it is an *initial* step in the Christian life, and must not for that reason be dissociated in thought or practice from the life and worship of the Church to which it leads. Failure to heed this fact will cause us to conclude that it is either a bare, meaningless ceremony, or that it must have some 'magical' effect upon the person concerned. Avoiding both of these extremes, we are in a position to understand what it meant in the early Church. We must think once again of the conviction the early Christians had, that the Church was the new Israel (*see* pp. 162f., above). Under the Old Covenant, the children of Abraham were heirs *by birth* of the promises of God, and members of His chosen People; and their membership was *sealed* by circumcision. Under the New Covenant, people became *by repentance and faith in Christ* members of the New Israel, the Church; they were *born anew* of the Spirit; and the *seal* of this membership was Baptism. Hence Baptism is the outward sign of entry into the Church, or, to express what this means in a different way, the outward symbol which signifies dying to sin, and rising again to righteousness, through communion with Christ.

In the New Testament, Baptism is associated with adults or believers. We can understand why this should be so. The Christian Church was just coming into being; accordingly those admitted into its fellowship were grown men and women, who had been converted by the preaching of the apostles and others. This still occurs on the mission field, when the Church adds to its company those who have no Christian ancestry. Accordingly, it was natural that the New Testament writers should state their doctrine of Baptism in terms corresponding to the baptism of adult believers who *already* had faith. Without that faith, the individuals concerned would not have wanted to come into the Church at all. For this reason, Baptism for them was always associated with a personal confession of faith. But we can understand that, as Church life became more settled, the Christian family came into view, and Christian parents felt that there was a positive blessing in the Sacrament which belonged to their *children* also (Acts 2^{39}). They too should be recognized as being in the Church. Just as Jesus had welcomed and blessed little children, so in baptism the children of believers were received into His company, and Baptism was *God's seal* upon the fact that they too were His children. Of course, the conscious response of children cannot be given at the time of their baptism; this must be completed by a later decision, and recognition of this by the Church. Yet, when this is subsequently made, it is only the personal response to those influences of grace to which the child has been subject since he was received into the Church of the New Covenant. Baptism therefore proclaims that the child is *inheritor* of God's promises in the Gospel; the later decision, conversion, and reception into full Church membership signify that he now *claims* his inheritance.

This leads us to understand in what sense Baptism is a *proclamation* of the Gospel to the person baptized. As, in preaching, God's Word comes through the preacher's words; so, in Baptism, the Gospel comes through human words and symbols. The words are, 'I baptize thee in the Name of the Father, and of the Son, and of the Holy Spirit' (which means into union with the Triune God); God takes these words, and through them *He* proclaims, '*This* man, *this* woman, *this* baby is My child'. Similarly, through our symbolic act of sprinkling with water, God proclaims that the promise of His cleansing and saving Spirit is for *him*. Thus Christ is the real minister in Baptism, which is the sign and seal of the blessings of the New Covenant in Him. The act of Baptism does not signify so much a change in the *nature* of the individual baptized as a sign of his new *status*. He is now definitely within the sphere of the Church's ministry, and has been taken into its fellowship, a fellowship in which Christ is present and active. (The practice of Infant Baptism in the Church today raises serious problems, if parents do not realize what is involved. The whole matter is discussed, along with safeguards which the Church ought to make, in Appendix VIII, *Minutes of Conference*, 1952.)

b. *The Lord's Supper*. As Baptism is the sign of entry into the Body of Christ, so the Lord's Supper is the Sacrament which nourishes our membership in that Body. The broken bread and poured-out wine are ordinary bread and wine; yet, within this ordinance, set apart by prayer and the words of Christ, their *purpose* is changed. Symbols of Christ's Body and Blood, when believingly received, they convey Christ to our souls through the action of the Holy Spirit. This is the essential Sacrament, the *approach* of God to us; while *our* part in the action is the expression of our individual and corporate *response to Him*. The complete service is indeed a dramatic representation of the historic redemptive Acts of Christ into which we, as members of His Church, are taken up. We can enumerate some of the essential points as follows:

(a) It is a *setting-forth* of the central facts upon which the Gospel is based—the passion, death *and* resurrection of the Lord Jesus.

(b) It is a *memorial* of the death of Christ on our behalf, when He ratified the New Covenant with His sacrificial Blood. We do it in remembrance of Him.

(c) It is the *Living Christ* who presides over and invites us to His Table, and we make our *response* to His invitation in penitence and faith. The Church is thus the company of forgiven sinners, whose trust is not in themselves but in Christ.

(d) As the bread and wine are *offered* to us (Mk $14^{22f.}$), so is God's grace in Christ.

(e) Our *taking* of the bread and wine is the outward sign of our receiving Christ by faith, to the nourishment of our Christian life.

(f) It is an action which must be shared with others, in which the *corporate nature* of the Church and the Christian life come to expression (1 Cor. 10^{17}).

(g) It is the realization, in miniature, of that *Christian Society* for which Christians must work in the world.

(h) It is a *foretaste* of the 'heavenly Feast', when God's Kingdom shall have been consummated, and Christ is revealed in power and glory (1 Cor. 11^{26}).

(i) In response to God's love, manifested towards us in Christ, we thankfully *offer ourselves*, body and soul, to Him for His service.

B. THE CHURCH IN HISTORY

We have reached a firm conclusion; the Church is a *divine* institution, called into being by God, whose function is to proclaim the eternal Gospel of salvation in Christ, which Gospel implies the formation of such a community. Therefore, it is also a *human* society, because made up of ordinary people; although these are being saved, they are not automatically made perfect (*see* p. 165). Consequently the Church, on its human side, has always been imperfect. In one sense, it is like a hospital, made up of those who are ill (and recognize the fact), and those who are being made better; nevertheless it possesses the means of healing, and its members know where their cure is to be found. While, therefore, we must take quite seriously the high terms in which the Church is spoken of in the New Testament, we must never idealise the actual institution as it appears in history. From the New Testament onwards, there has never been a perfect Christian community. It has always been composed of sinful and fallible people. At times its life has become particularly decadent, yet God has revived it; sometimes through groups of Christians, at times through individuals upon whom He had laid a difficult and unpopular commission. Accordingly there is always a tension within the Church, similar to that in the individual Christian's life. In one sense, the Christian, by faith and by his incorporation into Christ's people, has left his old life behind and entered upon a new life. Yet he has not automatically ceased to sin. Day by day, he 'must reckon himself dead to sin and alive unto God' (Rom. 6^{11}). He must see to it that he becomes increasingly what a member of Christ should be. Similarly the Church, as the fellowship of believers in Christ, is already one, because Christ is one; this unity could only be destroyed if the Church had several lords. Therefore the unity of the Church does not have to be created. It is already given in the fact of the Church; believers *are* one in Christ. 'There is one body, and one Spirit, even as also ye were called in one hope of your calling; one Lord, one faith, one baptism, one God and Father of all, who is over all, and through all, and in all' (Eph. 4$^{3-6}$). But in the Church as it appears in history, this unity has been broken. This does not destroy the real unity of the Church, but Christians must endeavour to 'keep the unity of the Spirit in the bond of peace' (Eph. 4^3). The Church as it actually appears is always under judgement, and must always be reforming itself. The high claims we make for it do not mean that every feature of Church life is thereby justified. There are those to whom the life of the Church has proved a stumbling-block. It was a great Christian who wrote, 'We may know people whose impression of the communion of saints is that it is a pack of petty, squabbling, jealous, uncharitable hypocrites'. The Church accordingly must continually subject itself to the judgement of Christ.

We have described the true life of the Church as a spiritual bond between Christ and His people. Although, in thought, we can distinguish this from its external organization, in actual fact the two can never be separated. The fellowship of the Church is always expressed in a visible organization. In history, the Church always appears as a community of people, which has signs by which it can be recognized. These are the proclamation of the Gospel in Word and Sacraments; the confession of faith in Christ as Lord; and a fellowship of people who, by their worship, lives and discipline, express their faith in God and their loyalty to the Gospel. The essential factor here is that the Gospel should be freely and clearly proclaimed.

This at once raises important questions. 'By what standard is the life of the Church to be judged? How do we know that the Gospel is being faithfully set forth? And, since the Church is an organism with a developing life in history, how can we judge whether changes or additions have been introduced which have no right to appear as part of the Gospel which is necessary for salvation?' The answer given by Protestantism is that the Scriptures are the supreme authority for the Church; that Christ rules in the Church through Holy Scripture. We must examine this answer more closely.

God acted in Christ. Through Him, the Church was gathered and formed. But Jesus left no written instructions. His teaching was given to His disciples by word of mouth, and during the first years of the Church the Gospel was proclaimed by living witnesses. By their testimony, men were converted and traditions about Jesus were passed on orally. The only Scriptures the Church possessed were what we call the Old Testament, which was interpreted by the Church as pointing forward to Christ. But gradually what Christians preached and taught about Christ was written down, either in letters or gospels. These, which now make up our New Testament, were accepted by the Church as a whole, but only gradually. What we know as the Canon of the New Testament (*see ANT*) was decided by the consensus of the Church, because it believed that it contained the true witness to the original tradition. The Church was thus responsible for the New Testament, but once this was accepted it became the authorititative witness to the Gospel of Christ. In this sense, the Church was now bound to the Scriptures. They now contained all that was necessary for salvation. 'But these are written, that ye may believe that Jesus is the Christ, the Son of God, and that believing ye may have life in his name' (Jn 20^{31}). 'That which we have seen and heard declare we unto you also, that ye also may have fellowship with us; yes, and our fellowship is with the Father, and with his Son Jesus Christ' (1 Jn 1³). The Church gave the New Testament to the world, but because it contains the earliest and most authentic witness to the Gospel of Christ, the Church is now subject to the New Testament, and must allow its witness to judge and determine its own life and witness.

The last sentence is not to be understood to mean that the New Testament is to be taken as a pattern for every detail in the organization of the Church today. As an institution, the Church always finds itself in a particular historic and social situation which is quite unlike that of the New Testament. It must serve its Lord by seeking to communicate its Gospel to people in terms which they understand, and must express its message in social terms which touch their lives; yet it may not change the content of the Gospel. Similarly, as we saw in *Study Nine*, different forms of the ministry have appeared during the Church's history. Most of those churches which call themselves Protestant do not agree that the form of the 'Catholic' ministry, with its three-fold order of bishop, priest and deacon, is a necessary part of the N.T. conception of the faith by which a man is saved; nor that it is to be found in the New Testament at all in the form which later became regulative in the Church, nor even during the period of the Church's earliest expansion. This is not to deny that episcopal ministries have played a valuable part in the life of the Church. It is merely to protest that they are not the only valid ones, and that other forms, such as are found in the non-episcopal Protestant churches, are equally legitimate expressions of the fundamental principles of the New Testament. Although none of the forms found in the Church today is precisely like that of the Church in the New Testament, this is no cause for reproach. The governing principle must be that nothing should constitute an absolute necessity in the Church today, which either contradicts or is not implied in the New Testament. It is by this standard that many of the features to be found in modern Roman Catholicism stand condemned in the eyes of a Protestant.

C. THE DIVISIONS IN THE CHURCH

The one Church appears in the world as divided into various 'churches'. These divisions must be regarded as a failure on the part of Christians; yet the blame for them cannot be laid on any particular group. It is quite wrong to imagine that one church—say the Roman Church—has always preserved the true faith, which has been reduced or changed by those who have broken away. That great Church must share in the common blame for many of the divisions, which were often due to its unwarranted pretensions and the additions to the apostolic faith which, it asserted, were necessary for salvation. Many historic reasons can be given for the various divisions which have taken place in the Church, not all of them theological ones. Often those who broke away did so in the cause of what they believed to be the truth. Our present-day awareness of the evils of the divisions in the one Body of Christ ought not to blind us to the fact that loyalty to the truth has the first claim upon a Christian; in many cases, no alternative to separation appeared to offer itself. A truer reading of the situation today is that *the whole Christian Church is in schism*, and that no one communion can claim to be the sole representative of the truth.

There were notable divisions in the Church during the 5th century, while in the 11th century the Great Schism took place between East and West—a schism which has persisted to this day. In 1054, the Pope of Rome excommunicated the Patriarch of Constantinople; today the Eastern Orthodox Church consists of about a score of independent national churches, which together constitute one body, the connecting link being provided by councils. The great division in the Western Church derives from the Reformation, inaugurated in the main by Martin Luther and John Calvin at the beginning of the 16th century. From this arose the great Protestant or evangelical communions, which can be grouped under their main confessional affirmations as Lutherans, Reformed or Presbyterian, Anglicans, Congregationalists and Baptists. All these are one in maintaining the general principles of the Protestant Reformation, and the repudiation of the supremacy of the Bishop of Rome. They include National Churches, episcopal and non-episcopal, as well as Independent or Free Churches.

The English Reformation Settlement was completed in the reign of Elizabeth I (1558–1603). The Church of England as established by law, which retained the government of the Church by bishops, in theory aimed at being the one Church for the English nation; but in practice this result was never achieved. A large number of people, known at the time as Puritans, desired a more radical reformation in the mode of Church government and

188 AN APPROACH TO CHRISTIAN DOCTRINE

worship; a mode more conformable in their view to the witness of the New Testament. From these sprang the Congregationalists, Baptists and Presbyterians. The last-named considered that the Church of England should be presbyterian in form, rather than episcopal: i.e. that the government of each church should be in the hands of its own minister and elders; that ministers should be appointed by the election of the Church; and that all ministers, including bishops, should engage in the ministry of the Word and prayer, and deacons in the care of the poor. The Congregationalists and Baptists take their origin from those who objected to the view that the Church should consist of the whole population (all being in practice baptized), rather than of those who have consciously dedicated themselves to Christ, who are 'gathered together' by God out of an unbelieving world, and who, as such, should be free from all outside interference. Consequently they formed separated churches and were known as Independents or Separatists, the local church being the unit of organization. Owing to persecution, many sought refuge abroad and found welcome in Holland, whence a group sailed to America in 1620, transferring to the *Mayflower* at Plymouth. In Holland, certain of these Independents became convinced of the necessity of believers' baptism, and in 1609 separated, forming the first English Baptist congregation. Meanwhile, in England, the Puritans suffered constant persecution, and many emigrated to the American Colonies between 1620 and 1640, to find religious freedom. Of those who did not emigrate, many who refused for conscience sake to conform to what they believed to be un-Christian practices were treated like criminals. Subsequently, under Cromwell, persecution of the Independents ceased, and they increased rapidly; but, when Charles II came to the throne in 1660, Presbyterians and Independents fared badly. In 1662 the Act of Uniformity required all ministers to be episcopally ordained, and to assent in all respects to the Book of Common Prayer. More than 1,600 ministers were ejected from their pastoral charges or academic posts for refusing to conform, representing one-fifth of the ministers in England, many of them among the most devoted and learned in the land. The plight of these 'Nonconformists' or 'Dissenters' was indeed sore; yet one result of this Act was to make religious Nonconformity a force in the life of England. The tide began to turn with the passing of the Toleration Act in 1689, which brought active persecution of Dissenters to an end, and accepted them as an element in the life of the nation. Equality with Anglicans was not yet won, however, and until comparatively recent times Nonconformists suffered certain disabilities.

Some acquaintance with the foregoing history is necessary in order to understand our present-day situation, social, political and religious. We must not judge our spiritual ancestors by our standards; toleration in the modern sense was largely unknown, and there were shortcomings on all sides. This is only to say that they were human, like ourselves. Yet we do well to remember the debt we owe to these early Nonconformists for our religious and political freedom. Our Parliamentary Democracy derives much of its strength from these conflicts, and our party system of government owes not a little to the two-fold factor of Church and Dissent. With the growth of religious toleration was won the right of an Opposition to exist; the struggle for this freedom in England started in the world of religion, and thence passed into politics.

One further fact must be emphasised. It is sometimes concluded, because the Protestant Reformers were led to oppose the Church of Rome, and the English Nonconformists came into conflict with the Established Church, that therefore their sense of the Church as such, and of the Apostolic Faith itself, was weak. Nothing could be further from the truth. Their opposition was to the Church as they saw it in the existing institution, but their protest was in the interest of establishing the Church as they believed it really ought to be. It was precisely because they believed so strongly in the essential place the Church holds in the Christian faith that they contended so strenuously, not for its abolition or its weakening, but for its reformation. They held that foreign elements had been allowed to obscure its true relationship to the Gospel and to the Apostolic Faith. For this reason, Protestants in general define the Church in relation to Christ, i.e. as the company of all believers in Him; rather than in terms of the papacy, or bishops, or the State, or any other element which may have appeared in the course of history. This fellowship of believers, which arises in response to the offer of God in Christ, and which confesses its allegiance to Christ as Lord, is not to be confined to any one branch of the Church today; rather it *is* the Catholic Church, even if it finds itself existing, so far as external organization is concerned, in a divided Body. This is the one, holy, catholic and apostolic Church of which the Creed speaks. 'The Church', in the Creeds, follows the confession of belief in the Holy Spirit, which means that God gathers the Church together in one spiritual fellowship through His Holy Spirit. More precisely stated, the Creed means, 'I believe in the Holy Spirit, and therefore also in the existence of the one, holy Church'. Everything in the Church depends upon the creative and sanctifying activity of the Holy Spirit; and in its fellowship we are forgiven and built up in holiness. The Church is holy, because it belongs to God, who has set it apart to do His work; it lives and works in this world, but is not of this world. It is catholic, i.e. 'universal', because it offers the whole Gospel of Christ to all men everywhere (*CAT* 20).

D. THE METHODIST CHURCH

No mention has been made in the preceding section of Methodism, one of the latest and largest denominations in Protestantism. The reason for this omission was that the existence of the Methodist Church presupposes the religious struggles of the two previous centuries, while its origin was in some sense different from that of the other great communions. Methodism arose, of course, from the great religious awakening in England, of which John Wesley and his associates were the instruments. Deeply grounded in the faith of the Church, they gathered together their followers into Methodist Societies, which had close associations with the Church of England, although they were never a part of that Church. Few of their members, before their conversion, had any vital connection with it; many were nominally associated with the Dissenting Churches. The majority, however, were 'lost sheep', brought for the first time into living communion with God. The Societies never formally separated from the Anglican Church, because they were already distinct organizations. No doubt a more sympathetic Anglicanism would have drawn them under its wing, as Wesley himself had desired. This did not happen, and Wesley took steps which made the independent development of their life inevitable. The great majority of his preachers were laymen. He refused to limit the work of God within the bounds of an inadequate organization; when the English Church was unwilling to ordain ministers for the administration of the Sacraments in the American Societies, Wesley took that step himself, being convinced that, in the primitive Church, bishops and presbyters were of the same order. Subsequently, the Methodist Conference authorized some of the preachers to administer the Sacraments. The truth is that the Methodist Church was created out of the Gospel, which went forth with such compelling power and claimed so evident a response. But, as a separate Church, it bore the marks of the ecclesiastical origin of its leaders. It gave primacy to the evangelical message of salvation for all men in Christ, but at the same time it gave equal weight to the communal life of the Christian fellowship, its worship and sacraments. For this reason, it took over the form of the Communion Service from the Church of England, and used in many instances the Order for Morning Prayer. Yet it also treasured, as means of grace, those forms which had proved so helpful in its own experience; the Covenant Service, the Class Meeting with its great spiritual ministry of Leaders, and the employment of 'laymen' as preachers. It preserved the communal sense, so strongly imparted to it by the organizing genius of John Wesley, and which was fostered by the annual Conference and the various meetings representative of circuit and local society.

As Methodism won for itself a distinctive place within the religious life of the nation, it was inevitable that it should range itself alongside the older Nonconformist Churches, which had already won their right to exist. For this, Methodism should not forget what it owes to them. Yet the dual existence of the Church of England and the Nonconformists, together with fresh outbursts of evangelistic work, produced certain tensions within Methodism which, although regrettable, were perhaps symptoms of its developing life. These led to some parallel and independent movements, represented in the main by the rise of the Methodist New Connexion (1797), the Primitive Methodists (1812), and the Bible Christians (1815). In no case was the separation due to doctrinal disputes, although organizational and political differences played their part. Each of the independent Methodist Churches did a noble work in the religious and social life of the nation, and each ought to be given the honour due; but happily the different streams came together in the Union of 1932.

The essential position of the Methodist Church is set forth in the *Deed of Union* (1932), and its words ought to be carefully marked:

'The Methodist Church claims and cherishes its place in the Holy Catholic Church which is the Body of Christ. It rejoices in the inheritance of the Apostolic Faith, and loyally accepts the fundamental principles of the historic creeds and of the Protestant Reformation. It ever remembers that in the providence of God Methodism was raised up to spread Scriptural Holiness through the land by the proclamation of the Evangelical Faith, and declares its unfaltering resolve to be true to its divinely appointed mission. The doctrines of the Evangelical Faith, which Methodism has held from the beginning and still holds, are based upon the divine revelation recorded in the Holy Scriptures. The Methodist Church acknowledges this revelation as the supreme rule of faith and practice. The Methodist Church recognizes two sacraments, namely, Baptism and the Lord's Supper, as of Divine appointment and of perpetual obligation, of which it is the privilege and duty of members of the Methodist Church to avail themselves.'

Let us underline the important points in this official declaration.

1. *Methodism is a communion within the Holy Catholic Church*

As such, it shares belief in the Apostolic Faith witnessed to in Scripture and in the historic creeds of the Church. It therefore takes its place within the main stream of Christian belief and doctrine, and is not a 'sect' with a peculiar set of tenets. The great creeds, formulated by the common mind of the Church, are not a different set of beliefs from those set forth in Scripture, but are comments upon and elucidations of the theology of Scripture made because the Christian doctrine of salvation was threatened by misconceptions which arose in the early centuries of the Church (*see* p. 108). Accordingly, they do not set up a standard other than Scripture, but are a defence of Scripture. It is a mistake to regard them as merely formal intellectual statements; rather they help us to see what is involved in our Christian Faith, when we ponder its meaning, or when we face the conflicting philosophies of the day. The creeds then become glorious affirmations of that trust in God upon which we base our lives. It should be noted how firmly the hymns of Charles Wesley are rooted in the faith of the whole Church; they proclaim the facts of the historic Faith, and our personal commitment to and experience of them. At a time when many Christians in 18th century England held only weakly to some of the essentials of the Faith, Methodism re-asserted these neglected truths with consistent vigour, and in its worship re-established the Sacrament of the Lord's Supper in its central place in the life of Christian believers.

2. *Methodism is a Protestant Evangelical Church*

It shares in the great doctrines of the Faith which were reaffirmed at the Reformation: the supreme authority of the

THE CHURCH (2) 193

Gospel, witnessed to in Holy Scripture and proclaimed in preaching and sacraments; Justification by grace through faith; the Priesthood of all Believers; and the Ministry of the whole Church (*CAT* 44—46). Within its ordered Church life, many services are open to its members, for all share in its one ministry, which is the function of the professing Christian rather than of the 'professional'. For the sake of order, the public preaching of the Word, and the administration of the Sacrament of the Lord's Supper, are confined to those who are conscious of a call from Christ which has been recognized by the whole Church, acting through its duly constituted representatives. Methodism's claim to continuity within the one Church of Christ does not admit that such a continuity is dependent upon an official succession of ministers, whether bishops or presbyters, from apostolic times, but rather is dependent upon fidelity to apostolic truth. This succession is handed on by any believer, whatever office he holds within the Church. 'If the Church resides in the successors of the Apostles, let us search for successors among those who have faithfully handed down their doctrine to posterity' (Calvin).

3. *Methodism is a distinctive community within the Church*

It believes that its origin was due to the agency of God (*CAT* 42). It is untrue to say that the Church was founded by John Wesley; he was rather the instrument used by God for His purposes. In addition to its re-assertion of the Apostolic Faith (as noted above) Methodism has its particular emphases, which together constitute a witness which is unique. These are, the gift of Assurance by the Holy Spirit, the power of the Holy Spirit to perfect us in love, and the practice and implications of Christian fellowship. This witness of Methodism can be popularly expressed in five universals: (i) Every man needs a Saviour; (ii) Every man can find a Saviour; (iii) Every man can know that he is saved; (iv) Every man can be saved to the uttermost; (v) Every man can witness to his Saviour. (On this section, *see* further *The Message and Mission of Methodism*, pp. 16–29.)

E. THE CHURCH TODAY

a. To the serious Christian, *the broken fellowship of the Church* in the world must appear as lamentable, and every effort must be made to heal it. Yet no one should desire union at the price of compromising the truth as he conceives it; nor can we lightly disregard past history, in which, despite man's self-will, God has been at work. It is quite possible to deplore the divisions in the Church, while admitting at the same time that we owe much to the insights and actions which sometimes brought them into being. Things being as they were, it is difficult to see how many of them could have been avoided; and it is not for us to adopt any lofty position of self-confidence, from which to judge our fathers in the faith. Perhaps the greatest evil lay, not in the divisions themselves, but in the bitterness and uncharitableness which so often accompanied them, and which caused such a succession of misunderstandings. This above all was a failure in Christian fellowship; we at least can seek to overcome this today, and ensure that we ourselves are not parties to such a spirit (*see* Wesley's *Sermons* XXXIII, *A Caution against Bigotry*, and XXXIV, *Catholic Spirit*).

b. *The future lies under the Hand of God.* We can gratefully acknowledge that the divisive movements of the past appear to have been halted, and that in the providence of God the separate non-Roman Churches are beginning to draw together in mutual understanding and co-operation. This is seen in what is known as the *Ecumenical Movement*, which finds its expression in the World Council of Churches, reaching down through the British Council of Churches to local Councils. Much has yet to be done, and many difficulties remain to be overcome; but already great discoveries have been made. In England, for instance, it has been realized amongst the great non-Roman communions that 'on the doctrines of God the Father, the Person and Work of Christ, the Person and Mission of the Holy Spirit, the Trinity and the Life Everlasting, we have found nothing which separates any one of these Communions from another. All acknowledge the Apostolic Faith as contained in the Scriptures and expressed in the Apostles' and Nicene Creeds' (Report on *Church Relations in England*, 1951).

c. *The true expression of Christian unity must be found in fellowship at the Lord's Table.* It should be noted that this already exists between the great majority of Protestant Christians today; for instance, among the Free Churches in England. Where it does not exist, the barrier lies in a doctrine of sacramental grace which is held to depend upon a succession of ministers through the historic episcopate. (For this doctrine of the Apostolic Succession, *see* p. 170.) Although many Anglicans do not accept this as final, it remains the stumbling-block on the Church of England side to inter-communion with Free Churchmen.

d. *Some major unions have already been achieved* in recent times: e.g. among Presbyterians in Scotland, and Methodists in Britain; the Methodists, Congregationalists and Presbyterians are now one in the United Church of Canada; and Anglicans, Presbyterians, Congregationalists and Methodists have come together in the Church of South India, which is the latest of the unions accomplished, and the most significant because it includes episcopal and non-episcopal traditions. It is not episcopacy *as such* which is likely to prove the main difficulty in the future, but rather that *interpretation* of the bishop's office which regards him as essential to the existence of a true Church—other non-episcopal ministries being regarded as in some way defective. Perhaps in the future Methodism may have a leading part to play in the achievement of such a union, since its organization includes features which approximate to both episcopal government and the presbyterian order. From our side, there is no obstacle to immediate inter-communion with members of other churches, including the Church of England. In the meantime, our catholic churchmanship must be expressed in grateful and loyal service within that Communion in which God has called us, or nurtured us, or given us our ministry. Through it, God has brought us into the Body of Christ, and all the heritage of Christian experience can be ours within its fellowship. Without such loyalty, any desire for a united Church of the future would become ineffective, while such a loyalty no more excludes love for the whole Church than attachment to a particular regiment precludes loyalty to the whole army, or affection for one's home-town the love of one's country. Within our own Church we can, by God's grace, exercise our ministry, and make it an increasingly effective instrument of His Will. Paul expresses the depth of personal faith when he wrote, 'He loved me and gave himself up for me'; but he also wrote, 'Christ loved *the church* and gave himself up for it' (Eph. 5[25]). Martin Luther called the Church 'the mother who bears and fosters every individual Christian' (*Larger Catechism*). The Christian will surely love his mother, even if sometimes she appears old, wrinkled, or slow.

SERMON XVIII. UPON OUR LORD'S SERMON ON THE MOUNT: DISCOURSE III

Three Sermons which deal largely with 'practical' subjects are set for study. This is a reminder that Wesley's *Standard Sermons* are a standard of *preaching*, not of doctrinal orthodoxy. Another reminder of the same principle is that there are in the 'Forty-Four Sermons' no sermons dealing expressly with such vital matters of belief as the divinity of our Lord, the Trinity, the Atonement, the Resurrection, the Holy Spirit, or the Church, though all these doctrines are presupposed and alluded to. Lying behind the *Standard Sermons* is the general presumption that the Methodist believes and preaches all the accepted doctrines of orthodox Christianity. Yet Wesley knew well that it was quite possible for those who are undeniably orthodox to fail in their evangelical witness through a variety of faults of emphasis or approach, such as cold formalism, failure to stress the need of a genuine change of heart, a presentation of faith as not more than 'a train of ideas in the head', neglect to summon the believer to search for Full Assurance and Perfection, or a lack of plainness in bringing home the ethical demands of the Gospel. The purpose of erecting the *Sermons* as a *Standard* is not the negative one of excluding heresy from Methodist pulpits, so much as the positive one of securing that, from among the whole body of orthodoxy, certain practical Gospel truths shall always receive due emphasis and clear statement. Hence it is natural to find that certain doctrines which were not particularly in dispute are passed over, while on the other hand, nearly half the *Sermons* are on practical and ethical matters. These sermons are just as important as the others. It is to be particularly noted that in Wesley there is never any sign of divorce between 'Gospel preaching' and 'ethical exhortation'. The reader will already have noticed that in a sermon on 'the religion of the heart' Wesley is always swift to press on from *Justification*, etc., to at least a brief practical application.

Theme of the Sermon. The life dominated by 'the Faith that works by Love': Christian Perfection.

EXPLANATORY OUTLINE OF THE SERMON

I. '*The Mind which was in Christ Impart.*' (1) The only secure foundation for love of man is love of God. (2) The love and fear of God casts out every base passion. (3) God requires inward purity as well as the outward good deed. (4) The Christian is to go to all lengths of self-discipline, that temptation be overcome. (5) The Christian marriage-law. (6) Those to whom God gives the gift of faith can see the marks of His greatness and goodness in the natural order, in (7) divine providence, and in (8) the means of grace. (9) An application of Christian purity of intention: the Christian's oath. (10) Argument (representing current Anglican methods of meeting the objections of Quakers and others, and not always very convincing today) concerning the rightness of an oath in a court of law. (11) Summary.

II. *'That all Mankind Thy Truth may see.'* (1) Christian experience is to show itself in open witness. (2) 'The peace of God.' (3) Portrait of a peace-maker. (4, 5) Unbounded devotion to good works. (6) But the chief delight of the child of God is to seek to bring others to a like experience. He knows that the conversion of sinners is God's work alone, but he knows that God uses human instruments, and he would be one such. (This very moving section runs far beyond the meaning of the text, of course.) (7) Those who make this witness will receive increase of grace.

III. *'From Doubt, and Fear, and Sorrow Free.'* (1) It might be supposed that the Christian would be loved for his pure goodness. (2) Actually the fallen world is such that the Christian will inevitably be persecuted. (3) The righteous are persecuted precisely because they are righteous. (There follows a portrait, magnificent in its irony and scorn, of the scoffer at eighteenth-century Methodism.) (4) There is a fundamental and complete 'incompatibility of temperament' between the worldly man and the believer. (5) God's providence can wonderfully overrule persecution for the advancement of the Gospel. (This is indeed true, and the comfort which it brought to the persecuted Methodist very obvious. However, Wesley surely goes too far in saying 'the ungodly are only a sword of His', as though wicked persecution could arise upon the divine initiative.) Historical survey of persecution. (The last paragraph refers to the reigns of Edward VI and of Queen Mary. It is a fact that, under the former, a government of greedy exploiters, sailing under the colours of 'Protestantism', goaded the people to such fury that they welcomed the Roman Catholic Mary. The resultant persecution saw simple and good men and women burning at the stake. It was popular reaction to this which, more than anything else, won

England for the Reformed faith.) (6, 7) More usually persecution is social and economic. (Wesley has the experience of early Methodists in mind.) (8) Worldly men may find it prudent to put honest Christian men in positions of trust, but they still hate them for their useful integrity. (There is sadly much truth in this. It is a counter-balancing principle to the often-canvassed opinion that the man who suffers for his principles 'comes out on top in the end'.) (9) The Christian is not to seek persecution, nor (10) to suppose that he can always avoid it, but (11) to rejoice in the blessing promised. ('They must blacken you to excuse themselves.' It is chiefly for this reason that the world criticizes the Christian. That the criticism is unjust is a comfort to the Christian. But he, for his part, is not to blacken the world, in order to excuse *himself*, for there are blots on the Church, which are a just offence to the outsider.) (12) The Christian is to return good for evil, with 'invincible meekness'. Yet he is also to exercise a certain degree of common sense in what he does. (13) Practical maxims for those who would be wholly devoted to the conversion of sinners.

IV. '*Now let me gain Perfection's Height.*' An invitation to share fully the excellence of the Christian religion.

TEST QUESTIONS

1. How would you define Christian Worship? Describe the chief means by which it is expressed.

2. 'The Methodist Church claims and cherishes its place in the Holy Catholic Church which is the Body of Christ'. How would you justify this statement from the Deed of Union?

3. Following Wesley's teaching, show briefly how 'the religion of the heart' is to work out in the Christian's life, and in his relations with others.

STUDY ELEVEN

Christian Ethics

A. WHAT IS ETHICS?

ETHICS is 'the science of morals', or 'the science of human duty'. It deals with the way in which human beings behave. The purpose of ethical analysis is to work out the principles of *right* behaviour, and so to construct a reliable or acceptable code of conduct.

It is true that, of the books which are nowadays being written on sociology, a great many deliberately refuse to tackle questions of 'right behaviour'. They are confined to dispassionate and impartial description of the ways in which people actually *do* behave. Religious activity is described, because religious activity happens; but no attempt is made to judge the comparative merits of, say, Roman Catholicism, Methodism, Shintoism or Ju-ju. Such cool descriptive studies are valuable, but they are not 'ethics'. But if the writer, on the basis of his observations, begins to suggest what seem to him to be commendable *changes* in the pattern of conduct, then he is moving into the realm of ethics.

Such a writer, for example, might undertake a careful sociological survey of a small town in one of the Southern States of the U.S.A. He would, among many other things, tabulate the money incomes of the citizens, and give representative family budgets. He would classify trades and occupations. He would tell us how many people went to the cinema and how often; how many went to the baseball game; how many to Church, and so on. He would describe the organization and meetings of the Elks, Lions, Kiwanis, Women's Christian Temperance Union, Knights of Pythias, Congress of Industrial Organizations, Chambers of Commerce, Y.M.C.A., and so on. He would indicate the changes that had occurred over the years. He would describe the effects of racial discrimination. If he knew his job, the result would be a clear and interesting portrait of a community.

But suppose that he went on to suggest one or two ways of reducing racial discrimination; changes in behaviour that seemed to him likely to improve the life of the community. He would then be discussing *ethics*—and we should want to know on what *grounds* he suggested this or that reform. (i) He might believe that some racial discrimination was justified, but that too harsh discrimination was economically unsound. (ii) He might have been convinced by his survey that discrimination has led to unnecessary unhappiness. (iii) He might hold the view that it was morally wrong.

B. ETHICS DEPENDS ON THEOLOGY

It is obvious that this third possible reason is based upon a *theological* judgement. It is equally true, though not so obvious, that so are the others. In fact, ethics depends on theology. Suggestions about human behaviour which assume that human beings are mere material creatures, or are dominated by economic self-interest, are based on theological convictions; bad theology, it may be, but still theology. 'Soviet morality' is based on the conviction that social life and personal character are finally determined by the prevailing ownership and organization of the means of production, that the destiny and nature of man only have meaning in terms of this material world, and that there is no God. Soviet ethics, in other words, is based on theological convictions.

This is bound to be so. Any attempt to estimate the value or the effectiveness of ways of behaviour necessarily involves an estimate of the nature of the '*right way*'—and that necessarily involves an opinion or a conviction about the destination. What is the goal and purpose of human life? Is it to transform the world into one political and economic unit, so organized that all the children of men may eat, drink and be merry, and live without fear of war or want? Do we seek security or liberty, or a compromise between the two? Is our goal to provide opportunity for all men for the fullest expression of human personality? Is the purpose one which can only be achieved in the far distant future, by some remote but fortunate generation, though all preceding individuals who have engaged in the pain and travail of the struggle will have perished as though they had never been? Is the goal entrance into the eternal Kingdom of God? The questions overlap, but they are basically different. We shall chart our way according to our answers, according to the faith which we hold.

C. CHRISTIAN FAITH AND CONDUCT

The way we shall follow in the rest of this Study is based specifically upon the *Christian Faith*. It accepts the Christian answer to the questions just posed, and is therefore linked with, and is a consequence of, the argument of the preceding *Studies* of this book. It is not something tacked on as an after-thought, to give a little light relief to the Local Preacher who likes occasionally to orate about social problems.

Though it may seem like labouring the obvious, it is of the utmost importance that the necessary relationship between faith and conduct, in which faith is primary, should be clearly recognized. Sometimes a rule of conduct may be presented and accepted as though it were an arbitrary decree, an imperial proclamation, which needed no justification. 'You must not drink alcohol and you must not gamble, if you become a Methodist', for example. If the Christian way of life is thought of like that—as a collection of arbitrary regulations which must be accepted, if one is to qualify for membership of the Christian community—it can become an intolerable burden. The joy departs, and only the burden remains. The result is a legalistic 'Christian Pharisaism' which breeds hypocrisy; it also breeds the subtle casuistry which so interprets the code of conduct, that complicated but logical reasons are found for my doing what I have been told not to do, while obeying the strict letter of the law (*see* Mk 7$^{5-14}$). Or else the result is a hardness edged with bitterness, a gnawing suspicion that those who do not walk by our rules are most unfairly enjoying life more than we do. If, on the other hand, to take a simple illustration, I refuse to gamble because I cannot reconcile gaining at another's loss with loving my neighbour as myself, my conduct springs from *my faith*, and is in harmony with it.

Here we touch on the old controversy between faith and works, and see the answer to it. The moral confusion of our age is a direct reflection and consequence of confused faith. The conduct we really approve indicates the faith we truly hold—the living faith, that is, and not only the doctrines to which we intellectually assent.

The point is best illustrated by a simple theological summary, personally applied. Let us begin with my unregenerate self. I am (let us suppose) an ordinary, reasonably decent sinner. I realize that there are many people more intelligent and more kindly than myself. I do not claim any notable merit, but I am quite sure that I am a pretty fair average. There are many, or so I flatter myself, more stupid and less charitable than I am. In fact, measuring myself against my fellows, and giving myself the benefit of the doubt, I am reasonably content. *And then I am challenged and transfixed by the Gospel.* I now have to measure myself against the purity and love of Jesus. I have to contrast the glory of God with my own littleness. In the cruel kindness of that majestic light, I can do no other than acknowledge my transgression and pray, 'Lord be merciful to me, a sinner'.

Sooner or later, I realize that the Lord is indeed merciful. I am a sinner, but He is a Saviour. Converted and justified, I enter into *a new relationship with God.* I enter also, of necessity, into a new relationship with *my fellow-man.* It is a fact of experience that, though I may believe with my mind that Christ is the Saviour of the world before I humble myself to acknowledge that He is *my* Saviour, it is only when I so acknowledge Him that I accept with my heart that He is indeed the Saviour of the world. There is now no personal possessiveness when I say '*Our* Father'. The man next door, and the stranger on the other side of the world, do really matter to Him as much as I do; no more and no less.

The nature of this process—sin, atonement, reconciliation, forgiveness, justification—has already been fully expounded in the previous *Studies*. This brief summary is here included so that you may see clearly that it is vital to an understanding of Christian ethics. What it comes to is, as our Lord Himself has told us, that the rule of our life is that we should love God with all our heart and mind and soul and strength, and love our neighbour as ourselves. This is the 'Law of Christ'. We demonstrate that this is indeed our guiding law when, not with a resentful acceptance of uncongenial obligations, nor with a nicely calculated decision as to how little we can do to evade the wrath of God, we 'bear one another's burdens' (Gal. 6^2).

D. THE RANGE OF 'THE LAW OF CHRIST'

The next question we have to consider is, '*How far does this three-fold relationship*—this inter-connecting relationship between God, my neighbour and myself—*extend?*' For the fact is that there are many who have fully accepted the theological statement, but deny that it has other than a 'spiritual' meaning. This new relationship, they say, means that I must pray for my neighbour and seek after his salvation. It means that together we worship and adore our Maker. It does not mean that we soil ourselves by involving ourselves in political and economic disputes, for they are the things which belong to this perishing world, and are of no importance to those whose eyes are fixed upon the eternal Kingdom.

This is altogether too limited and inadequate a conception of the range of God's dominion. It is not 'wrong'. To pray for the salvation of others, and to love them in the context of worship, is indeed part of our Christian duty, and apt to be overlooked in an age which sets too high a value on material things. But the 'Law of Christ' covers more than this. (Before going further, carefully read Rom. 12.) The strength of Christian faith is in the fact that it is rooted and grounded in reality; in the reality of God and man, of eternity and time, of spirit and body. It is not such a faith as atheistic Marxism, which endeavours to exalt the *material* by denying the spiritual, and ends by building a barrier against truth. It is not such a faith as 'Christian Science', which seeks to exalt the *spiritual* by denying the material, and ends in a thin and insubstantial unreality. We believe that the Word was made flesh. We know that 'man shall not live by bread alone', but we know also that our own daily bread is real enough for us to bring our need for it to God in prayer. Material things are real; this is one of the consequences of Incarnation theology (*see Study Six*). And because material things are real, the way we use or misuse them is in itself a reflection of our relationship with God; we are gladly accepting His Law, or rebelling against it.

In other words, we are not permitted by our faith to limit the Law of Christ to what is commonly known as 'personal piety'. Nor, on the other hand, are we permitted to evade the demand for personal dedication by manifesting a 'zeal for righteousness' which is *solely* concerned with social problems and material needs. A 'social Gospel' which is a substitute for the real thing, all 'social' and no 'Gospel' because it concentrates on the Sermon on the Mount, and forgets that the Preacher of that Sermon died and rose again for man's redemption, is perhaps a greater heresy than is self-regarding piety.

The mistake of both extremes is that they emphasise halves of a truth which should not be divided. Christian moral duty, or rather the privilege and the joy of the man who is reconciled to God in Christ, is personal *and* social, spiritual *and* material—it is, in fact, related to the unity of life.

The pattern is made plain in *Ephesians*. This tremendous Pauline letter begins with the will of God as it was before the foundation of the world, and ends with advice to parents and to children as to how they ought to treat one another. It deals with the battle against spiritual wickedness in the high places, but brings the fighting line into a very practical place where masters and servants meet one another in the daily business of life. The theme of *Ephesians* is 'reconciliation'. The reason is in the mercy of God, the method is in the sacrifice of Christ, and the fulfilment is in the conduct of those who join themselves to their Lord.

To sum it all up, this is God's world, linked by His will and by the death and resurrection of Jesus to the eternal realm. In this world, which is part of the universal dominion of God, *all things* are either according to His will (and so under His approval), or in rebellion against His will (and so under His judgement). All things—family life, entertainment, work, Sunday School Teachers' Training Class, international relations, or trade union organizations. In this world, the Christian is God's fellow-worker, the servant of the good news of the Gospel. His aim is to advance in all things the true welfare of his fellow-men, and to maintain his own growth in grace. His strength and his guidance are from God.

E. APPLICATION

All this is very well and raises no awkward problems, so long as it is confined to vague generalisations. Conduct, however, cannot be so confined. It has to be *practical*. Problems of behaviour crowd urgently in upon us in every waking moment, and the decision as to how we shall behave in any particular situation has to be made here and now.

1. *Difficulties*

The making of such ethical decisions is not easy. It might be, indeed we believe it would be, if we lived always in unclouded fellowship with God. Brief moments of such fellowship we may experience, but—for most of us—they are fleeting and rare experiences. For the most part we struggle against the sins that do so easily beset us. We are moving on to perfection, but we have not so low an estimate of perfection as to claim that we have already attained it. The sin that is in us has two consequences.

In the first place, it means that we do not always do the things that we know we ought to do. In the second place, it means that we sometimes do not even know what are the things we ought to do.

For some things, even a doubtful and feeble hold upon the Faith is enough to give us a clear answer. We know that we ought not to murder or to rob. We know, even though we struggle against the temptations they offer, that envy and malice are wrong. But there are some great questions which still divide the minds of the most earnest and sincere believers. We know, for example, that the evil and mass destruction of *war* is contrary to the will of God. But what is the duty of a Christian man in a war which he has neither sought nor desired? Ought he to defend his country against a tyrannous aggressor? Ought he to resolve to have neither part nor lot in war? Again, we know that *murder* is wrong. But what should be done with a caught and convicted murderer? Ought he to die by verdict of the law, as a grim warning to other would-be offenders? Or is it murder to take his life for the life he himself has taken? These questions are posed as questions, because there is as yet no answer that would carry the consent of the whole Christian community. On each of them I can say, 'I believe that this way is right, and that that way is wrong', but to none dare I say, 'In these circumstances, a Christian must . . .'

Because we live in a sinful world, we live in a world where all too often we must choose, not between the altogether right and the altogether wrong, but between the slightly better and the slightly worse. Because we live in a world of intricate relationships, we are sometimes caught in a tangle of conflicting loyalties. Suppose that I am a loyal member of my trade union, and that I am called out on strike against a grievance which does not seem to me fully to justify strike action. How far does my loyalty to my fellow-workers, on which the whole strength of union bargaining depends, over-ride my loyalty to my family, or even to my individual conscience?

The difficulties are there, and must frankly be realized. They are not surprising. When we are still far from giving to our God the entire devotion of heart and mind and soul, we should not anticipate the clarity of judgement that can only come from the undimmed brightness of His wisdom. At the least, the awareness of our own imperfection should guard us against hasty dogmatisms and uncharitable judgements.

How, then, are we to bring the Gospel to bear on daily life? One way is to ask, either by majority decision or under the guidance of experts, for a code that will cover all emergencies. But this way brings us back to the spirit-stifling legalism of the Pharisees. Or are we to leave all decisions about conduct to the conscience and judgement of the individual—an individual who might well confuse his own desires with the will of God? The answer, I believe, is that we are not in fact confronted with a choice between two such extreme and opposed solutions. We do not have to choose between the rigid law or the uncontrolled individual. Life is always tension. The tug-of-war between the claims of liberty and justice, between adventure and security, between social and individual—this is part of the tension between the temporal and the eternal. We have to live by the light that is in *us*, by the guidance that is granted to *us*, and by the wisdom and experience of *others*.

2. Clear Judgements

This section on the difficulties of Christian ethics has been given some emphasis, in order that we should not be looking for a neat and tidy little statement on 'What Every Young Christian Ought To Know'! Nevertheless, there are many things on which a clear Christian judgement *can* be given, and it is to these that we must now turn.

a. *The Christian Doctrine of Man* is at the heart of our theology (*see Study Four*). Man is a sinner, made in the image of God and capable, by the grace of God, of redemption and restoration. All men are equal before God, who is no respecter of persons. It follows from this doctrine that we ought not to favour unduly the rich and the important in the organized life of the Church (*see* Jas 2). It follows, too, that we must care for our brother in distress, even though he belongs to a commonly despised group, or—which is even harder to bear—even though he belongs to a group which commonly despises us. We remember the parable of the Good Samaritan. It follows, also, that laws and customs and traditions which deny the proper dignity of man are to be condemned by the followers of Christ. The racial discrimination, which acts on the supposition that a part of the human race is of necessity inferior to the rest, pleasantly gratifies the sinful pride of many, but the Christian finds no satisfaction in it. We may give thanks that in our day the Christian Church is speaking clearly and unmistakably on this issue. It follows, also, that the newer tyrannies of our modern world, those which deal with men and women as 'expendable units', and as 'an undifferentiated jelly of socially necessary labour power', are equally to be condemned. The individual, created by God in order that he might know Him and enjoy Him for ever, is not to be battered and moulded into the monolithic structure of a super-State.

b. *The doctrine that we are members one of another*, and that we are bound together in closest relationship through our relationship to God, has a direct bearing on *industrial relations*. It is probable that there will always be conflicts of interest within the world of industry, trade and commerce, but it is not necessary that there should be automatic conflicts of power. The simple picture of the massed might of Capital ranged against the massed might of Labour is too readily accepted, even by those within the fellowship of the Church. It must be because they have not thought out the consequences of their faith. Sooner or later, we must learn that management and labour belong together, necessary partners, and not rivals, in a joint enterprise. It is good that, of recent years, increasing care and thought are being given to the question of human relations within industry. It is good that, more and more, it is being understood that the personnel manager is a key man. It is good that the heresy of describing human beings as 'hands' is fading away.

c. *The Christian's attitude to Work*. Industrial relationships, of course, are not ends in themselves. People do not come to work merely in order to enjoy rather queer and limited fellowship with other people. To take the argument one step further, they do not go to work in order to earn money. At least, if that is the personal reason which moves any individual to go to work, it is not the reason for the whole organization of the industry. The purpose of work is to provide the goods and services which men and women need, or think they need, in order to satisfy the material demands of existence. The very remarkable world-wide network, that links each one of us in a thousand different ways with other people, is itself but an example of the basic truth that we are members one of another. Much of the frustration, much of the bitterness or apathy about work, is caused by a total misconception of its purpose. There is no likelihood, in the foreseeable future, that all the dirty or monotonous or unpleasant jobs will be lifted from our shoulders and undertaken by unthinking machines, but there is no reason why the Christian should not at once be able to discover that, as he goes to his daily work, he may indeed be serving there, because he is helping his fellow-men. Work has always been emphasised in Christian ethics. Too often, I suspect, the emphasis has been upon work for its own sake, as a discipline of the proud and rebellious spirit of man. I would suggest that we would do well to work out in greater detail the ethical demands that follow from accepting the view that work is really a part of the service we offer to God for the welfare of His human family.

d. *The Christian's use of Time.* The questions just considered are the big questions which confront us as members of an industrialised community. Very often, it must be confessed, though we have done our best and sought to use our influence as Christians, we have been unsuccessful. The general pattern of relationships within the factory is poor, and all that we can do is to try to make it work a little better by our personal example. We are overruled by majority decisions, and have to try to live as Christians in a largely un-Christian world. But there are some areas of life which are, generally speaking, entirely under our own control. There is, for example, the whole period of *our free time*. With the general reduction in the hours of work, a reduction which has come belatedly but steadily even to the agricultural worker—at least to those who are paid directly for the hours of work they do —most people have now three times as much free time as they have of paid working time.

This time, precious hours at our disposal, is as it were the investible capital of our lives. It can be frittered away. It can be used so badly that it falls under the paralysing dominion of evil. It can be so clumsily managed that, though our intentions are the noblest, somehow we never seem to accomplish anything. Or it can be used with wisdom and with gratitude as a gift of God.

e. *The Christian's use of Sunday.* There can be no doubt that our spare time comes under the Law of Christ. We must use our leisure for rest, for relaxation, for re-creation, for voluntary service in the Church and in the community, and for worship. *Sunday* is a day on which most of us are 'free'. (Those of you who are Local Preachers in wide country circuits will look a little doubtful at that word 'free', but it is still true that the crowded hours you spend on Sundays are hours which you have voluntarily given to God's service.) Mention of Sunday brings up the whole subject of the right use of Sunday—and that will emphasise the relevance of the points which we discussed earlier. All too frequently, the question is asked, 'Is it right to do this or that or the other on Sunday?' It is the form of the question that is itself wrong, for it implies that, once a certain minimum obligation has been satisfactorily complied with, the rest of the day is at your discretion. The fact of the matter is that the whole of the day is at our disposal, and that it is to be seen in relation to all the rest of our available free time. I can understand that those who have spent six days hard at work, from dawn to dusk, might justly ask for an hour or two of physical recreation on Sunday afternoons. But when Sunday is seen as twenty-four hours in a total of approximately one hundred and twenty in the week that we can use as we wish, it would seem that there supremely, in the hours of Sunday, is the opportunity for worshipping God and learning more of Him.

The compulsory observance of Sunday can be a deadly thing. The thoughtless neglect of Sunday can be even worse. But the Christian, in such measure as he is near to his God, is not likely to waste that day, nor does he need to be compelled to use it.

f. *The Christian's use of Money*. What we have said about time also applies to money and abilities. Money is an impersonal agency, but it is a very powerful agent. It can be either the messenger of healing, or the chariot of death. In point of fact, the way in which I use my money has probably a more direct impact upon the lives of my fellow-men than any other action of my life. Some great saint of the last century, a wise warrior whose name I forget, once said, 'I know that people are really converted to a cause when their hands go to their pockets'. There is much shrewd wisdom in the observation. There is, indeed, a rough and ready (but fairly reliable) guide for us, as to the priority of our convictions, in the disposal of our budget. How much do we spend a week on food? How much on entertainment? How much on the work of the Church?

The Christian attitude to money raises at once the allied problem of the Christian attitude to *gambling*. There again, I suspect that it is a problem to many because the wrong sort of question is asked. Put in the form, 'I give generously to the Church and to charity, and I take ample care of my wife and family. I don't miss two shillings a week. Why should I not amuse myself by a harmless flutter?', the practice seems innocuous enough. And, if we are basing our Christian ethics upon 'a nicely calculated less or more', there is no real answer to it. But if we base our ethics upon love to our neighbour, the whole thing is seen in an entirely different light. That which differentiates gambling from every other sort of financial transaction is that one man's gain inevitably involves another man's loss. The Christian will not refrain from gambling because he is afraid to lose two shillings. He refrains because, loving his neighbour, he will not profit at his neighbour's loss.

g. *Other questions.* The application of our faith to conduct, summarized in the illustrations just given, has not of course been fully covered by those illustrations. This is not a text-book on ethics, but rather an attempt to indicate the theological bases of conduct. You will undoubtedly be able to think of many other practical questions which need a similar examination. One of them is the attitude of the Christian towards the drinking of alcoholic beverages. (How can we reconcile the drinking of a narcotic drug with loving God with all our mind?) Another is the Christian view of the family. (The social group nearest to the heart of any individual, and the one in which most immediately love of others should be manifest.) The purpose of this survey will have been accomplished, if it has convinced you that the way we behave and the way we believe are indissolubly joined—and that the way we believe comes first.

F. CONCLUSION

If I do not drink, and do not gamble, and do not smoke, and do not swear, and live peaceably at home, minding my own business, it does not automatically follow that I am either a good Christian, or a candidate certain to be accepted into the everlasting Kingdom of God. I may be too mean to spend my money, and too timid to commit the sins I should dearly love to commit. Turn back, if you will, to the beginning of this *Study*, and to the questions which were there put, about the nature and purpose of our lives. Because we believe in God through Jesus Christ, we know the way we should go. We know that it is a road on which we never journey alone, for it is a road on which our Lord walks with us. More than that, it is a road along which His strength sustains us, on which we stumble and fall continuously, unless supported by that strength. The manner of our journeying is Christian ethics. The strength for the journey is the grace of

Christ. Let us, to whom has been granted the inestimable honour of preaching the unsearchable riches of Christ, strive faithfully to proclaim both the manner of the journeying and the strength which God supplies to those who start on pilgrimage.

Sermon XIX. upon our lord's sermon on the mount: discourse iv

Theme of the Sermon. The Christian life of practical service, public witness, and open allegiance to the Church. A check to that Christianity which is so absorbed with the delights of 'religious experience' that it makes light of the moral demands of God's law (Antinomianism), and to the error of those who, while they wait for a Christian experience, neglect the discipline of Christian worship and service (Quietism).

EXPLANATORY OUTLINE OF THE SERMON

Introduction. The Snare of Purely Inward Religion (1) The religion which promises so to transform the soul of man that it shows forth the glory of God, cannot fail to attract any awakened spirit. (For the Scripture reference see the opening verses of *Hebrews*. The two citations of the Greek are translated in the words immediately following.) (2) But some will say, 'If the religion of the heart is so rapturous and delightful, why cannot we just enjoy what God has given us? Why need we fill our lives with anxiety and labour by bothering with an ungrateful and difficult world?' (3) Some seemingly spiritual men have indeed argued thus (Quietists and Antinomians), but (4) this deceptive argument is Satan's masterpiece for deluding those who have made a good start in true spiritual religion. (5) Christ has most plainly warned us against it.

I. *The Christian must go to the World.* (1) For the Christian to yield to the temptation to isolate himself from worldly men, and thus to neglect the attempt to influence them for good, will shipwreck his faith. On the other hand, contact with unspiritual men is likewise an unhelpful influence. Therefore there is a necessary time for private devotion. (2) But devotion must not be such as to leave no time for witness and service. (3) Cross-bearing and (4) the doing of good presuppose contact with human society. (5) Paul teaches us that we must not make familiar friends with evil men, and yet must not leave them to their own devices. (6) To be put to the necessity of returning good for the evil which worldly men will offer is an essential part of the Christian discipline. (7) Christ calls us to be the salt of the earth, and (8) those who do not try to pass on their religion are in a desperate state. (9) The awful sin of apostasy.

II. *The Christian must make an Open Witness.* (1) Some argue: 'Our Christian witness ought to be very private and discreet, so as to cause no annoyance to those who do not agree with us.' (2–4) Christ has forbidden this plausible argument. Real religion makes so great a change that it cannot but be conspicuous. (5) Proof from the word of Christ, and (6) the experience of His heroes. (7) However, Satan is ingenious with plausible excuses for secret or semi-secret religion.

III. *Current Excuses for Secret Discipleship Exposed.* (The argument is set in terms of the controversy of those days, but human nature is still the same, and if what Wesley says is translated into present-day terms his advice is more than apposite in these times when there are so many who are disinclined 'to make themselves conspicuous' for the sake of Christ.) (1) It is objected that true religion is in the heart, not in outward works. This is true, but the root of heart religion must produce the fruit of good works. (2) Love is indeed 'the fulfilling of the law' but by enabling us to keep it, not by releasing us from it. (3) 1 Cor. 12^{31} does not teach that love is more excellent than obedience. (4) Practical, outward obedience ought not to take the mind from spiritual religion. 'Consequently, one branch of the worshipping God in spirit and in truth is, the keeping of His outward commandments.' (5) It is not necessary to be a recluse to cultivate spiritual contemplation. (6) The great reason for lapsing into a purely inward religion of 'experience' divorced from service, is reaction against a purely formal religion. (7) Various excuses overturned. (8) The Christian does indeed sometimes find that his attempt to be an evangelist has only resulted in fretting his own soul. (This can be a devastating temptation to sincere believers who are of a sensitive frame of mind, who are disinclined to controversy, and who do not want to be guilty of an improper attempt to 'push themselves on folk'. Many would-be evangelists have been disillusioned by the experience that their well-intentioned attempts have resulted in the disturbing of their own religious faith.) The guard against disillusionment here is to remember that while it is the Christian's calling to preach the Gospel, the response to it is the concern of God. The evangelist is to be bold, but discreet and humble.

IV. *The Invitation to Christianity in Earnest.* (1) The believer is to let his light shine in his passion for souls, but (2) is to be on his guard against the temptation in this to have an eye to his own reputation for holiness. (3) He is to let his light shine in a manifestly honest, open, and upright character, and (4) to this end is not to shrink from standing alone if need be, and from a life of strict self-denial.

TEST QUESTIONS

1. How does 'the Law of Christ' illustrate the connection between ethics and theology?

2. In what respects should our Christian faith influence (i) our attitude to our fellow-man, and (ii) our use of our leisure?

3. 'Social, open, active Christians' (II. 7). Is being a 'social Christian' the same thing as being 'an open, active Christian'? What light does your answer throw on the place of the Church in the Christian life?

STUDY TWELVE

*The Last Things**

A. THE GOD WHO COMES

THERE is one great difference between what you have considered in previous *Studies* and the theme of the 'Last Things', to which we now turn. In this *Study*, the emphasis is upon an event (the Final Coming of our Lord) and an experience (life after death) which have not yet happened to us. Does this mean that we must rest content with saying, 'Ah well, we cannot know anything about them until they happen?' No, it does not mean that, for—as we shall see—the Christian's beliefs about things that have not yet occurred are *rooted in events that have already happened*. God has revealed Himself in His deeds in the past, and thus throws light on His action in the future. There are some facts concerning the Final Coming and the Life Beyond about which we can be quite sure. But on the other hand, we shall be wise if we mingle with our certainties a proper humility in the face of the mysteries of God.

1. *Time and Eternity*

We have just said that Christian thought about the Last Things is both confident and humble. A second paradox should now be noted. *The future is regarded by the Christian bi-focally*—in terms of Time and of Eternity. This may sound puzzling at first but it will become clearer as we proceed. For the moment it is enough to say that, as we look *forward* into the years still to come in this world of space and time, it is for the Lord's Final Coming that we look; and as we turn our minds *inwards*, to consider the unseen world of spiritual reality in which we already experience Christ here and now, it is to another kind of future that we are looking, the Heaven of His presence. Both views are needed, if we are to see clearly the range of God's activity on this earth and beyond.

2. *The God who will come—has come*

We have said that 'the Christian's beliefs about things that have not yet occurred are rooted in events that have already

* In this chapter, I have freely used material from my articles on the same theme in *PH* (3).

happened'. We only have the right to speak like that because of the central Christian claim that God has revealed His nature and will in the sacred events of the Bible pages; in His dealings with the People of Israel at home and in exile, in His Coming in Jesus Christ, and in His Spirit-filled Church. As our whole theology teaches us, the God who has thus revealed Himself is self-consistent; He does not change in character or intention.

a. *The same God.* So we declare that the God who will come at the last is the same God as the One who created all things 'in the beginning', and who in Christ reconciled all things unto Himself. However obvious this statement may appear to be, it carries important consequences for the way in which we may expect God's purposes to be fulfilled. (i) For example, it is plain, from what we have written above, that when the world ends, Time will not just peter out casually, but events will culminate under God's hand in clear meaning. It was this conviction that led the Jewish apocalyptic writers (in *Daniel, Enoch,* etc.) to cling fiercely to the view that God would vindicate Himself in history, even if that meant a triumphant upheaval at its close. We must never leave out of account the solemn yet bracing fact that at the End, as at the Beginning, God will be there; and where God is, there is meaning and holy love. (ii) Or, looking at the future from another point of view, the miracle of *Pentecost* declared that the God of the ages, who had come to men through the Incarnation and the Cross, now entered the very heart of believers in the fullness of His resurrection power and of the Holy Spirit. Christ dwells in the Church for ever! Thus His outward Coming at the end will only fulfil what is going on all the time through His Church, by way of mercy and judgement. Having entered history, He remains in it until He fulfils it. (iii) Similarly, we can be certain that in the experience which lies beyond death—whether issuing in Heaven or Hell—men will encounter the same God who has revealed Himself on the earthly stage. The One beyond the grave will bear the features of Jesus Christ, 'the same yesterday and today, yea and for ever'.

In these and other ways, the historic Coming of Christ among men throws shining light on His future dealings with us, when Time is no more. He is the same God, and is faithful to the end. He cannot deny Himself (2 Tim. 2^{13})!

b. *The God who ever comes.* It is important that we stress this 'comingness' of God. He is the God who ever comes. He does not just 'exist' in an abstract way. It is because men have often thought so, that God's purpose through history on the stage of Time has seemed to them unlikely to have any real climax or final meaning. The Bible calls us away from such feeble thinking. He who led Abraham into the land of promise (Gen. 12^1), and called Moses to deliver His oppressed people (Exod. 3^{10}), shaped that people of promise until the Day broke when—in spite of their blindness—Christ came into their midst. When they had crucified Him, He still came; in resurrection force and the Holy Spirit's coming. God was in the midst of His Church, and will be to the end of time, proclaimed by Word, and Sacraments and godly life. And all the time, meanwhile, He is coming in the personal spiritual life of those who are 'hid with Christ in God' (Col. 3^3). Thus Time and Eternity are inter-blended by the God who comes!

When we turn to a more detailed study of such matters as the Final Coming of Christ, the meaning of Heaven and Hell, and the Christian way of living in the light of the Last Things, we shall bear in mind the fact that He is always the same God, and the God who always comes. He is Alpha and Omega, the beginning and the end; from everlasting to everlasting, He is God.

B. THE FINAL COMING OF CHRIST
1. *Maran Atha*

This Aramaic phrase occurs in 1 Cor. 16^{22}, and means 'Our Lord cometh'. It stands at the end of this letter of Paul as a reminder to the Corinthians—and to us—that Christ will one day *return in finality*. In other passages, Paul affirms this same truth, and the same assertion is to be found (as we shall see) in many other parts of the New Testament. But the reason we have begun with Maran Atha is because this alien phrase from another tongue stands as a symbol to us of the fact that this doctrine of Christ's Final Coming is at first *foreign* to our modern ways of thinking; it challenges us to convey its meaning to our hearers by translating its sense into 20th-century terms which they can grasp. In order to do this, we shall first face some difficulties which the doctrine of the Parousia raises for some minds; then note the main things which the New Testament has to tell us about it; and finally observe that, if this doctrine is to live in our theology, it must live as a vivid certainty in our hearts.

2. Three difficulties

a. *Why need Jesus come?* 'After all', some thoughtful Christians say, 'Jesus has already come and brought us salvation through His Cross, His Resurrection and the coming of the Holy Spirit. What need is there for any further coming?' They point out, too, that in one of the greatest books of the New Testament (John's Gospel) there is much more stress on the eternal life that Christ can give *now*, than on any vindication of His glory at the end of the world. 'Surely', they add, 'there is no need for people of all generations to be rallied from the dead, to join the final generation of men in one great outward act of Judgement and Glory? Why can't the last of mankind meet God individually when they die, as all previous men have done, without this drawing of everyone together?' Some would reply with the simple answer that the Final Coming of Jesus is widely foretold in the New Testament—and that that settles the matter. But more may be said. The reason why the New Testament insists so strongly on the Final Coming of Christ seems to lie in the immense stress which the Bible lays on the sacredness of time, and on the oneness of the entire human race in God's purposes. Having begun a process of time with the personal act of creation, He will conclude it with His personal presence among men. And among *all* men—not merely the last generation. For the pattern which will then be revealed affects the whole race. So will Christ come, and in His Coming sum up the happenings of Time.

b. *And what about Science?* Scientists sometimes write of the possible end of this planet in extreme heat or cold; others make more general comment (which any of us might make) about the unpredictable end to which man's atomic control may lead. Now the question is, 'If the world is moving towards gradual or speedy annihilation, how are such tendencies related to the Final Coming?' To this we make the following answer. There is much, Jesus told us, that we *cannot* know about the time of His Coming (*see* Mk 13^{32}, Acts 1^7; and *ANT*), but of this we can be sure: that the times and seasons are 'within the Father's own authority'; *He* will determine whether to allow full span to the life of the planet, or to let man cut it short by his own sin and folly. He who is Lord of Lords is not at the mercy of human sin. The scientists have the right to make their estimate of the *physical* ends towards which this section of the universe is tending, so far as can be humanly judged; but they, like the rest of us, have to acknowledge ignorance of all the imponderable spiritual factors which lie deep in the heart and knowledge of God.

c. *Isn't Adventist teaching unbalanced?* A great deal of it is. The subject of the Last Things has often become the happy hunting-ground of religious cranks. The result has been that this doctrine (like the doctrine of Christian Perfection) has tended to be either ignored or caricatured. Every preacher knows how fatally easy it is to isolate texts of Scripture and make them mean what we want them to mean. This mistake has been sadly and repeatedly made in the treatment of the doctrine of the Final Coming. T. F. Glasson, in *His Kingdom and His Appearing*, has given us a list of these mistakes which makes sorry reading. Again and again, Christian thinkers have neglected our Lord's word about our essential ignorance of the date of His Coming, and have sought to interpret the various signs that are mentioned in the Gospels, the Epistles and *Revelation* (not to mention *Daniel*) in terms of *their* age and its events, saying, 'His Coming is about to take place'. We Christians today have less excuse than any of our predecessors for making this mistake, for Biblical scholarship has shown plainly that the passages which are most often used by such Adventists do not carry a distinctively Christian meaning about the End. In some cases they predict the Fall of Jerusalem (A.D. 70); in some cases they refer to the Coming of Christ at His Resurrection or at Pentecost (*see ANT, para.* 166); in other instances the passages are part and parcel of the first-century Jewish way of thinking of God's defeat of evil powers—a way of thinking which has produced such phrases as 'the man of sin', 'the abomination of desolation', and 'the thousand years'. The last group of passages should fall into the background of the Christian picture. This does not mean that we shall be any less *certain* of Christ's Coming, but only that we shall be more modest about claiming to know *when* it will be.

3. *The New Testament's witness*

New Testament study in recent years has firmly underlined the *unity* of the New Testament theology. This holds true in the main of its teaching about the Last Things, and about the Final Coming of Jesus in particular, despite differences of approach, expression and—most important—emphasis. The doctrine of the Final Advent does not hang on a few texts in Paul's earlier letters, with the energetic support of *Matthew* and *Revelation*. The chord 'Christ will come' rings right through the New Testament. It is organically part of the whole Book. In confirmation of this, notice the wide range of texts and passages mentioned in the course of the four declarations expounded below. At the risk of a little oversimplification, it can be said that the New Testament pages declare four great truths concerning Christ's Final Coming.

a. *He will come—to judge men.* One of the most solemn sentences in the Bible is found in 2 Cor. 5^{10}: 'For we must all be made manifest before the judgement-seat of Christ'. Whatever else our Lord will come to do, it will be to judge the hearts of men. This note is sounded throughout the New Testament. It is difficult to be sure whether this or that passage represents our Lord's own word, or whether it has been partly modified by the convictions of the writer; but there can be little doubt that this emphasis springs from Jesus Himself. Men's attitude to Him will determine their future destiny (Mt 10$^{32f.}$=Lk 12$^{8f.}$). Therefore they must ever be alert for His coming (Mt 24^{44}=Lk 12^{40}). It will have for them the solemn meaning which men attached in Old Testament times to 'the Day of Yahweh' (e.g. in Isa. 66^{18}; Zech. 14$^{3-5}$; Ps. 50$^{3-6}$, 96$^{10-13}$), although their Christian expectation will be purified by the kind of Lord they know Him to be.

The final judgement will be the same in principle and working as the verdict which began to operate when Jesus first came among men, and men refused the Light, preferring the darkness (Jn 3^{19}). No wonder that Paul calls his readers to cast off the works of darkness, since 'the day is at hand' (Rom. 13^{12}; and *see* 1 Thess. 1^{10}, 5^9; Rom. 1^{18}, 5^9; Phil. 1^{10}). This same message of coming judgement centring in Jesus, which we have noted in the Gospels and Paul's letters, runs through the other strands of the New Testament. We find it in Acts 10^{42}; 1 Pet. 4^5; Heb. 10^{29}; Revn. 5^9. Just 'because he is the Son of Man' (Jn 5^{27}), He 'shall judge the quick and the dead' (2 Tim. 4^1).

b. *He judges—because He loves.* If only men had always remembered the motive of divine judgement! There is no vengeful spirit in God; only a great longing to redeem, even at the cost of the bearing of sins (ponder Jn 3$^{17ff.}$). A man will be judged according to the light he has received. But if a man refuses such light, the love of God shines in judgement upon that refusal. Such loving judgement is more thorough and persistent than any lesser, harsher kind. Our Judge will not let us go. He who has suffered at the Cross with desolated heart will not rest content until men's guilt has been forgiven, and purged as well as exposed! What this may mean in terms of the place and purpose of Hell in God's purposes will be discussed later. This searching, importunate, seeking Love of God will—by its very nature—be more generously just in its judgements than any formal, impersonal Justice could prove to be. For example, there may well be instances in which human judgement on our fellows has been more stringent than the judgement of the most holy God. For He knows the opportunities which the criminal never had, and the immensely evil influences to which his soul, at an early uncared-for period, was dangerously open. We must not sentimentalise the love of God, but neither must we degrade His judgement till it seems compounded of something less than justice and something less than love. There are passages in the New Testament which represent a lower standard of spiritual insight than the rest. Such passages as Revn. 21⁸, 2 Thess. 1⁸, and certain verses of the Parable of the Sheep and the Goats (Mt 25³¹ff.) are dangerous if they are isolated. (On this subject, *see PH* (3) pp. 52–3, 67).

But the loving God is searching in His judgement. Pride, bitterness (*see* Mt 6¹⁵), lovelessness and all the sad and sordid 'works of the flesh' (Gal. 5¹⁹ff.) will be revealed for what they are. Nothing will escape His eye; and no genuine desire towards goodness and truth, in whatever unexpected quarter, will escape His mercy. The 'wrath of God' (*see ANT, para.* 451) is never at variance with His love; for divine wrath resists the power of evil, *at all co to Himself as well as to its objects*. He will not let us go, till we are purged and clean. 'It is a fearful thing to fall into the hands of the living God' (Heb. 10³¹); until you hear Him say, 'Him that cometh to me I will in no wise cast out' (Jn 6³⁷).

c. *He will come with glory.* One of the strangest and most important Gospel sayings is found in Mk 14⁶²: 'Ye shall see the Son of Man sitting at the right hand of power, and coming with the clouds of heaven' (*see ANT*). It strikes a note which the New Testament often sounds about His coming; it will be with power and triumph.

'The power and the glory' of the Coming of Christ (Mk 13²⁶) caught the eager imagination of the Christians through the centuries; but His coming may be quieter than we think. His power and His glory are eternally humble. He who stooped to die, and

THE LAST THINGS 221

found His glory in the Cross, does not change. It would seem that this final splendour of Christ will lie in the revelation, in all its magnificence, of *what it means to love the world*. The Lamb is in the midst of the throne (Revn. 5⁶). It is because His divinity and humbleness are held so closely together, that the New Testament can attribute to Jesus all the glory of the Lord, of Yahweh, of 'the God who comes'—as we have described Him. It is against this inspired spiritual background that the celestial desscription of 1 Thess. 4¹⁶f. and 1 Cor. 15⁵¹ff. must be set. The shout, the voice of the archangel, the trump, the clouds convey the thought of the very Presence of God.

d. *He will not come alone.* The New Testament does not isolate Jesus from His Church, at any stage. The Son of Man and the Church are visibly drawn together at the end, as they have been inwardly one through all the years in Christian history. The Church has been the Bride of Christ (Eph. 5²⁵ff.), has indeed been the Body of Christ (1 Cor. 12¹²; Eph. 1²²f.; *see* pp. 164f., above) all through the centuries. By her Sacraments and her membership in Christ, she stands as a living witness to the supernatural work of her ascended Lord, 'till he come' (1 Cor. 11²⁶). At His Coming, she will be joined to Him for all to see, an immense multitude of 'the church of the firstborn' (Heb. 12²³). This does not excuse the Church from the searching judgement of her Lord. Those who are nearest Him will be the most willing to be weighed and sifted by such love. And judgement begins with the household of God (*see* 1 Pet. 4¹⁷ and pp. 183.f, above). But in the very act of judging His believing people, He gathers them to Himself. They will need no word of command to muster to Him. They have been 'in Christ' on earth, they will be with Him after death; and now, united with the last generation of Christians on the earth (*see* 1 Thess. 4¹⁴ff.; 1 Cor. 15⁵¹ff.), they see each other and themselves in company with the Son of Man. Only such a vista suffices to describe either the Church or the Son of Man. Even He is not His completed person, save with His people. How could it be otherwise?

These, then, are four of the great New Testament declarations about Christ's Final Coming. In the light of the difficulties with which we began, and these declarations which we have just studied, are we now in a position to believe and expound this doctrine with the confidence of our fathers? To this question, we now turn.

4. *A Humble, Vivid Certainty*

It is clear that this doctrine finds a strong place in the New Testament, and this ought to make us accept it as part of our heritage. But do we receive it with eagerness and gratitude? Is it a vivid certainty, as well as a formally acknowledged doctrine? Our answer may well depend on further factors which we must now briefly mention.

a. The doctrine of the Final Coming of Jesus grows in significance for us, the more we ponder the deep meaning of His *First Coming*. If we regard the end as merely a 'happy ending', to prove rather belatedly to the world that Pilate was wrong and that Jesus was right—then, while that is good, it does not go very deep. But if we see that, by His Incarnation, Jesus was already *'breaking the back' of history by coming as a Man among men*, then the subsequent story of the Church presents, for all eyes to see, the work of the victorious Lord. In among all our Church divisions and individual disloyalties, One is at work who raised Christ from the dead, and has smitten the powers of evil a blow which is eternal (*see* pp. 74f. and 79f., above). The Final Coming is then discovered as the last of a series of Mighty Acts, gathering up the noticed and unnoticed triumphs of God in a final, meek, but absolute disclosure of His Person and His Grace.

b. The other point affecting the vividness of our confidence is a psychological one. When men think of God's dealings at the end of Time, they are inclined to picture Him in cold and cruel terms. R. H. Charles well described this human tendency when he wrote, 'Eschatological beliefs' (i.e. beliefs about the End) 'are universally the last of all beliefs to be influenced by the loftier conceptions of God'. We must allow, then, for this inclination of the mind as it considers the majesty of Christ's Coming. Although the thought that He will come is a sobering one, recalling us to the fact that we are 'unprofitable servants', it is also a joyous expectation! It is Jesus Christ who will come! Infinitely tender as well as utterly holy, His gentleness is eternal. Once we lose this warm, sweet, tender note from our theology of the End, we have lost its very heart.

We can be certain, then, of the Coming of our Lord. Firmly rooted in the New Testament, re-interpreted in terms of our own day, this doctrine proclaims to men the truth that History will not be allowed to peter out; that Jesus will be central at the End, as at the Beginning; and that all the Church of believers will be joyfully united in Him. 'In His own way and in His own time God will finally judge the world through Christ, sum up all things in Him, and establish His Kingdom for ever' (*CAT* 16). Humbly, yet vividly, we can pray, 'Come, Lord Jesus'.

C. HEAVEN

As we have said (*see* p. 214), the Christian looks at the future bi-focally. Having considered the Final Coming, we now turn to the question of *Heaven*, and in the next section to that of *Hell*.

1. *Heaven is the Presence of God*

We must define in simple terms what we mean by Heaven. It is the place where God dwells. This may sound an over-simplified description, and in one sense it is misleading to call Heaven a place, for—by its very nature—it occupies no geographical position in time or space; but it reminds us that the essence of Heaven is not what we feel or know, but the objective fact that *God is there*. 'Fullness of life and eternal joy with all believers' is 'in the Presence of God, which is Heaven' (*CAT* 39). And as the Presence of God is focussed for Christians in the Presence of Christ, we may further say that by Heaven we mean 'the near presence of God in Christ, shared and known by believers'.

It is plain that, in a real sense, Heaven has already begun for the Church on earth. Christ has come to men; in His life and death and resurrection, the light has already shined (2 Cor. 4^6), and the Kingdom has arrived. Now that the Holy Spirit has been received, Christ dwells and works in men's believing hearts. No wonder that Paul talks of Christians living in 'heavenly places' (Eph. 2^6), and that John reports the promise of Jesus that we can abide in Him, here and now (Jn 15^4), and enter into eternal life (Jn 3$^{15f.}$, 6^{47}). Although we have not the privilege of the early disciples in knowing Jesus in the flesh, yet we know Him in the power of His resurrection and the fellowship of His sufferings (Phil. 3^{10}), and have been called by Him out of darkness into His marvellous light (1 Pet. 2^9). Peter can write to his readers of the Christ 'whom, not having seen, ye love' (1 Pet. 1^8). Although we are still on earth, with its limitations and frailties, we are already citizens of Heaven (Phil. 3^{20}; Lk 10^{20}).

If all this begins to be true *now*, how infinitely more wonderful will be the full experience of Heaven. If to live is Christ, death means more Christ (Phil. 1^{21}). But how can we begin to portray the glories of Heaven? In the interests of clarity, we must try to say what it will mean, but we must remember that, in the experience of meeting God in Christ, there will be elements of poetry and joy which no words can express.

2. *Heaven will mean unfettered Adoration*

Here on earth we live by faith, there we shall see Him 'face to face' (1 Cor. 13^{12}); here we seek to know His truth and beauty, there we shall meet them with glad delight. Here we try to give ourselves to Him, there we shall lose ourselves in the wonder of self-giving. We shall see Him even as He is (1 Jn 3^2), and worship and *adore*. As individuals, but much more as a company in Christ, we shall 'cry with a great voice, saying, Salvation unto our God which sitteth on the throne, and unto the Lamb' (Revn. 7^{10}).

3. *Heaven will mean a deep fellowship with one another in Christ*

That sentence is an attempt to convey the idea of a supernaturally wonderful comradeship with Christ, and in Him with one another. Our fellowship in Him here below is only a foretaste and first instalment of our communion with Him in Heaven. The barriers of our earthly sin and ignorance will be swept away. Men and women of all nations and all generations will find their centre *in Him*. What a vivid, joyous and colourful assembly it will be! Each one will bring his own precious quota—himself—to the scene, and all will be enriched by all. 'All are yours; and ye are Christ's; and Christ is God's' (1 Cor. 3$^{22f.}$).

4. *Heaven will mean the perfect delight of doing God's Will*

Just as Jesus called His men in Galilee, both that they might be with Him and that they might work for Him (Mk 3$^{14f.}$), so in Heaven worship and activity will be one. Some speak as though Heaven means doing nothing for ever and ever. Peace there will be certainly, in wondrous depths; but, just because we are in peaceful harmony with God, we shall want to serve Him and *work* as joyous sons. He is a God who works (Jn 5^{17}), and we are His servants, His friends. Shall we wish to sit idle, while He toils alone? And if we are asked what kind of work it will be, we would answer that it will include the fulfilling of all satisfying and creative work that man has known—and, further, that it will have at its heart prayer and seeking love. There may well be a profound sense in which Heaven's work may share God's travail over unredeemed souls.

These are some of the plain glories of Heaven; everything centring in adoration ... and in Jesus ... in doing God's will ... and the whole, over-arched and under-girded by the love of God. But it is of the very nature of Heaven that we can only partly describe it. 'It is not yet made manifest what we shall be' (1 Jn 3^2). We walk by faith, not by sight (2 Cor. 5^7). Much of Heaven is 'beyond words' (2 Cor. 12^4; 1 Cor. 2^9). We are conscious of this as we try to express a further truth which we can dimly see.

5. *In Heaven, we shall have Spiritual Bodies*

Here we are reminded of Paul's answer to the question, 'What happens to our bodies after death?' When our natural, material bodies are laid aside at death, they are replaced by their *spiritual counterparts*; it is these that are raised at the last day. 'It is sown a natural body; it is raised a spiritual body' (*see* 1 Cor. 15^{44}, and *ANT*). The striking phrase 'spiritual body' serves to emphasise three things. (i) In Heaven life will not be ghostly. The Bible does not think of the body as belonging only to our earthly life; its spiritual equivalent is ours for ever. We shall be *persons*, there as here, each with our own self, distinct and real. (ii) In the Heavenly life, we shall be able to communicate with each other. Just as on earth the physical body provides the means (mouth, ears, eyes, hands, etc.) by which we have communication with each other, so in Heaven those who are in Christ will be in full conversation with each other, and able to talk, and laugh, and listen. (iii) Heaven is not only as real as, but *more real than* the life of earth. This truth is firmly underlined in *Hebrews*. The unseen world is the real world. And, of course, a spiritual body is more real than a physical one.

The question may arise, 'What will happen to those whose earthly bodies were maimed or shattered?' That question has only to be asked, to be *partly* answered—for our 'spiritual bodies' will not depend on the condition at death of their earthly counterpart.

Again, we may be asked, 'Will people appear or a certain age or aspect in their spiritual bodies? Will a mother know her son as a baby, or as a man? And what of the baby whose full personality never unfolds on earth; or the person whose mind is slow in developing?' All such questions, when reverently asked, demand the outline of an answer, if we can give it. We can surely say that 'up there' personality will not be tied to time. We shall not appear old or young, but rather *alive*—with the vitality of youth and the maturity of age; and the more we advance in spiritual wisdom, the more we shall develop the two qualities of vitality and maturity. As regards the child who is not fully-grown, or the person who is mentally retarded, can we believe anything less than that God will give to them (as He will to those who have never heard His name on earth) full opportunity to develop in mind and soul? Those who are 'little ones' in mind or body must be specially dear to His heart.

When all has been thought and said, the chief wonder and reward of Heaven is that we shall be with God in Christ. All else is centred in that. The unfading crown of glory (1 Pet. 5^4), the wreath that does not fade (1 Cor. 9^{25}), the treasure in Heaven (Mt 5^{12}, $6^{1, 4, 6, 18, 20}$; Lk 6^{35}), is the presence of the King of Love and the Shepherd of our souls.

Note on Spiritualism

There seems to be a fairly widespread feeling that Spiritualism has something constructive to offer in this field. But, however natural it may be for those who have been bereaved to turn to any source which proffers comfort or seeks to lift the veil, it must be said, and emphatically, that the Christian Church does not look in this direction for its solaces, but to the revelation of God in Christ. While spiritualistic phenomena are a proper field of enquiry for scientific research, and for those who are suitably equipped and mentally balanced, they do not offer lasting spiritual assurance and comfort. In *Psychology, Religion and Healing*, Leslie D. Weatherhead confirms the judgement expressed in an earlier book, that 'Spiritualism has not made a single definite, valuable, or original contribution to Christian thought concerning that life' (i.e. life after death).

Note on Immortality

Quite good reasons can be brought forward to support belief in survival after death. For example, it is hardly likely that God would create human souls to live for only a few years on earth, and then to flicker out. Again, beyond the grave, injustices on earth could be remedied. But the *Bible* speaks in terms of Eternal Life, rather than of bare survival.

D. HELL

Here too we must begin with a definition of what we mean by the word. In our A.V. Bibles, the word 'Hell' is used rather confusedly for two Greek words, 'Hades' and 'Gehenna'; but in the Revised Version the proper distinction is made. *Hades* means the 'after-life' in general terms, and is roughly equivalent to 'Sheol' in the Old Testament; a shadowy sub-existence after death for good and bad people alike. It was mainly in the period between the Testaments that the distinctions between Heaven and Hell emerged clearly in Jewish thought. *Gehenna* is the word which will concern us here. Hell, or Gehenna, can be described as 'the place after death where a man begins to feel the force of his unrepented sins in terms of the holiness of God'. As when talking of Heaven, we must add at once that the word 'place' in that sentence has no geographical meaning, but describes a relationship outside time and space.

Already we are in the midst of our subject, for at once questions are raised in our minds. 'How does this experience relate to the love of God?' 'What happens to people in Hell, if they do not repent?' 'Isn't Hell to do with refusing the Gospel of Christ, rather than with just repenting of our general sins?' We shall bear such questions in mind, both as we consider men's hesitations about the doctrine, and as we ponder the teaching itself.

1. *Hesitations about the Doctrine of Hell*

Many preachers hesitate to preach about Hell; and indeed there are at least two good reasons for such hesitation.

a. *Preaching about Hell has often been exaggerated*; so exaggerated that it has become a caricature of the New Testament message. Doctrines have been proclaimed as Christian which have in fact been cruel and unjust. This mistake has often been made by isolating very severe texts (e.g. Revn. 20^{15}; 2 Thess. 1^8) from the complete New Testament witness. In violent reaction to such abuses, many have thought that the subject of Hell is best left alone, and have not preached about it; but such a view swings to the other extreme. There is no doubt, as we have seen (pp. 219f.), that God's judgement awaits men after death. The exaggerations, mentioned above, would not have been preached if men had not credited God with motives or actions which would be considered unworthy of a good man.

b. *The word Hell (Gehenna) is not a common New Testament word.* This is true; except for one passing reference (Jas 3^6), the word is not used in the New Testament outside the pages of the Gospels. Indeed, even in the Gospels, it is only found in four contexts: Mk $9^{43ff.}$ and parallels; Mt 10^{28}=Lk 12^5; Mt 5^{22}; Mt $23^{15, 33}$. (The one Scripture reference to Hell, given in the *Senior Catechism*, is the passage in Mk 9.) This fact in itself should make us pause before speaking dogmatically about the *details* of Hell. As Reinhold Niebuhr says, with a touch of humour, 'It is unwise for Christians to claim any knowledge of either the furniture of heaven or the temperature of hell'.

This does *not* mean that we should dismiss this doctrine as unimportant. The Gospel references are sayings of Jesus Himself; though it should be noted that, in one or two of these quoted sayings, non-Christian influences have affected their present form. Again, though Paul and other New Testament writers do not use the word 'Gehenna', they most certainly emphasise the judgement of God after death. Let us, therefore, try to interpret the message concerning Hell in the New Testament. It seems to involve four main truths.

2. *Four Truths about Hell*

a. *A man faces his self-centredness after death.* Hell is the pain of being accused as guilty before God after death. This is the truth of the *pangs* of Hell. In their zeal, earnest Christians have sometimes seized on vivid Biblical phrases, like 'where their worm dieth not and the fire is not quenched', to suggest that Hell means physical fire and anguish. Not only is such an idea degrading to the love of God, but it obscures the fact that spiritual pains are more searching, just because they are gentler, than violent physical inflictions. No wonder that Paul warns his readers against such an experience (Rom. 2^5); or that our Lord warns men so sternly against the same tragedy. The main passage we must study has already been mentioned; Mk 9^{43-8}. There Jesus says that it is better for a man to enter into the life of the Kingdom of God with one hand, one foot, one eye, rather than to go to Gehenna entire and unmutilated. What do these solemn words describe? 'Jesus used an accepted idea of His time. He is not to be credited with later ideas of eternal punishment which are alien to His teaching concerning God and man; but, on the other hand, His words must not be explained away as a picturesque metaphor. By contrast with the phrase 'to enter into life', the words 'to go into Gehenna' indicate spiritual ruin and perhaps destruction' (Vincent Taylor*). It is this peril that faces those who allow one aspect of life ('hand', 'foot', 'eye') to gain the priority over God, and thus to turn them away from the road to life eternal. Their self-centredness has to be faced after death in the presence of God. This is more than remorse, which can be a self-centred emotion. It is the pronouncement of guilt.

b. *Hell is not the automatic destiny of the non-Christian.* Who, then, is destined to go to Hell, according to the Bible? Is 'the wrath to come' (Mt 3^7; Lk 3^7) only avoided by those who trust in Christ? This strict view has certainly been widely held, and it reminds us of a very important truth—that a man's soul cannot reach pardon and life except in Jesus Christ. But the harsh statement that every one who (for whatever reason) has not yet accepted Jesus Christ will go straight to Hell at death cannot be said to be widely accepted today as representing the message of the Bible. It is too sweeping, and, although it may seem to find support from a few individual texts, it does not do justice to the range of God's grace and justice. It over-simplifies the issue. For example, what of the people, including those who lived before His time, who have never even heard of Jesus Christ? And again, what of those who have heard of Him—vaguely, perhaps—but have never had the Gospel plainly and winsomely presented to them? And what of those who, having heard the Gospel, have seen the insincerity of so-called Christians, and have reached the wrong conclusion—that 'there's nothing in it'? Further, what of those who, through illness, extreme poverty, mental slowness or other factors, have been (partially at least) hindered from making the Gospel their own?

These questions, and others like them, remind us that only an unjust God would send every unbeliever to Hell. We have touched upon one or two of these questions when referring to the 'spiritual bodies' of believers (p. 225). Two further comments may be added. (i) It seems quite plain from the Scriptures that the Old Testament patriarchs, who of course had never heard of Jesus, are with God in Heaven (Lk $13^{28\text{ff.}}$; Mk $12^{26\text{f.}}$). They responded to the light which they had received with boldness and faith (Heb. 11). (ii) It surely springs from the very heart of the Gospel that all those who, for reasons outside their personal control, have not heard the Good News of Christ will be given

* *The Gospel according to St Mark*, p. 411.

the opportunity to hear and understand in the world beyond death. It does not follow that all such will say 'Yes' to the revelation of God's grace. Because of the character of God, we may be sure that, even in eternity, the Gospel will be proclaimed to such people in such a way that they will be *free* to say 'Yes' or 'No' to God's offer of Eternal Life.

We must never forget that our God is always just and more than just. Although He never ceases to be completely holy, He is never anything less than loving. It may suit our tidy minds to put all people into two categories—going straight to Heaven, or Hell—but life is not so simple as that.

What, then, is the principle by which, humanly speaking, we can know who is tending towards Hell? Remembering our Lord's warning to us about judging others (Mt 7[1]), we may declare that Hell is for those who refuse the light that reaches them. The more light we have, the graver our responsibility (Mt 11[21ff.]=Lk 10[12ff.]). Any man who is shown any truth at all is in danger of some form of Hell after death, if he does not accept and embrace that truth (Rom. 2[1]). Truth is sacred, and of God; and men are responsible beings. When we preach an amazing Gospel of the redeeming love of God in Christ, we should ask people to pause long—before glibly accepting it, or lightly passing it by. For here is sacred truth incarnate! To receive or to deny Him is to receive or deny God. The salvation which shines so brightly from the Cross casts the darkest shadow on those who pass it by. It is a grave responsibility, as well as a high privilege, to hear the Gospel.

c. *The purpose of Hell is redemptive.* At first sight this seems a strange statement, and yet it springs from the very heart of the Gospel. The pains of Hell are a judgement (p. 228). They are part of the experience of being shown or discovering the reality of guilt. What follows, then? If God were an unfeeling Judge, bare justice could be satisfied by the sentence and the punishment; but the Judge is a Saviour. He cannot, therefore, by His very nature, stop short of any action which may bring His rebellious child back to Him. Having led His stubborn sons and daughters towards a sense of guilt, can He refrain from offering them pardon also? If, therefore, our preaching is to be fully Christian, we must declare that, even while men are suffering in Hell, God is loving them still. It is largely because theologians have not kept closely linked the doctrines of Hell and the Love of God,

THE LAST THINGS

that abuses and neglects have crept in. The Roman doctrine of purgatory as the place where the faults of backsliders are punished and the penitents are duly purified (aided by prayers, 'indulgences' and the celebration of the Mass by those still alive) is not acceptable to us because of its superstitious errors and abuses; *but* at least it stands as a protest (however limited and perverted) against confining the influences of grace within the bounds of Heaven.

We have said that the purpose of Hell is redemptive; we must add, however, that there is little *detailed* evidence by way of texts to support and amplify that statement. There is one passage (1 Pet. $3^{18\text{ff.}}$) which *may* describe the love of Christ as seeking men after death—but its meaning is not certain (*see* p. 75n.). There is, too, Paul's conviction that the day will come when all things will be summed up in Christ (1 Cor. 15^{22}; Rom. 11^{32}; Phil. 2^{10}), which may imply that all *men*, as well as all *things*, will finally be purged and redeemed. But the main reason for our statement lies in the Cross itself, and the whole direction in which redemption moves. God cannot deny Himself; and God loves men with a deathless love. Such love cannot shrug its shoulders and cease to care. He will love men to the end.

d. *Hell may lead to spiritual Death.* Does this seem to contradict what we have just said? Surely, you may say, if God loves men to the end, that settles the matter, and all men will finally be redeemed. If we came to such a conclusion, we should be less than fair, either to the New Testament, or to the freedom of man's will. What we have said in the previous section concerns the motive and intention of God in permitting the pangs of Hell. And we may indeed *hope* that men will so respond that no one will finally be unredeemed. But there is the dread *possibility* that some, like the Elder Brother of the Prodigal, may refuse to come in; in which case, they are moving towards spiritual death or destruction. The New Testament warns us of such a danger. The process can begin on earth, and no doubt continues beyond death. Perdition is a real possibility for men (Phil. 3^{19}; *see* also Mt 7^{13}; Jn 15^6; Rom. 2^5; 2 Thess. 1^9; Heb. 6^8). And when our Lord solemnly warns men of the sin against the Holy Spirit (*see ANT, para.* 113), He is speaking in similar vein. The human spirit, it seems, can sin so often against goodness that in the end it may sin against the *very idea of goodness*; so that, even when all the glories of Heaven's joys and the splendour of God's self-giving are placed before it, it turns stiffly and proudly away.

Just as the 'spiritual bodies' of those who are in Heaven find their vitality in Christ, so the spiritual equipment of the hard, bitter, self-centred man will grow increasingly weak and poor, if he persists in the refusal of goodness and God—until *he may cease to be*. The final tragedy of Hell is not anguish, but the missing of the life and glory of God.

In discussing such a grave subject, we are bound to include a measure of speculation. The preacher is advised to take these thoughts as a basis of reflection, and to turn back in the light of them to the Bible itself, looking up the references which have been given. (You will notice, by the way, that the Bible is much more concerned with the positive joy of Heaven, than with the exact destination of every non-believer.) As you consider this subject, the controlling figure in your thought must be the God who gives us free-will, and who gave Himself for the world.

E. LIVING IN THE LAST DAYS

So far, we have been thinking of the Last Things as doctrines; but *doctrine is to be lived as well as believed*.

For us, as Christians, the centuries between the First and Last Coming of Christ are only an interval, bridging the hidden triumph of the Cross and the obvious victory of Christ when all things are completed in Him. And the Christian Church is the Community of this Interval. How, then, should this Christian Community live 'in the last days'?

1. *Be ready!*

The Church should never forget that Christ has said, 'Watch therefore: for ye know not when the lord of the house cometh' (Mk 13^{35}). It is so easy for the Church to be less than the Church; to become conventional, unevangelical, exclusively denominational, petty. We rise towards our full status when we recall that the Church acts its role within the drama which Christ began and which He will close. In this lies the glory and the awful challenge of the Church's position. Upon it the 'ends of the ages are come' (1 Cor. 10^{11}). 'Wherefore', adds Paul, 'let him that thinketh he standeth take heed lest he fall.'

2. *Be Spirit-filled!*

The Church and the Christian alike need no longer remain in spiritual despair and weakness, for the Spirit has come. This was

a gift that belonged very much to the 'last days' (Acts 2¹⁶ᶠ·).
The Church of the Interval has the gift, till the between-time is
over, and the Lord finally comes. In some centuries, she lets the
Spirit fill her with great power; at other periods she flags and
fails, weak and divided: but the energising, unifying Spirit is
always there—if she will receive Him. When she does, her goodness is no longer a list of purely negative virtues, but is the harvest
of the Spirit, sown and matured by the love of God. So let the
Holy Spirit fill the Church!

3. *In the struggle with evil—rejoice!*

It is because the Church bears the Kingdom of God to men
that it becomes involved in combat with evil. 'Rejoice, and be
exceeding glad . . . for so persecuted they the prophets which
were before you' (Mt 5¹²). Let us be under no illusion. If we
represent Christ faithfully, we shall be in conflict with the evil
powers. Surrounded by an interceding Church, the persecuted
believer prays to stand fast, remembering that our 'redemption
draweth nigh'.

4. *Expect problems of compromise*

The word 'compromise' is used in two different senses. For the
first, the lowering of standards of truth or goodness to win cheap
approval, the Church can have no use. But the second meaning,
in a Christian context, is very different, and much nobler: the
bringing of the challenge of the Gospel so close to the complex
problems of life, that new questions of how to apply it are created,
and (at the time maybe) only partially solved. For example, it is
easy to exhort one another to love our fellow-man; but how hard
it is to express that love in real terms, if our 'neighbour' is on the
other side of a political and economic curtain of mistrust. There
will be times when we shall almost despair—both as individuals,
and as a society of Christians in a non-Christian world—as we
seek to apply the Christian way of life to situations which are
complicated by human rebellion and folly. We must *share* in the
sense of human sinfulness which such situations involve; but we
must never forget the supernatural challenge, 'Ye therefore shall
be perfect' (Mt 5⁴⁸). In humble dependence on God, we seek
to bring His Kingdom to the world, praying both 'Forgive us
our trespasses', and 'Thy kingdom come!'

Sermon XXVIII. UPON OUR LORD'S SERMON ON THE MOUNT: DISCOURSE XIII

Theme of the Sermon. To show that the religion of the Sermon on the Mount is founded on the religion of the heart.

EXPLANATORY OUTLINE OF THE SERMON

Introduction. The Text. (1–3) Our Lord's conclusion to His Sermon on the Mount is cited, and is to be expounded.

I. *What it is to say: 'Lord, Lord.'* (1) This includes all religion, however sincere, which is merely in the mouth: orthodoxy, the saying many prayers, preaching, including even earnest preaching which may convert many sinners. (Notice Wesley's modest spirit in the last sentence of this paragraph.) (2) It includes blameless conduct, and (3) many sincere works of piety and charity. (4) Those who are astonished to hear it said that a man can do all this without being Justified before God do not understand the essential principle of the Christian faith. (5, 6) Jesus emphasized this very principle, and insisted that the heart must be right with God. (Some may find it almost self-contradictory that Wesley can speak of a man having a heart not right before God, i.e. not possessed of 'the faith which works by love', who is yet *sincere* in his good works, piety, and Gospel preaching. Admittedly Wesley is trying to make his point plain by an extreme example, but the truth he is driving at has already been observed in the sermon on 'The Almost Christian'. It is a Christian commonplace that God requires not only obedience, but obedience from the right motive. Wesley insists that this 'right motive' must be nothing less than that of warm personal love toward God. This alone is 'a heart right with God', 'the faith that works by love' and 'altogether Christianity'. That stern sense of duty which prompts a man diligently to apply himself to the service of God may be quite sincere, but stern duty alone is only 'the faith of a servant', not 'the faith of a son'. It is 'almost Christianity'. In his earnestness to enforce what is admittedly the *full* Christian experience, and the proper aspiration of the awakened Christian, Wesley at times seems to speak as though the 'almost Christians', with their lower order of 'sincerity', were not in possession of Justifying Faith, and were not in the Kingdom. However, he does not really intend to preach the damnation of such. The *interest* of his argument is not to damn 'almost Christians' in their admitted goodness, but to spur them on to the full evangelical experience. It has to be admitted that not a few upright, useful, and honoured members of the Church are 'strangers to the whole religion of Jesus Christ' as defined in (4).

II. *What it is to be 'Built upon the Rock'.* (1, 2) This man has been deeply convicted of the guilt and power of sin, he is humble and patient, the love of God is shed abroad in his heart, God is his sole treasure. (3) His sole hope is in the grace of God, and in the atoning work of Christ. (4) He will certainly be tempted, but in this strength will not fall.

III. *A Summons to the Religion of the Heart.* (1) The vanity of trusting for salvation in orthodoxy or sound Church principles, in (2) a harmless life, in (3) the use of the means of grace, in (4) works of charity and of evangelism. Does your preaching result in conversions? You still need to make sure that you yourself have saving faith. (5) Yet the most perilous snare of all is 'faith' which does not issue in sanctification, which does not produce works. (6, 7) The call to conviction of sin, and penitence, (8) to inward and outward meekness, and (9) to the laying up treasure in heaven. (10) The call to love of all mankind, (11) to purity and humility. (12) The appeal: 'let thy religion be the religion of the heart.'

NOTE

In order that you may have time for the adequate revision of your previous work, no Test Questions are included in this final *Study*.

REMINDER

You are reminded that, before you can be received on Full Plan, you must have read the 'Forty-Four Sermons of Wesley' (and not only the 12 Sermons selected for special study), and be able to give general approval to them as a standard of faith.

Appendix

BELIEF IN GOD

There are two alternatives. *Either* the universe is the work of a creative, purposive Mind, *or* it is the result of the play of mindless, physical forces. Which alternative is the most adequate explanation of the world we know? The following lines of thought suggest an answer.

1. *The evidence from Nature*

There are two traditional lines of reasoning for the existence of God. The first seeks to answer the question, 'How did the *world* of nature come into being at all?' The second, in its modern form, stresses the order and design in nature, and reasons that these are evidence that the world is not the product of blind, capricious forces, but is the creation of a supreme, *purposive* Mind.

a. The former argument affirms that, as we go back farther and farther in time to explain the existence of the universe, we must at last suppose a first cause—and that cause must be a creative spirit, God. It has always been recognized that this line of thought would be immeasurably strengthened if evidence could be secured which would show that there was a time when the natural world did not exist, and that it has come into being by some act or process of creation. It is just this evidence which modern research is supplying. Two scientific doctrines of creation has been advanced in the last quarter of a century. The first asserts that the universe had a beginning in time, about ten thousand million years ago. The second asserts that Creation is continually taking place as new atoms are formed. In either case, the question remains: 'How did or does the act of creation take place? Where did or does the creative impulse come from?' The religious mind asserts that it could only come from the creative Mind, God.

This argument becomes more emphatic when we recognize that Creation involves the creation of *life* itself, with all that life involves at its highest levels, of thought, of emotion, of the forming of judgements of values, and of the ability to undertake acts of will. If the atheist says that life simply came out of dead matter, he is not solving the puzzle, but only re-stating it. The theist, i.e. the man who believes in God, asserts that mindless forces could not have produced life; that only a living God, Himself the source of all life, could have created it.

b. The second argument starts from the fact of the world's orderliness, and reasons that this is indicative of *purpose*, and that purpose implies a Mind, in which it is born and by which it is made effective.

The strength of this argument can be understood even more clearly when we consider the suggestion, made by some people, that the universe is a *great machine*, subject to unbreakable laws, and that therefore it must exclude God. This is a completely wrong conclusion, for the evidence on which the argument is built points unmistakably to a Creator. Machines are not made by chance but only by purposive minds. The simplest tool, the flint handaxe of primitive man, is a witness to the mind which created it. The way in which it is chipped shows that it was not made by the chance rubbing of stone on stone, but that it was fashioned deliberately by a man who had a purpose in view. The complex machines of modern times witness even more emphatically to the fact that minds conceived and created them. Blind forces could not have smelted the ores, refined the metals, gathered them at the right spot at the right time, moulded, forged and cut them into shape, and then assembled the parts into the complicated machine. Every machine is a witness to the fact that designing minds conceived it and directed the work which produced it. The orderly nature of the machine—the fact that it both works according to natural laws, and also uses such laws to do useful work for man—is to us the evidence that some designer made it. As we look at the universe, then, and see its order and dependability, so like a great Machine, we are impressed with fresh evidence that it is the handiwork of a purposive Mind.

Many find their belief in teleology strengthened by the theory of *Evolution*. This theory, briefly stated, holds that the varied species of living things were not created separately, one by one, but that the more complex developed from the more simple by the transformation and transmutation of species already existing. The critical point in the conception of evolution is that the later forms of life are more complex in every way than the earlier;

and that in time *man himself* has emerged, with all the complexity of mental and spiritual equipment which marks him off from the beasts.

No one can say how the changes have occurred, or why, or what forces helped to bring them about; but of the broad principle of evolution there would seem to be little doubt. The principle leaves us with a problem. Where did the impetus come from which first created life, and then worked in and through the emergence of ever more complex forms of living things, until mankind at last came into being? Dead matter cannot provide an explanation. The only reasonable explanation lies in a *purposive Mind*, the source of life, whose ways of working the evolutionary process makes a little clearer.

The fuller implications of this line of reasoning will now be seen, as we proceed to consider the spiritual values which guide and inspire our human life.

2. *The existence and compulsion of Spiritual Values*

When man emerged in the world, there appeared a creature with the power to appreciate *spiritual values*, and to feel the inward *compulsion to seek them* at whatever cost. These values are aptly summarised in the familiar triad of Truth, Beauty and Goodness. They are only meaningful for conscious, rational and responsible beings, and point to a Creative Mind from whom they come; a Mind also conscious, rational and responsible.

a. *Their existence*. We can distinguish between *truth* and falsehood. When we admit that we have told a lie, when we say that a speech has been accurately reported or that a scientific theory is in strict agreement with all the observed facts, we recognize that there is difference between what is true and what is false. Any particular scientific theory may be 'true' to all the observed facts, even though all the related facts have not been noted. Nevertheless, scientific advance depends on the conviction that there is ultimately a 'true' picture of the universe, actually corresponding to *all* the facts. Further, we can appreciate *beauty*. We inwardly respond to the peace or grandeur of a landscape, the loveliness of a face in the glow of youth or in the serenity of age, the spell of haunting music, or a great work of art; and we know that there is a difference between beauty and ugliness. In man, again, there has emerged a creature who can distinguish between *goodness* and moral evil, and with a conscience which shows him the difference between what is right and what is wrong in conduct; and this power to distinguish between good and evil, right and wrong, does not depend on the conventions of society, or what at any time men may think *is* good and right.

If, then, these supreme spiritual 'values' of Truth, Beauty and Goodness are not transitory, accidental illusions of the human mind, but 'absolute' values—i.e. part of the very nature of things and grounded in the structure of ultimate reality—does it not follow that the source of these values is a divine Being who confers absolute worth upon them? Does it not follow that our apprehension of truth, our appreciation of beauty, and our achievement of goodness are only imperfect images of a perfection which is in God Himself?

b. *Their compulsion.* But these supreme values exercise a silent, yet insistent authority over us. We know that we *ought* to speak the truth, and not to tell lies. When scientists, teachers and theologians speak of 'the sacredness of truth', they are recognizing that a *compulsion* is laid upon them to pursue their search for truth with sincerity and devotion, and fearlessly to proclaim what they discover; that, for truth's sake, old ideas and prejudices must be set aside, and danger and ostracism must be dared. So, too, the artist knows that beauty lays a sense of duty upon him. When he speaks of 'the sacredness of beauty', he knows that he *ought* to create and preserve the beautiful, and to seek to destroy all that is ugly. And every one of us knows that goodness lays upon us an *obligation* to seek to achieve it, and to do the right at whatever cost to ourselves. Conscience speaks to us with the voice of authority: 'Thou shalt'! 'Thou shalt not'! It may cause a man to set himself against the laws of the community, and lead him to sacrifice his material interests, and even his very life, for what he believes to be a higher moral obligation than his duty to himself or to his society.

How, then, can we explain the authority and compulsion which these spiritual values bring to bear upon us? Is it not unreasonable to suppose that they are the product of dead matter and a mindless universe? Is it not much more reasonable to believe that this compulsion to seek Truth, Beauty and Goodness is the pressure upon the human spirit of the supreme Being, God, who is Himself the source of these values and of their authority?

It is sometimes argued that the opposites of these values exist—falsehood, ugliness and evil—and that these deny the kind of

God in whom the Christian believes. Here, however, we have to make a choice of beliefs. Is it harder to believe in a good God who has created a world in which are the possibilities of falsehood, ugliness and evil, than to believe in a godless world where truth and beauty and goodness are found? It is true that the first alternative presents us with a problem; but the second alternative seems to be an impossible one.

3. *The evidence of History*

In every race there has been found some sort of belief in God. Indeed, as our knowledge of primitive races has increased, we have discovered that, along with much that is primitive and crude in religion, belief in a 'High God' constantly appears.* The idea of God has not only been found everywhere; it has also been a power in shaping the destinies of individuals and nations.

The existence of belief in God takes on a deeper significance when we study the lives of those in whom devotion to God has burned most brightly. They form a chain of witnesses of singular strength and impressiveness. With a depth of conviction even greater than that of those who composed it, we can sing the lines of the *Te Deum*:

The glorious company of the Apostles praise Thee:
The goodly fellowship of the Prophets praise Thee:
The noble army of Martyrs praise Thee:
The Holy Church throughout all the world doth acknowledge Thee . . .

because, since the early days of the Church, so many more can now be included in their scope. The devotion to God shown by so great a company has been a driving force in every branch of life. Social and political life has felt its impact. It has created the noblest architecture, art, music and literature. It has inspired the exploration of unknown lands, the practice of medicine and surgery, and a host of other activities.

Where has this dynamic power come from? Is its source—belief in God—purely an illusion? Does it arise merely from some strange outworking of the material particles of the brain?

---

* By a 'High God' we mean a supreme God who, though He may be overlooked in the common worship of a people, is yet held to exist and to be the creator and source of all life and of all authority. Belief in such a God is so common amongst primitive peoples that some scholars have thought that the most primitive form of religion was Monotheism.

We cannot dismiss these questions by saying that 'mankind is incurably religious', for that is the very fact which calls for explanation. Surely there can be only one cause adequate to produce such a result; the fact that belief in God is inspired by God Himself.

We might carry this argument a little further. Again and again, we trust our native instincts and emotions; e.g., those of self-preservation and love. Why should we not trust that natural reaching-out to God which is almost universal?

The lines of evidence we have been considering are not meant as independent 'proofs' of God's existence. They are given to show that the world of nature leads us along different avenues of thought towards belief in its Creator, God.

To Be Continued

Even if you have now completed this particular course of study, you will remember that this is only a beginning. The wise—and humble—Christian student knows that there is always more, so much more, to learn and by which to be further enriched and better equipped. And so he is well content to remain to the end of his days 'a scholar in God's school', always a learner—which is what 'disciple' means.

If we can help you in your continued studies we shall always be glad to do so. Suggestions for further reading are given in the appended 'Books for Further Study' (see opposite page). Always at your service too, is our Local Preachers' Library. And do not forget the further correspondence courses ('continuation' courses, and also for the L.P. Diploma) about which further information is available to all who are interested.

D. N. F.

The Local Preachers Department
  of the Methodist Church.

Books for Further Study

(Books marked with an asterisk (*) are for the more advanced student)

GENERAL

*G. Aulén, *The Faith of the Christian Church* (Muhlenberg).
E. Brunner, *Our Faith* (Harpers).
S. Cave, *The Doctrines of the Christian Faith* (Independent).
H. M. Hughes, *Christian Foundations* (Epworth).
C. S. Lewis, *Mere Christianity* (Bles).
*N. Micklem, *What is the Faith?* (H. & S.).
A. Nygren, *The Gospel of God* (S.C.M.).
O. C. Quick, *Doctrines of the Creed* (Nisbet).
J. G. Riddell, *What we Believe* (Church of Scotland).
A. R. Vidler, *Christian Belief* (S.C.M.).
J. S. Whale, *Christian Doctrine* (C.U.P.).
The Message and Mission of Methodism (Epworth).
The Senior Catechism of the Methodist Church (Epworth).
Relevant articles in the various issues of *The Preacher's Handbook* (Epworth).

STUDY ONE

TWB, Articles on Faith, Revelation, Inspiration.
J. Baillie (ed.), *Revelation* (Faber & Faber).
J. Baillie, *The Idea of Revelation in Recent Thought* (O.U.P.).
John Mackay, *A Preface to Christian Theology* (Nisbet).
*W. R. Matthews, *God in Christian Thought and Experience* (Nisbet).
A. Richardson, *Christian Apologetics* (S.C.M.).

STUDY TWO

TWB, Articles on God, Miracle, Providence.
J. Baillie, *Our Knowledge of God* (O.U.P.).
*E. Brunner, *The Christian Doctrine of God* (Lutterworth).
D. S. Cairns, *The Faith that rebels* (S.C.M.).
*H. H. Farmer, *The World and God* (Nisbet).
C. Gore, *Belief in God* (Murray).
C. S. Lewis, *The Problem of Pain* (Bles).

C. S. Lewis, *Miracles* (Bles).
A. Richardson, *Science, History and Faith* (O.U.P.).
*Sir E. Whittaker, *Space and Spirit* (Nelson).
G. E. Wright, *God who Acts* (S.C.M.).

STUDY THREE

TWB, Articles on God, Choose, Covenant, Holy, Righteous, Loving kindness, Grace, Love, Redemption, Sacrifice, Remnant, Kingdom of God, Servant.
A. W. F. Blunt, *The Prophets of Israel* (O.U.P.).
W. N. Clarke, *The Christian Doctrine of God* (T. & T. Clark).
*J. K. Mozley, *The Doctrine of the Atonement* (Duckworth).
*Oesterly and Robinson, *Hebrew Religion, its origin and development* (S.P.C.K.).
E. B. Redlich, *Introduction to Old Testament Study* (Macmillan).
*H. W. Robinson, *The Religious Ideas of the Old Testament* (Duckworth).
T. H. Robinson, *Prophecy and the Prophets in Ancient Israel* (Duckworth).
W. L. Wardle, *The History and Religion of Israel* (Clarendon Bible).
G. E. Wright, *The Old Testament against its Environment* (S.C.M.).

STUDY FOUR

TWB, Articles on Adam, Sin, Grace, Justify, Faith.
B. Citron, *The New Birth* (Nelson).
F. Greeves, *The Meaning of Sin* (Epworth).
*R. Niebuhr, *The Nature and Destiny of Man*, 2 vols. (Nisbet).
*J. Oman, *Grace and Personality* (C.U.P.).
C. Ryder Smith, *The Bible Doctrine of Man* (Epworth).
C. Ryder Smith, *The Bible Doctrine of Sin* (Epworth).
H. Wheeler Robinson, *The Christian Doctrine of Man* (T. & T. Clark).

STUDY FIVE

TWB, Articles on Save, Cross, Atonement, Victory, Reconcile, Redeem, Sacrifice, Suffer, Forgive, Repent, Punish.
F. W. Dillistone, *The Significance of the Cross* (Lutterworth).
H. A. Hodges, *The Pattern of Atonement* (S.C.M.).
*L. Hodgson, *The Doctrine of the Atonement* (Nisbet).
G. W. H. Lampe, *Reconciliation in Christ* (Longmans).

BOOKS FOR FURTHER STUDY 245

W. R. Maltby, *The Meaning of the Cross* (Epworth).
W. R. Maltby, *The Meaning of the Resurrection* (Epworth).
C. F. D. Moule, *The Sacrifice of Christ* (H. & S.).
V. Taylor, *Jesus and His Sacrifice* (Macmillan).
*V. Taylor, *The Atonement in New Testament Teaching* (Epworth).
H. G. Wood, *Why did Christ Die?* (Epworth).

STUDY SIX

TWB, Articles on Christ, Preach, Reveal, Reconcile, Son of God, Son of Man, Lord, Virgin Birth.
*D. M. Baillie, *God was in Christ* (Faber & Faber).
J. W. Bowman, *The Intention of Jesus* (S.C.M.).
C. H. Dodd, *The Apostolic Preaching and its Developments* (H. & S.).
F. Greeves, *Jesus, the Son of God* (Epworth).
H. E. W. Turner, *Jesus, Master and Lord* (Mowbray).
J. W. C. Wand, *The Four Great Heresies* (Mowbray).

STUDY SEVEN

A. *Salvation*

TWB, Articles on Save, Forgive, Just, Adoption, Redeem, Free, Reconcile, Peace, Fellowship, Birth, Saint, Sanctify, Grace, Determinate, Faith, Repent.
B. Citron, *The New Birth* (Nelson).
A. Raymond George, *Communion with God* (Epworth).
H. Lindström, *Wesley and Sanctification* (Epworth).
W. E. Sangster, *The Path to Perfection* (Epworth).
*V. Taylor, *Forgiveness and Reconciliation* (Macmillan).

B. *The Holy Spirit*

TWB, Article on Spirit.
J. E. Fison, *The Blessing of the Holy Spirit* (Longmans).
Headingley Lectures, *The Doctrine of the Holy Spirit* (Epworth).
A. L. Humphries, *The Holy Spirit in Faith and Experience* (Hammond).
G. F. Nuttall, *The Holy Spirit and Ourselves* (Blackwell).
T. Rees, *The Holy Spirit* (Duckworth).
*H. W. Robinson, *The Christian Experience of the Holy Spirit* (Nisbet).

STUDY EIGHT

TWB, Article on God.
*D. M. Baillie, *God was in Christ* (Faber & Faber)
P. Harthill, *The Unity of God* (Mowbray).
L. Hodgson, *The Doctrine of the Trinity* (Duckworth).
C. W. Lowry, *The Trinity and Christian Devotion* (E. & S.).
*W. R. Matthews, *God in Christian Thought and Experience* (Nisbet).
*A. E. J. Rawlinson (ed.), *Essays on the Trinity and Incarnation* (Longmans).

STUDIES NINE AND TEN

TWB, Articles on Church, Fellowship, Minister, Thank, Baptism, Worship.

A. *The Nature of the Church*

Davies and Flew (ed.), *The Catholicity of Protestantism* (Lutterworth).
The Nature of the Christian Church according to the Teaching of the Methodists (Epworth).
*L. Newbigin, *The Household of God* (S.C.M.).
*P. Carnegie Simpson, *The Evangelical Church Catholic* (H. & S.).

B. *The Teaching of the New Testament*

R. Newton Flew, *Jesus and His Church* (Epworth).
A. M. Hunter, *The Unity of the New Testament* (S.C.M.).

C. *The History of the Church*

*R. H. Bainton, *The Reformation of the Sixteenth Century* (H. & S.).
S. C. Carpenter, *Christianity* (Pelican Books).
Horton Davies, *The English Free Churches* (Home University).
Horton Davies, *Christian Worship* (R.E.P.).
B. Manning, *Essays in Orthodox Dissent* (Independent).
D. J. Stephen, *Outline History of the Christian Church* (S.P.C.K.).
V. E. Walker, *A First Church History* (S.C.M.).

D. *Methodism*

F. Baker, *A Charge to Keep* (Epworth).
J. Bishop, *Methodist Worship* (Epworth).

H. Carter, *The Methodist Heritage* (Epworth).

H. Watkin-Jones, *Methodist Churchmanship and its Implications* (Epworth).

E. *The Sacraments*

*W. F. Flemington, *The New Testament Doctrine of Baptism* (S.P.C.K.).

*Y. Brilioth, *Eucharistic Faith and Practice, Evangelical and Catholic* (S.P.C.K.)

STUDY ELEVEN

F. R. Barry, *What has Christianity to say?* (S.C.M.).

*E. Brunner, *Christianity and Civilization*, 2 vols. (Nisbet).

T. E. Jessop, *Social Ethics: Christian and Natural* (Epworth).

*R. Niebuhr, *An Interpretation of Christian Ethics* (Nisbet).

C. A. Anderson Scott, *New Testament Ethics* (C.U.P.).

J. F. Sleenan, *Basic Economic Problems* (S.C.M.).

C. Ryder Smith, *What Do Ye?* (Epworth).

E. C. Urwin, *The Way of the Christian Citizen* (C.C. Dept).

E. C. Urwin, *Religion and the Common Man* (Epworth).

The Declarations of the Methodist Church on Social Questions (Epworth).

STUDY TWELVE

TWB, Articles on Time, Prophecy, Judge, Glory, Kingdom of God, Heaven, Hope, Body, Hell, Death, Perdition, Church.

J. Baillie, *And the Life Everlasting* (O.U.P.).

T. F. Glasson, *The Second Advent* (Epworth).

T. F. Glasson, *His Appearing and His Kingdom* (Epworth).

H. A. Guy, *The N.T. Doctrine of the Last Things* (O.U.P.).

J. A. T. Robinson, *In the End, God . . .* (J. Clarke).

L. D. Weatherhead, *After Death* (Epworth).

Index of Subjects

ADOPTION, 12, 99, 117, 122
Adventism, 218
Agnostics, 19
Alcohol, 201, 210
Anthropomorphism, 34
Apostolic Preaching, 10, 95ff., 126, 162
Apostolic Succession, 170, 194
Arianism, 145, 147
Armenianism, 119f.
Assumptions, 12f.
Assurance, 12, 123, 127, 132f., 193
Atheists, 19, 237
Atonement:
   Tests of true doctrine, 76ff.
   Theories of the,
      Christ our Champion, 79ff.
      Satisfaction, 81f.
      Moral Influence, 82f.
      Sacrifice, 44, 83ff.
      Completion of Penitence, 85f.
   No complete theory, 73, 76, 88

BIBLE, THE, 6ff., 10, 179, 185
Birth, The New, 112f., 117f., 181
Bodies, Spiritual, 225, 229, 232

CALVANISM, 119
Chalcedon, 108f., 110, 146, 148, 150
Christ:
   Ascended, 96, 103, 126, 141, 142
   Exalted, 103, 128
   His Death, *see* Cross
   His glory, 220f.
   His Life, 7, 73f.
   His Person, 94-112
   His Work, 72-90, 95f.
   Lord, 102f., 136, 142, 162
   Messiah, 101f., 137, 159
   Not two Persons, 105f.
   Reconciler, 97f., 140, 142
   Redeemer, 9, 79ff., 83, 117, 142
   Representative, 79, 80, 84, 86, 121
   Revealer, 77, 97f., 136f., 139ff.
   Risen, 7, 73ff., 79f., 89, 96, 103, 141
   Saviour, 10, 72ff., 95f., 110
   Son of God, 94f., 98ff., 101, 102, 105ff., 111, 138f., 147
   Son of Man, 47f., 99f., 102
   Teacher, 137f., 159f.
   Truly God, 98-103
   Truly Man, 103-7
   Truly God, Truly Man, 107-12
   Word, 102.
Christology, 94, 106
Christian Science, 203
Church, the, 10f., 157-73, 177-95
   in Teaching of Jesus, 159ff.
   after Pentecost, 161ff.
   in rest of N.T., 164ff.
   Fellowship of Believers, 122, 127, 165ff., 189, 193f.
   its Divisions, 186-90
   its History, 183-6
   its Ministry, 169-73
   its Purpose, 158, 164, 165, 168f.
   its Growing Unity, 193ff.
   its Worship, 177-83
   the Body of Christ, 11, 122, 164ff., 169f., 172, 221
   the New Israel, 7, 159ff., 162f., 181
   under Judgement, 183f.
Church of England, 187ff., 190f., 194f.
Communion of Saints, 166
Communism:
   Christian, 163f.
   Marxist, 3, 4, 14, 53, 200, 203
Compromise, 233
Conscience, 53, 239
Conversion, 116
Copernicus, 12f.
Covenant:
   Old, 36, 41f.
   New, 42, 137, 161, 183
Creation, 38f.
Creeds, 1, 10f., 104, 147, 162, 192
   Apostles' Creed, *opp.* 1, 11, 126, 129, 194
   Nicene Creed, 11, 129, 146, 151, 153, 194

INDEX OF SUBJECTS

Cross, The, 7, 27ff., 76f., 78-89, 95f., 139f., 183

Day of Yahweh, 219
Days, Living in Last, 232f.
Death, 29
  Spiritual, 231f.
Deed of Union, 191f.
Depravity, Total, 64
Devil, the, 79, 89f.
Double Procession, 129
Dying with Christ, 117

Eastern Church, 129, 170, 187
Ecclesia, 157f.
Ecumenical Movement, 194
Eternity, 214
Ethics, 199-211
  and Theology, 4f., 200ff., 206
  its Difficulties, 204ff.
Evangelism, 40, 111, 168f., 191
Evils, Physical, 26-9
Evolution, 54, 237f.
Experience, Personal, 1f, 11f.
Exodus, The, 6, 24, 32f., 37, 44f.
Expiation, 83

Faith, 1, 9, 16f., 67ff., 95, 120, 146, 155f.
  the, 2, 9ff., 65f., 137, 193, 201
Family, the, 210
Fellowship with God, 122
Fellow-workers with God, 204
Flesh, the, 60, 91
Forgiveness, 4, 77f., 86f., 116, 155
Free Churches, 188ff., 191, 194f.
Free Will, 53f., 56
Future, regarded bi-focally, 214

Gambling, 201, 209f.
Gehenna, 227f.
Gnostics, 145, 147
God:
  His Existence, 236-41
  His Judgement, 219f.
  His Orderliness, 21f.
  His Redeeming Purpose, 7, 8f., 25f., 41-8
  in Nature, 19-30
  in the O.T., 32-48, 51f.
  in Teaching of Jesus, 137ff.
  is Creator, 38f., 236f.
  is Father, 35, 138f.
  is Holy, 34f., 85, 141
  is Love, 36f., 82, 141
  is One God, 37f., 141
  is Personal, 20f., 33f., 141
  is Righteous, 36f., 82, 141
  Is Sovereign of all, 39f., 59, 141
Gospel, the, 3, 158, 167, 178ff., 206
  the Social, 203
Grace, 12, 65ff., 73, 119f.
Guilt, 61, 75f., 82, 83f., 122, 228, 230

Hades, 227
Heaven, 89, 223-6
Hell, 227-32
Homo-ousios, 109

Image of God, 20, 57, 64
Immortality, 226
Incarnation, the, 79, 98, 103f., 142
'In Christ', 89, 91, 121, 166f.
Industry, 207
Inspiration, 7f.

Judgement, Present, 219
  the Final, 219f.
Justification, 67f., 116, 118f., 121, 153ff.

Kenotic Christology, 106f.
Kingdom of God, 46f., 101, 137f., 159, 200, 210.
Knowledge of God, 5ff., 19, 53, 147

Law of Christ, 202ff.
'Laws' of Nature, 21ff.
Life Eternal, 94, 217
Local Preachers, 171f., 173, 191
Love to God, 202
Love to Neighbour, 123, 202
Loyalties, Conflicting, 205

Man, 51-8
  Materialistic view of, 52f.
  Christian view of, 53ff.
  his Failure, 57f.
  his Fall, 63ff.
  needs a Saviour, 154

Maran Atha, 216
Means of Grace, 66, 122, 173f., 177f.
Messianic Hope, 46f., 51
Methodism: 11, 190-3
  its Divisions, 186f.
  its Doctrine, 118, 120, 123f., 191f., 193
  its Ministry, 171f.
  its Place in the Universal Church, 192f.
  its Origin, 11, 167, 190, 193
  its Worship, 179f., 192f.
Methodist Union, 191f.
Miracle, 23ff., 100, 105
Monotheism, 38, 97, 102, 103, 142
Money, 48f., 209

NATURE, ITS NEUTRALITY, 27
Need, Modern, 3
Newton, Sir Isaac, 13

OLD TESTAMENT, Christ and, 137

PARABLES, 67, 101, 139
Paraclete, 128f.
Pelagianism, 67, 119
Pentecost, 126, 129f., 145, 161ff., 170
People, the Chosen, 32, 36f., 40, 44f., 137
Perdition, 231
Perfection, 123f., 193, 204
Pharisaism, 201, 206
Piety, Personal, 202f.
Prayer, 21, 26, 132, 147, 164, 177
Preaching, 2f., 72f., 179f.
Priests, 38, 42f.
Prophets, 32, 34, 36, 38f., 44, 51
Propitiation, 83f., 155
Protestantism, 7n., 11, 185ff., 189
Providence, 25ff.
Punishment, 4, 86ff.
  Capital, 205
Purgatory, 124
Puritans, 187f.

RANSOM, 81
Redemption, in O.T., 8f., 40-8
  in N.T., *see* Christ.
Reconciliation, 42f., 84, 117

Reformation, The, 7n., 11, 67f., 153, 167, 171, 187
Regeneration, *see* New Birth.
Relationships, Personal, 56f.
Remnant, Saving, 46, 164
Repentance, 4, 85f., 120
Revelation: *see* Christ.
  General, 5f.
  Special, 6f.
  its Purpose, 9
  and Reason, 12ff.
Roman Catholicism, 13, 170, 186f., 189

SACRAMENTS, 172, 177, 180f., 192f.
  Baptism, 66, 121, 164, 180f., 188, 192
  Lord's Supper, 164, 182f., 192f.
Sacrifice, 43f., 83ff.
Salvation, 16ff., 72, 115f.
Sanctification, 117f., 122ff., 130f., 190
Science, 13f., 53f., 217f.
  Christian, 203
Sermon on Mount, 100, 160, 203
Sin, 57-65
  Actual, 63
  Original, 60ff.
Spirit, the Holy, 6, 9, 73, 115, 124-32, 142f., 162f., 166, 190, 193, 216, 232f.
  in O.T., 125
  in Synoptics, 126
  in Acts, 126f.
  in Paul, 127f.
  in John, 128f.
  Fellowship of, 127n., 163, 165f.
  Work of, 130f., 142f., 147, 161f., 163, 172f.
Spiritualism, 226
Suffering, 28f., 88f.
Suffering Servant, 47, 84, 102, 159
Sunday, 208f.

Te Deum, 240
Theology:
  and Ethics, 200f., 206
  and Preaching, 2f.
  its Importance, 1ff.
  its Sources, 9ff.
Time, 214f.
  Use of, 208

INDEX OF SUBJECTS

Trinity:
  Doctrine of the, 108, 110, 111, 125, 128, 143-53
    Controversies about, 145f., 148f.
    its Formation, 144f., 147
    its Mystery, 151f.
    its Necessity, 147f.
  and Worship, 152f.
  Generation of the Son, 151
  in the N.T., 143f.
  Persons in the Godhead, 149f.
  Procession of the Spirit, 151

UNIVERSE, THE, 21ff., 237f.

VALUES, SPIRITUAL, 53, 238f.
Venite, 87
Vicarious Penitence, 85f.
Victory of the Cross, 74f., 79ff. 140f.
Virgin Birth, 111f.

WAR, 27, 205

Wesley's Sermons:
  I. 16, 120
  II. 30
  V. 116, 118, 153f.
  VIII. 91
  IX. 68f., 117
  X. 123, 132f.
  XII. 123, 173f., 177
  XIV. 117
  XV. 112f., 117
  XVIII. 196f.
  XIX. 211f.
  XXVIII. 234f.
  XXXIII. 194
  XXXIV. 194
  XXXV. 124
  XXXIX. 117
  XLIV. 48f.
Witness of Spirit, *see* Assurance.
Witness to Others, 168f.
Work, 207f.

YAHWEH, 33f., 35

Index of Authors

Abelard, 82
Anselm, 81
Athanasius, 80
Augustine, 67

Baillie, D. M., 110
Baillie, J., 8
Barth, Karl, 147, 150
Brunner, E., 51

Calvin, 57, 65, 67, 119, 187, 193
Campbell, J. M., 85
Charles, R. H., 222

Denney, J., 95
Dodd, C. H., 96, 101

Glasson, T. F., 218
Greeves, F., 95

Hunter, A. M., 159
Hodgson, L., 87

Irenaeus, 79

Lewis, C. S., 60, 63, 105, 148

Lewis, G. P., 112
Lowrey, C. W., 153
Luther, 57, 68, 80, 120, 187, 195

Manson, T. W., 138f.
Moberly, R. C., 85

Oman, J., 67

Quick, O. C., 112

Rupp, E. G., 96

Sayers, Dorothy, 105

Taylor, Vincent, 84, 85, 229
Temple, Wm., 106
Turner, H. E. W., 99, 102

Weatherhead, L. D., 226
Welch, C., 151
Wesley, Charles, 2, 11, 192
Wesley, John, 2, 11, 15f., 117, 123f. 133f., 167, 190f., 193
Whale, J. S., 100

Index of Bible Passages

Genesis
1-2³...38
1¹...38
1²...125
1²⁷...57
2⁴, ⁷...38
3⁸...34
6⁵...234f.
6¹³...34
8²¹...43
11⁵...34
11³¹ff....6
12¹...216
15¹⁸...41
17⁷f....41
18¹...34

Exodus
3¹⁰...216
3¹³⁻¹⁷...32
4²⁴ff....32
20²²-23³³...41
21³⁰...40
24⁷...41
29³⁸ff....43
34...128
34²⁰...40

Leviticus
4-5¹³...43
5¹⁴-6⁷...44
6¹⁻⁵...44
17-26...42
25⁴⁸...40

Deuteronomy
2³⁴...32
12²³...84
23²ff....158
26¹⁷f....42
30¹⁹...119

Joshua
7...8
10¹²ff....13

Judges
11²⁹⁻⁴⁰...8

17⁵...43

1 Samuel
2¹⁵...43
10⁶, 10...125
15...32
23⁶⁻¹²...43

2 Samuel
12¹⁻¹⁵...36
21⁹...8

1 Kings
19¹⁸...46
21¹⁻¹⁶...36

2 Chronicles
28⁸...158

Nehemiah
13¹...158

Psalms
8...39
8⁵...58
19...39
24...39
50³ff....219
51...59
51⁴f....60f.
51¹¹...125
73...28
96¹⁰ff....219
104³⁰...125

Isaiah
1²⁵...46
4²f....46
6...35
8¹⁶ff....160
9⁶f....46
10⁵...39
11¹...46
11²...125
40¹²⁻²⁶...38
40¹⁸...34
41¹⁸ff....38

43¹⁰...38
45¹⁻⁴...40
45⁷...38
49⁶...40, 45
52¹³-53¹²...47
60²f....40
60¹¹f....45
61¹...125
61⁵f....45
66¹⁸...219

Jeremiah
31³¹ff....42

Ezekiel
34¹², ¹⁶, ²³...159

Daniel
7¹³...47f.

Hosea
2⁸f....39
2¹⁹...37
11¹⁻⁴...34
11⁸...37
11⁹...34

Joel
2²⁸...125

Amos
1-2...39
5²⁰...45
5²²...44
9⁷...39

Micah
2⁵...158
5²ff....159

Zechariah
9⁹...47
14³ff....219

Malachi
3⁷...173f.

Matthew
1^{21}...116
3^7...229
4^{1-11}...90
4^{17}...101
5-7...160
5^{8-12}...196f.
5^{12}...226, 233
5^{13-16}...211f.
5^{22}...228
5^{24-38}...100
5^{45}...67
5^{48}...233
6^1...226
$6^{4\mathrm{ff.}}$...226
6^9...138
6^{15}...138, 220
$6^{18\mathrm{ff.}}$...226
7^1...230
7^{7-11}...160
7^{13}...231
$7^{24\mathrm{ff.}}$...100
10^{28}...228
$10^{32\mathrm{f.}}$...219
$11^{21\mathrm{ff.}}$...230
11^{27}...99
12^{28}...100f.
13^{41}...100
16^{18}...159
18^{20}...165
23^{15}...228
23^{33}...228
24^{44}...219
$25^{31\mathrm{ff.}}$...220
$26^{26\mathrm{ff.}}$...180
26^{39}...21
28^{19}...144, 180
28^{20}...165

Mark
1^8...126
1^{9-11}...84, 86, 102, 126
$1^{14\mathrm{f.}}$...101, 120
2^{1-12}...102
2^{1-22}...100
2^{10}...100
2^{28}...100
$3^{14\mathrm{f.}}$...224
3^{29}...231
$4^{3\mathrm{ff.}}$...101
7^{6-14}...201
8^{27-37}...84, 100, 102
8^{38}...100
$9^{43\mathrm{ff.}}$...228
10^{27}...160
10^{45}...81, 117, 159
$11^{23\mathrm{f.}}$...160
12^{1-12}...139
$12^{26\mathrm{f.}}$...229
12^{28-34}...137
13^{26}...220
13^{32}...217
13^{35}...232
$14^{22\mathrm{ff.}}$...180, 183
14^{24}...161
14^{25}...101
14^{36}...141
14^{58}...161
14^{62}...218, 220

Luke
1^{26-38}...111
1^{35}...126
3^7...229
4^1...126
6^7...160
6^{35}...226
$8^{1, 10}$...101
10^1...160, 170
10^9...101
$10^{12\mathrm{ff.}}$...230
$10^{17\mathrm{ff.}}$...170
10^{18}...90
10^{20}...223
10^{22}...99
10^{25-37}...138
12^5...228
12^{32}...160
12^{40}...219
$13^{28\mathrm{ff.}}$...229
14^{12-24}...138
$15^{3\mathrm{ff.}}$...138, 160
16^9...234f.
18^8...100
$18^{10\mathrm{ff.}}$...66
19^{10}...138
$22^{15\mathrm{ff.}}$...180
22^{31}...90
23^{34}...75

John
1^1...102
3^{1-15}...117
3^5...128, 130
3^{16}...73, 223
$3^{17\mathrm{ff.}}$...219
3^{19}...219
4^{24}...129
5^{17}...224
$5^{19\mathrm{ff.}}$...99
5^{27}...100, 219
6^{37}...220
6^{46}...99
6^{47}...223
7^{39}...128, 130
8^{34}...59
$10^{4\mathrm{f.}}$...160
$10^{30\mathrm{f.}}$...99
11^{52}...160
12^{32}...82
$14^{6\mathrm{ff.}}$...99
14^9...141
14^{10}...141
14^{16-26}...128, 165
15^4...223
15^6...231
15^{13}...141
$15^{26\mathrm{f.}}$...128
16^{7-15}...128
16^{14}...129
20^{22}...129
20^{31}...94, 185
21^{17}...160

Acts
1^{4-8}...126
1^7...217
$1^{21\mathrm{f.}}$...171
2...126
2^{14-39}...96
$2^{16\mathrm{f.}}$...233
2^{33-8}...103, 126
2^{39}...181
2^{40}...162
2^{42}...163
$2^{46\mathrm{f.}}$...164
3^{13-36}...96, 164
$3^{25\mathrm{f.}}$...162
$4^{10\mathrm{ff.}}$...96
5^3...90
5^{11}...158
$5^{30\mathrm{ff.}}$...96
6...169
$6^{3, 5}$...127
7...164
7^{57}...103

INDEX OF BIBLE PASSAGES

Acts—cont.
8^3...158
8^{14-17}...126
9^{1-19}...116
9^{31}...158
10^{36-43}...96
10^{38}...140
10^{42}...219
10^{42}...219
10^{47}...126
11^{19-23}...162
$11^{27f.}$...127
13^{17-41}...96
14^{14}...170
15^{28}...127
16^{28}...30f.
$16^{30f.}$...119, 120
19^{1-7}...126
20^{28}...158

Romans
1^{1-4}...96
1^4...102
1^{17}...68
1^{18}...219f.
$1^{18}-2^{29}$...60, 220
1^{18}...219
2^1...230
2^5...228, 231
2^{16}...96
3^{21-6}...83, 116
4^3...121
4^5...116, 153f.
$5^{6ff.}$...66, 73
5^9...219
$6^{4, 6}$...117
6^{11}...184
7^{14-24}...59
8...127
8^1...91f.
8^{1-15}...127
8^{12-17}...12
8^{14}...130
8^{15}...68f., 117
8^{16}...123, 132f.
8^{26}...127
8^{34}...96, 103
$10^{8f.}$...96
11^{32}...231
11^{36}...153
12...203
12^{4-7}...169

$12^{5ff.}$...165
13^{12}...219
16^7...170

1 Corinthians
1^9...122
1^{18}...115
2^9...225
3^5...172
3^{15}...115
$3^{22f.}$...224
5^7...83
6^{11}...144
7^5...90
8^6...102
9^1...170
9^{25}...226
10^{11}...232
10^{16}...122
10^{17}...183
$11^{23ff.}$...180
11^{25}...161
11^{26}...183, 221
$12-14$...127
12^3...127, 130, 146
$12^{4ff.}$...144
12^{4-28}...169
$12^{12ff.}$...165, 169, 221
12^{28}...130, 158
12^{31}...212
13^{12}...224
15^{1-11}...96, 170
15^3...72
15^7...170
15^{10}...148
15^{22}...231
15^{44}...225
$15^{51ff.}$...221
16^{22}...216

2 Corinthians
$1^{21f.}$...144
3^{17}...128
4^5...172
4^6...223
5^7...225
5^{10}...219
$5^{18ff.}$...73, 117, 140, 142
5^{21}...86
8^9...66, 107
8^{23}...170
12^4...225
13^{14}...122, 127n., 144

Galatians
2^{16}...120
2^{20}...78, 117
3^1...141
4^{4-7}...117
5^1...117
5^{16-26}...91
$5^{19f.}$...60, 220
5^{22}...123, 127
6^2...202

Ephesians
$1-6$...204
$1^{22f.}$...221
2^{1-10}...12
2^{1-18}...110
$2^{5f.}$...117, 223
2^8...16f, 115, 119
$2^{14ff.}$...117, 128
$4^{3ff.}$...184
$4^{11f.}$...172
$5^{25f.}$...195, 221

Philippians
1^{10}...219
1^{21}...224
2^{1-11}...103, 106f., 146
2^1...122, 127n.
2^{10}...231
2^{11}...146
3^{10}...122, 223
3^{14}...124
3^{19}...231
3^{20}...223

Colossians
1^{16}...102
$2^{12f.}$...117
2^{15}...79
2^{20}...117
3^1...117
3^3...216

1 Thessalonians
1^{10}...219
$4^{14ff.}$...221
5^9...219

2 Thessalonians
1^8...220
1^9...227, 231
2^{13}...127

2 Timothy
2^{13}...215
3^{16}...132
4^1...219

Titus
2^1...2

Hebrews
1^{1-4}...10
6^8...231
7^{25}...103
9^{14}...144
10^{29}...144, 219
10^{31}...220
11...229
11^{8-12}...6
12^{14}...124
12^{23}...221

James
1^1...94
$1^{13f.}$...63
2...206
2^1...94
2^{26}...120
3^6...228

1 Peter
1^2...144
1^8...223
$1^{18f.}$...117
2^9...223
2^{23}...75, 87
$3^{18ff.}$...231
4^5...219
4^{10}...169
4^{17}...221
5^4...226

1 John
1^3...186
1^7...84
2^1...128
2^2...84
3^2...224f.
3^9...112f.
3^{24}...128
4^2...128
$4^{7f.}$...141
5^{20}...102

Revelation
5^6...221
5^9...219, 122
7^{10}...224
20^{15}...227
21^8...220

www.ingramcontent.com/pod-product-compliance
Lightning Source LLC
Chambersburg PA
CBHW050343230426
43663CB00010B/1964